DATE DUE

GAYLORD   PRINTED IN U.S.A.

Future Babble

Future BABBLE

Why Expert Predictions
Are Next to Worthless,
and You Can Do Better

Dan Gardner

DUTTON

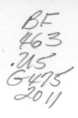

DUTTON
Published by Penguin Group (USA) Inc.
375 Hudson Street, New York, New York 10014, U.S.A.
Penguin Group (Canada), 90 Eglinton Avenue East, Suite 700, Toronto, Ontario M4P 2Y3, Canada (a division of Pearson Penguin Canada Inc.); Penguin Books Ltd, 80 Strand, London WC2R 0RL, England; Penguin Ireland, 25 St Stephen's Green, Dublin 2, Ireland (a division of Penguin Books Ltd); Penguin Group (Australia), 250 Camberwell Road, Camberwell, Victoria 3124, Australia (a division of Pearson Australia Group Pty Ltd); Penguin Books India Pvt Ltd, 11 Community Centre, Panchsheel Park, New Delhi—110 017, India; Penguin Group (NZ), 67 Apollo Drive, Rosedale, North Shore 0632, New Zealand (a division of Pearson New Zealand Ltd); Penguin Books (South Africa) (Pty) Ltd, 24 Sturdee Avenue, Rosebank, Johannesburg 2196, South Africa

Penguin Books Ltd, Registered Offices: 80 Strand, London WC2R 0RL, England

Published by Dutton, a member of Penguin Group (USA) Inc.

First printing, March 2011
10   9   8   7   6   5   4   3   2   1

LIBRARY OF CONGRESS CATALOGING-IN-PUBLICATION DATA
Gardner, Dan, 1968–
   Future babble : why expert predictions are next to worthless, and you can do better / Dan Gardner.
    p.   cm.
Includes bibliographical references and index.
ISBN 978-0-525-95205-3 (hardcover)
1. Uncertainty.   2. Fallacies (Logic)   3. Thought and thinking.   4. Perception.   I. Title.
BF463.U5G475   2010
303.4909—dc22   2010041293

Printed in the United States of America
Set in Minion Pro
Designed by Daniel Lagin

For Mum and Dad, who gave me a future,
and for Victoria, Winston, and MacDougall, who are the future

Contents

Preface

As I read the newspaper this morning, I became engrossed in a story about what would happen in the future.

The story said the latest economic forecast of the Organization for Economic Cooperation and Development (OECD) showed growth over the next couple of years would be stronger than previously projected. I read every word avidly. Like most people these days, I'm worried about the economy. The last few years have not been good ones. There was a calamitous credit crisis, the puncturing of real estate bubbles in one country after another, and a global recession worse than anything since the Second World War. Then came a weak recovery, debt crises, and fears of inflation. Or deflation. Take your pick. Who knows what will come next? Not me, although I very much want to. So when my morning newspaper delivered the knowledge I crave, from the esteemed experts at the OECD no less, it had my full and enthusiastic attention. Growth will be better than expected! Fabulous!

But then I realized something. The phrase *better than expected* means there was a forecast that preceded this one, and by issuing a new and different forecast, the OECD was conceding that the latest information suggested the earlier forecast was wrong. If the first forecast could fail, so could the second, and yet I had reacted to the second forecast as if it were a sure thing. It was also a little sobering to recall that the OECD had forecast smooth sailing in 2008 and 2009. Hurricane? What hurricane?

And I remembered something else. I had just finished writing a book about how awful experts are at predicting the future and how psychology compels people to take predictions seriously anyway.

Case in point: me.

I mention this because the mistakes and delusions I chronicle in this book are *human* follies. We are all susceptible to them, even authors who write about the mistakes and delusions of others. The goal of this book is not to mock particular individuals. Nor is it to scorn the category known as "experts." It is to better understand the human desire to know what will happen, why that desire will never be satisfied, and how we can better prepare ourselves for the unknowable future.

Although most of the issues discussed in this book are very much in the news today—from the economy, to oil prices, to environmental catastrophe—I generally don't examine current predictions for the simple reason that no one really knows if they are accurate or not. I may feel that a prediction is sensible or silly, but others may feel differently, and arguing about it will get us nowhere. Only the passage of time can settle it. And so I focus on recent history: If, for example, someone predicted a second Great Depression would start in 1990 (as one economist did in a wildly popular book), then I can say with considerable confidence that he was wrong. And no reasonable person will disagree.

I should also note that while I have tried to be fair in portraying what experts predicted and how accurate those predictions were, I often had to condense entire books to a few sentences and sum up complex evidence with equal brevity. Inevitably, these summaries are full of subjective judgments: Do not take what I say as the final word. Most of the papers and articles discussed here are available on the Internet; all the books can be found in libraries and used book stores. Have a look and decide for yourself. I know that reading old predictions about a future that is now the past may sound hopelessly dull, but it's not. In fact, it's surprisingly enjoyable and rewarding. It's raw history, after all. There is no better way to climb inside a moment in time and see the world from that perspective. Or to realize that while the future we face may be disturbingly uncertain, 'twas ever thus—which is oddly reassuring.

My profound thanks to Philip Tetlock, for doing the demanding research that is the foundation of this book and for being generous and helpful at an unimaginably difficult time in his life. A gentleman and a scholar, indeed.

Also thanks to my research assistant, Courtney Symons, and my marvelous editors, Susan Renouf at McClelland & Stewart and Stephen Morrow at Dutton. Many others contributed one way or another to the book in your hands, including Scott Gilmore, Rudyard Griffiths, Liam Scott, Bruce Schneier, and my longtime friends and colleagues David Watson and Leonard Stern. A special thanks to Paul Slovic, John Mueller, Marc Ramsay, and Barry Dworkin for reading early versions and providing invaluable thoughts and suggestions. Of course, having been written by a fallible human, this book will contain errors—for which the author is solely responsible. All corrections and constructive criticism will be gratefully received.

And finally, thanks to my wife, Sandra, without whom I could do, and would be, nothing.

Future Babble

1

Introduction

The end of everything we call life is close at hand and cannot be evaded.

—H. G. WELLS, 1946

George Edward Scott, my mother's father, was born in an English village near the city of Nottingham. It was 1906. We can be sure that anyone who took notice of George's arrival in the world agreed that he was a very lucky baby.

There was the house he lived in, for one thing. It was the work of his father, a successful builder, and it was, like the man who built it, correct, confident, and proudly Victorian. Middle-class prosperity was evident throughout, from the sprawling rooms to the stained-glass windows and the cast-iron bathtub with a pull-cord that rang a bell downstairs. A maid carrying a bucket of hot water would arrive in due course.

And there was the country and the era. Often romanticized as the "long Edwardian summer," Britain at the beginning of the twentieth century was indeed a land of peace and prosperity, if not strawberries and champagne. Britain led the world in industry, science, education, medicine, trade, and finance. Its empire was vaster than any in history, its navy invincible. The great and terrible war with Napoleon's France was tucked away in dusty history books and few worried that its like would ever come again.

It was a time when "Progress" was capitalized. People were wealthier. They ate better and lived longer. Trade, travel, and communication steadily expanded, a process that would be called, much later, globalization. Science advanced briskly, revealing nature's secrets and churning out technological marvels, each more wonderful than the last, from the train to the telegraph to the airplane. The latest of these arrived only four years before George Scott was born, and in 1912, when George was six, his father gathered the family in a field to witness the miracle of a man flying through the air in a machine. The pilot waved to the gawkers below. "Now I've seen it," George's grandmother muttered. "But I still don't believe it."

And the future? How could it be anything but grand? In 1902, the great American economist John Bates Clark imagined himself in 2002, looking back on the last hundred years. He pronounced himself profoundly satisfied. "There is certainly enough in our present condition to make our gladness overflow" and to hope that "the spirit of laughter and song may abide with us through the years that are coming," Clark wrote. The twentieth century had been a triumph, in Clark's imagining. Technology had flourished, conflict between labor and capital had vanished, and prosperity had grown until the slums were "transformed into abodes of happiness and health." Only trade had crossed borders, never armies, and in the whole long century not a shot had been fired in anger. Of course this was only to be expected, Clark wrote, even though some silly people in earlier generations had actually believed war could happen in the modern world—"as if nations bound together by such economic ties as now unite the countries of the world would ever disrupt the great industrial organism and begin fighting."

At the time, Clark's vision seemed as reasonable as it was hopeful, and it was widely shared by eminent persons. "We can now look forward with something like confidence to the time when war between civilized nations will be as antiquated as the duel," wrote the esteemed British historian G. P. Gooch, in 1911. Several years later, the celebrated *Manchester Guardian* journalist H. N. Norman was even more definitive. "It is as certain as anything in politics can be, that the frontiers of our modern national states are finally drawn. My own belief is that there will be no more wars among the six Great Powers."

One day, a few months after H. N. Norman had declared the arrival of eternal peace, George Scott fetched his father's newspaper. The top story was the latest development in the push for Irish home rule. Below that was another headline. "War Declared," it read.

It was August 1914. What had been considered impossible by so many informed experts was now reality. But still there was no need to despair. It would be "the war to end all wars," in H. G. Wells's famously optimistic phrase. And it would be brief. It has to be, wrote the editors of *The Economist*, thanks to "the economic and financial impossibility of carrying out hostilities many more months on the present scale."

For more than four years, the industry, science, and technology that had promised a better world slowly ground millions of men into the mud. The long agony of the First World War shattered empires, nations, generations, and hopes. The very idea of progress came to be scorned as a rotten illusion, a raggedy stage curtain now torn down and discarded.

In defeated Germany, Oswald Spengler's dense and dark *Decline of the West* was the runaway best seller of the 1920s. In victorious Britain, the Empire was bigger but the faith in the future that had sustained it faded like an old photograph left in the sun. The war left crushing debts and the economy staggered. "Has the cycle of prosperity and progress closed?" asked H. G. Wells in the foreword to a book whose title ventured an even bleaker question: *Will Civilization Crash?* Yes to both, answered many of the same wise men who had once seen only peace and prosperity ahead. "It is clear now to everyone that the suicide of civilization is in progress," declared the physician and humanitarian Albert Schweitzer in a 1922 lecture at Oxford University. It may have been "the Roaring Twenties" in the United States—a time of jazz, bathtub gin, soaring stocks, and real estate speculation—but it was a decade of gloom in Britain. For those who thought about the future, observes historian Richard Overy, "the prospect of imminent crisis, a new Dark Age, became a habitual way of looking at the world."

My grandfather's fortunes followed Britain's. His father's business declined, prosperity seeped away, and the bathtub pull-cord ceased to summon the downstairs maid. In 1922, at the age of fifteen, George was apprenticed to a plumber. A few years later, bowing to the prevailing sense that Britain's decline was unstoppable, he decided to emigrate. A coin toss—heads Canada, tails Australia—settled the destination. With sixty dollars in his pocket, he landed in Canada. It was 1929. He had arrived just in time for the Great Depression.

A horror throughout the industrialized world, the Great Depression was especially savage in North America. Half the industrial production of the United States vanished. One-quarter of workers were unemployed. Starvation was a real and constant threat for millions. Growing numbers of desperate, frightened people sought salvation in fascism or communism. In Toronto, Maple Leaf Gardens was filled to the rafters not for a hockey game but for a Stalinist rally, urging Canadians to follow the glorious example of the Soviet Union. Among the leading thinkers of the day, it was almost a truism that liberal democracy and free-market capitalism were archaic, discredited, and doomed. Even moderates were sure the future would belong to very different economic and political systems.

In 1933, the rise to power of the Nazis added the threat of what H. G. Wells called the "Second World War" in his sci-fi novel *The Shape of Things to Come*. Published the same year Adolf Hitler became chancellor of Germany, *The Shape of Things to Come* saw the war beginning in 1940 and predicted it would become a decade-long mass slaughter, ending not in victory but in the utter exhaustion and collapse of all nations. Military analysts and others who tried to imagine another Great War were almost as grim. The airplanes that had been so wondrous to a young boy in 1912 would fill the skies with bombs, they agreed. Cities would be pulverized. There would be mass psychological breakdown and social disintegration. In 1934, Britain began a rearmament program it could not afford for a war that, it increasingly seemed, it could not avoid. In 1936, as Nazi Germany grew stronger, the program was accelerated.

A flicker of hope came from the United States, where economic indicators jolted upward, like a flat line on a heart monitor suddenly jumping. It didn't last. In 1937, the American economy plunged again. It seemed nothing could pull the world out of its death spiral. "It is a fact so familiar that we seldom remember how very strange it is," observed the British historian G. N. Clark, "that the commonest phrases we hear used about civilization at the present time all relate to the possibility, or even the prospect, of its being destroyed."

That same year, George Scott's second daughter, June, was born. It is most unlikely that anyone thought my mother was a lucky baby.

The Second World War began in September 1939. By the time it ended in 1945, at least forty million people were dead, the Holocaust had demonstrated that humanity was capable of any crime, much of the industrialized world had been pounded into rubble, and a weapon vastly more destructive than anything seen before had been invented. "In our recent history, war has been following war in ascending order of intensity," wrote the influential British historian Arnold Toynbee in 1950. "And today it is already apparent that the War of 1939–45 was not the climax of this crescendo movement." Ambassador Joseph Grew, a senior American foreign service officer, declared in 1945 that "a future war with the Soviet Union is as sure as anything in this world." Albert Einstein was terrified. "Only the creation of a world government can prevent the impending self-destruction of mankind," declared the man whose name was synonymous with genius. Some were less optimistic. "The end of everything we call life is close at hand and cannot be evaded," moaned H. G. Wells.

Happily for humanity, Wells, Einstein, and the many other luminaries who made dire predictions in an era W. H. Auden dubbed "the Age of Anxiety" were all wrong. The end of life was not at hand. War did not come. Civilization did not crumble. Against all reasonable expectation, my mother turned out to be a very lucky baby indeed.

Led by the United States, Western economies surged in the postwar decades. The standard of living soared. Optimism returned, and people expressed their hope for a brighter future by getting married earlier and having children in unprecedented numbers. The result was a combination boom—economic and baby—that put children born during the Depression at the leading edge of a wealth-and-population wave. That's the ultimate demographic sweet spot. Coming of age in the 1950s, they entered a dream job market. To be hired at a university in the early 1960s, a professor once recalled to me, you had to sign your name three times "and spell it right twice." Something of an exaggeration, to be sure. But the point is very real. Despite the constant threat of nuclear war, and lesser problems that came and went, children born in the depths of the Great Depression—one of the darkest periods of the last five centuries—lived their adult lives amid peace and steadily growing prosperity. There has never been a more fortunate generation.

Who predicted that? Nobody. Which is entirely understandable. Even someone who could have foreseen that there would not be a Third World War—which would have been a triumph of prognostication in its own right—would have had to correctly forecast both the baby boom and the marvelous performance of postwar economies. And how would they have done that? The baby boom was caused by a postwar surge in fertility rates that sharply reversed a downward trend that had been in place for more than half a century. Demographers didn't see it coming. No one did. Similarly, the dynamism of the postwar economies was a sharp break from previous trends that was not forecast by experts, whose expectations were much more pessimistic. Many leading economists even worried that demobilization would be followed by mass unemployment and stagnation. One surprise after another. That's how the years unfolded after 1945. The result was a future that was as unpredictable as it was delightful—and a generation born at what seemed to be the worst possible time came to be a generation born at the most golden of moments.

The desire to know the future is universal and constant, as the profusion of soothsaying techniques in human cultures—from goats' entrails to tea leaves—demonstrates so well. But certain events can sharpen that desire, making it fierce and urgent. Bringing a child into the world is one such force. What will the world be like for my baby? My great-grandfather undoubtedly asked himself that question when his little boy was born in 1906. He was a well-read person, and so he likely paid close attention to what the experts said. George Edward Scott was a very lucky baby, he would have concluded. And any intelligent, informed person would have agreed. Thirty-one years later, when my grandfather held his infant daughter in his arms, he surely asked himself the same question, and he, too, would have paid close attention to what the experts said. And he would have feared for her future, as any intelligent, informed person would have.

My great-grandfather was wrong. My grandfather was wrong. All those intelligent, informed people were wrong. But mostly, the experts were wrong.

They're wrong a lot, those experts. History is littered with their failed predictions. Whole books can be filled with them. Many have been.

Some failed predictions are prophecies of disaster and despair. In the 1968 book *The Population Bomb,* which sold millions of copies, Stanford University biologist Paul Ehrlich declared "the battle to feed all of humanity is over. In the 1970s, the world will undergo famines— hundreds of millions of people will starve to death in spite of any crash programs embarked upon now." But there weren't mass famines in the 1970s. Or in the 1980s. Thanks to the dramatic improvements in agriculture collectively known as "the Green Revolution"—which were well under way by the time Ehrlich wrote his book—food production not only kept up with population growth, it greatly surpassed it. Ehrlich thought that was utterly impossible. But it happened. Between 1961 and 2000, the world's population doubled but the calories of food consumed per person increased 24 percent. In India, calories per person rose 20 percent. In Italy, 26 percent. In South Korea, 44 percent. Indonesia, 69 percent. China had experienced a famine that killed some thirty million people in the dark years between 1959 and 1961, but in the forty years after that horror, China's per capita food consumption rose an astonishing 73 percent. And the United States? In the decades after *The Population Bomb* was published, fears that people would not get enough to eat were forgotten as American waistlines steadily expanded. The already-substantial consumption of the average American rose 32 percent, and the United States became the first nation in history to struggle with an epidemic of obesity.

In 1977, President Jimmy Carter called for the "moral equivalent of war" to shift the American economy off oil because, he said, the production of oil would soon fail to keep up with demand. When that happened, oil prices would soar and never come down again—the American economy would be devastated and the American dream would turn brown and die like an unwatered suburban lawn. Eight years later, oil prices fell through the floor. They stayed low for two decades.

A small library could be filled with books predicting stock market crashes and economic disasters that never happened, but the giant of the genre was published in 1987. The hardcover edition of economist Ravi Batra's *The Great Depression of 1990* hit the top spot on *The New York Times* best-seller list and spent a total of ten months on the chart; the paperback stayed on the list for an astonishing nineteen months. When the American economy slipped into recession in 1990, Batra looked prophetic. When the recession proved to be mild and brief, he seemed less so. When the 1990s roared, he looked foolish, particularly when he spent the entire decade writing books predicting a depression was imminent.

In 1990, Jacques Attali—intellectual, banker, former adviser to French president François Mitterrand—published a book called *Millennium,* which predicted dramatic change on the other side of the year 2000. Both the United States and the Soviet Union would slowly lose their superpower status, Attali wrote. Their replacements would be Japan and Europe. As for China and India, they "will refuse to fall under the sway of either the Pacific or the European sphere," but it would be hard for these desperately poor countries to resist. Catastrophic war was "possible, even probable." However, Attali cautioned, this future isn't quite chiseled in stone. "If a miracle were to occur" and China and India were to be "integrated into the global economy and market, all strategic assumptions underpinning my prognostications would be overturned. That miracle is most unlikely." Of course, that "miracle" is precisely what happened. And almost nothing Attali predicted came true.

Even economists who win Nobel Prizes have been known to blow big calls. In 1997, as Asian economies struggled with a major currency crisis, Paul Krugman—*New York Times* columnist and winner of the Nobel Prize in 2008—worried that Asia must act quickly. If not, he wrote in *Fortune* magazine, "we could be looking at a true Depression scenario—the kind of slump that sixty years ago devastated societies, destabilized governments, and eventually led to war." Krugman's prescription? Currency controls. It had to be done or else. But mostly, it wasn't done. And Asia was booming again within two years.

Pessimists have no monopoly on forecasting flops, however. Excited predictions of the amazing technologies to come—Driverless cars! Robot maids! Jet packs!—have been dazzling the public since the late nineteenth century. These old forecasts continue to entertain today, though for quite different reasons. And for every bear prophesying blood in the stock markets, there is a bull who is sure things will only get better. The American economist Irving Fisher was one. "Stock prices have reached what looks like a permanently high plateau," the esteemed economist assured nervous investors. "I do not feel there will soon be, if ever, a fifty- or sixty-point break from present levels, such as they have predicted. I expect to see the stock market a good deal higher within a few months." That was October 17, 1929. The market crashed the following week. But that crash was none of Britain's concern, the legendary John Maynard Keynes believed. "There will be no serious consequences in London resulting from the Wall Street Slump," Keynes wrote. "We find the look ahead decidedly encouraging." Shortly afterward, Britain sank with the rest of the world into the Great Depression.

Another bull market, this one in the late 1990s, produced a bookshelf full of predictions so giddy they made Irving Fisher sound like Eeyore. The most famous was the 1999 book *Dow 36,000* by James Glassman and Kevin Hassett. "If you are worried about missing the market's big move upward, you will discover that it's not too late," Glassman and Hassett wrote. Actually, it was too late. Shortly after *Dow 36,000* was published, the Dow peaked at less than 12,000 and started a long, painful descent.

Paul Ehrlich can also take consolation in the fact that many of the optimists who assailed his writing were not much better at predicting the future. "The doomsayers who worry about the prospect of starvation for a burgeoning world population" will not see their terrible visions realized, *Time* magazine reported in 1966. The reason? Aquaculture. "RAND experts visualize fish herded and raised in offshore pens as cattle are today. Huge fields of kelp and other kinds of seaweed will be tended by undersea 'farmers'—frogmen who will live for months at a time in submerged bunkhouses. The protein-rich underseas crop will probably be ground up to produce a dull-tasting cereal that eventually, however, could be regenerated chemically to taste like anything from steak to bourbon." The same RAND Corporation experts agreed that "a permanent lunar base will have been established long before A.D. 2000 and that men will have flown past Venus and landed on Mars." Herman Kahn, a founder of the Hudson Institute and a determined critic of Ehrlich, was similarly off the mark in a thick book called *The Year 2000,* published in 1967. It is "very likely," Kahn wrote, that by the end of the century, nuclear explosives would be used for excavation and mining, "artificial moons" would be used to illuminate large areas at night, and there would be permanent undersea colonies. Kahn also expected that one of the world's fastest-growing economies at the turn of the millennium would be that of the Soviet Union.

So pessimists and optimists both make predictions that look bad in hindsight. What about left versus right? Not much difference there either. There are plenty of examples of liberal experts making predictions that go awry, like Jonathan Schell's belief that Ronald Reagan's arms buildup was putting the world on course for nuclear war. "We have to admit that unless we rid ourselves of our nuclear arsenals a holocaust not only *might* occur but *will* occur—if not today, then tomorrow; if not this year, then the next," Schell wrote in 1982. "One day—and it is hard to believe it will not be soon—we will make a choice. Either we will sink into the final coma and end it all or, as I trust and believe, we will awaken to the truth of our peril . . . and rise up to cleanse the earth of nuclear weapons." The stock of failed predictions on the right is equally rich. It was, for example, a "slam dunk" that Saddam Hussein's weapons of mass destruction would be discovered following the American invasion of Iraq in 2003 and that, as Vice President Dick Cheney said, American soldiers would be "greeted as liberators" by the grateful Iraqi people. "A year from now," observed neoconservative luminary Richard Perle in September 2003, "I'll be very surprised if there is not some grand square in Baghdad named after President Bush."

So the inaccuracy of expert predictions isn't limited to pessimists or optimists, liberals or conservatives. It's also not about a few deluded individuals. Over and over in the history of predictions, it's not *one* expert who tries and fails to predict the future. It's whole *legions* of experts.

Paul Ehrlich's bleak vision in *The Population Bomb* was anything but that of a lone crank. Countless experts made similar forecasts in the 1950s and 1960s. In 1967, the year before Ehrlich's book appeared, William and Paul Paddock—one an agronomist, the other a foreign service officer—published a book whose title said it all: *Famine 1975!* When biologist James Bonner reviewed the Paddocks' book in the journal *Science,* he emphasized that "all serious students of the plight of the underdeveloped nations agree that famine among the peoples of the underdeveloped nations is inevitable." The only question was when. "The U.S. Department of Agriculture, for example, sees 1985 as the beginning of the years of hunger. I have guessed publicly that the interval 1977–1985 will bring the moment of truth, will bring a dividing point at which the human race will split into the rich and the poor, the well-fed and the hungry—two cultures, the affluent and the miserable, one of which must inevitably exterminate the other. . . . I stress again that all responsible investigators agree that the tragedy will occur."

There was also an expert consensus in support of Jimmy Carter's prediction of perpetually rising oil prices. And Jacques Attali's belief that Japan and Europe would eclipse the United States and dominate the world economy in the twenty-first century was standard stuff among strategic thinkers. As for Jonathan Schell's fear that Ronald Reagan's policies would plunge the world into a nuclear inferno, it dominated university faculties and brought millions of protestors to the streets. And, as easy as it is to forget now, support for the invasion of Iraq was widespread among foreign policy analysts and politicians, most of whom were confident weapons of mass destruction would be uncovered and American forces greeted as liberators.

We are awash in predictions. In newspapers, blogs, and books, on radio and television, every day, without fail, experts tell us how the economy will perform next year or whether a foreign conflict will flare into war. They tell us who will win the next election, and whether the price of oil will rise or fall, housing sales will grow or shrink, stock markets will soar or dive. Occasionally, the experts lift their eyes to more distant horizons. I recently read a cover story in *Time* magazine that claimed the first ten years of the twenty-first century were "the decade from hell" and went on to explain "why the next one will be better." But what made the "decade from hell" what it was? Events that confounded the expectations of most experts. The 9/11 terrorist attacks. The debacle in Iraq. Hurricane Katrina. The financial crisis of 2008 and the global recession. If the previous decade was shaped by uncertainty and surprise—and no one can seriously argue it was not—why would we expect the next ten years to be so much more predictable? But simple questions like that are

seldom asked. Instead, the predictions are churned out, one after another, like widgets on an assembly line. I recently read a description of
the Chinese economy in 2040. And American suburbs in 2050. And
now I'm reading an article that explains "why Europe will outshine
North America in the twenty-first century." There are apparently no
limits to the vision of these wise men and women. Experts peer into the
distant future and warn of great wars and conflicts. They tell us what's
in store for the climate, globalization, food, energy, and technology.
They tell us all about the world of our children and our grandchildren.
And we listen.

Economists, in particular, are treated with the reverence the ancient
Greeks gave the Oracle of Delphi. But unlike the notoriously vague pronouncements that once issued from Delphi, economists' predictions are
concrete and precise. Their accuracy can be checked. And anyone who
does that will quickly conclude that economists make lousy soothsayers:
"The record of failure to predict recessions is virtually unblemished,"
wrote IMF economist Prakash Loungani in one of many papers demonstrating the near-universal truth that economists' predictions are least
accurate when they are most needed. Not even the most esteemed economists can claim significant predictive success. Retired banker and
financial writer Charles Morris examined a decade's worth of forecasts
issued by the brilliant minds who staff the White House's Council of
Economic Advisors. Morris started with the 1997 forecast. There would
be modest growth, the council declared; at the end of the year, the
American economy had grown at a rate more than double the council's forecast. In 1998, the story was much the same. And in 1999. In
2000, the council "sharply raised both their near- and medium-term
outlooks—just in time for the dot-com bust and the 2001–2002 recession." The record for the Bush years was "no better," Morris writes. But
it was the forecast for 2008 that really amazes: "The 2008 report expected slower but positive growth in the first half of the year, as investment
shifted away from housing, but foresaw a nice recovery in the second
half, and a decent year overall. Their outlook for 2009 and 2010 was for

a solid three percent real growth with low inflation and good employ-ment numbers," Morris writes. "In other words, they hadn't a clue."

And they weren't alone. With very few exceptions, economists did not foresee the financial and economic meltdown of 2008. Many econo-mists didn't recognize the crisis for what it was *even as it was unfolding.* In December 2007—months after the credit crunch began and the very moment that would officially mark the beginning of the recession in the United States—*BusinessWeek* magazine ran its annual chart of detailed forecasts for the year ahead from leading American analysts. Under the headline "A Slower but Steady Economy," every one of fifty-four econo-mists predicted the U.S. economy wouldn't "sink into a recession" in 2008. The experts were unanimous that unemployment wouldn't be too bad, either, leading to the consensus conclusion that 2008 would be a solid but unspectacular year. One horrible year later—as people watch-ing the evening news experienced the white-knuckle fear of passengers in a plunging jet—*BusinessWeek* turned to the economists who had so spectacularly blown that year's forecast and asked them to tell its readers what would happen in 2009. There was no mention of the previous year's fiasco, only another chart filled with reassuringly precise numbers. The headline: "A Slower but Steady Economy."

By definition, experts know much about their field of expertise. Econ-omists can—usually—look around and tell us a great deal about the economy, political scientists can do the same for politics and govern-ment, ecologists for the environment, and so on. But the future? All too often, their crystal balls work no better than those of fortune-tellers. And since rational people don't take seriously the prognostications of Mysterious Madam Zelda or any psychic, palm reader, astrologer, or preacher who claims to know what lies ahead, they should be skeptical of expert predictions. And yet we are not skeptical. No matter how often expert predictions fail, we want more. This strange phenomenon led Scott Armstrong, an expert on forecasting at the Wharton School of the University of Pennsylvania, to coin his "seer-sucker" theory: "No matter how much evidence exists that seers do not exist, suckers will pay for the existence of seers." Sometimes we even go back to the very people whose predictions failed in the past and listen, rapt, as they tell us how the future will unfold.

This book explains why expert predictions fail and why we believe them anyway.

The first part of the answer lies in the nature of reality and the human brain. The world is complicated—too complicated to be predicted. And while the human brain may be magnificent, it is not perfect, thanks to a jumble of cognitive wiring that makes systematic mistakes. Try to predict an unpredictable world using an error-prone brain and you get the gaffes that litter history.

As for why we believe expert predictions, the answer lies ultimately in our hardwired aversion to uncertainty. People want to know what's happening now and what will happen in the future, and admitting we don't know can be profoundly disturbing. So we try to eliminate uncertainty however we can. We see patterns where there are none. We treat random results as if they are meaningful. And we treasure stories that replace the complexity and uncertainty of reality with simple narratives about what's happening and what will happen. Sometimes we create these stories ourselves, but, even with the human mind's bountiful capacity for self-delusion, it can be hard to fool ourselves into thinking we know what the future holds for the stock market, the climate, the price of oil, or a thousand other pressing issues. So we look to experts. They must know. They have Ph.D.'s, prizes, and offices in major universities. And thanks to the news media's preference for the simple and dramatic, the sort of expert we are likely to hear from is confident and conclusive. They *know* what will happen; they are *certain* of it. We like that because that is how we want to feel. And so we convince ourselves that these wise men and women can do what wise men and women have never been able to do before. Fundamentally, we believe because we want to believe.

We need to see this trap for what it is, especially at this moment. Over the last several years, we have experienced soaring prices for commodities, food shortages, talk of an "age of scarcity," the bursting of a real estate bubble that ruined millions of middle-class homeowners, growing evidence of environmental catastrophe, a financial crisis that upset conventional economic wisdom, and a global economic recession the like of which has not been seen since the Second World War. Uncertainty? The air is electric with it. It's precisely in times such as these that the desire to know what the future holds becomes a ravenous hunger. We've seen it happen before. The 1970s may be remembered as the era of disco and bad fashion, but it was, in reality, a tumultuous and unsettling time that created an enormous demand to know what lay ahead. The result was a profusion of detailed and compelling expert predictions, many of them involving the very same issues—oil, food, terrorism, recession, unemployment, deficits and debt, inflation, environmental crisis, the decline of the United States—we are grappling with today. Most of them turned out to be wrong, some hilariously so. That doesn't prove that similar predictions in the present will also fall flat, but it does provide a valuable reminder to be skeptical when experts claim to know what lies in our future.

That sort of skepticism doesn't come easily, but it is possible. As natural as it is to want to hear predictions, and to believe them, we do not have to. With effort, we can learn to accept reality when we do not, and cannot, know what lies ahead.

Of course, that still leaves us with a big problem because, in our lives and businesses, we all have to make plans and forecasts. If the future is unpredictable, doesn't that mean all our planning and forecasting is pointless? Not if we go about it the right way. Certain styles of thinking and decision making do a far better job of groping amid the inky blackness of the future to find a path ahead. These styles can be learned and applied, with results that are positive, although far from perfect. And that leads to the ultimate conclusion, which is one we do not want to accept but must: There are no crystal balls, and no style of thinking, no technique, no model will ever eliminate uncertainty. The future will forever be shrouded in darkness. Only if we accept and embrace this fundamental fact can we hope to be prepared for the inevitable surprises that lie ahead.

ARE EXPERTS REALLY SO BAD?

But now I have to pause and make an admission: My whole argument is based on the belief that expert predictions have a lousy track record. But I haven't actually proved that, at least not yet.

So far, I've presented a number of expert predictions that failed. Or rather, I've presented a number of expert predictions that I think failed. But not everyone would agree. Many people insist even today that Paul Ehrlich was essentially on the mark in *The Population Bomb*. One of those people is Paul Ehrlich. In a 2009 essay, Ehrlich acknowledged that the book "underestimated the impact of the Green Revolution" and so the starvation he expected wasn't as bad as he predicted. But the book's grim vision was basically accurate, he insisted. In fact, its "most serious flaw" was that it was "much too optimistic about the future."

I'll take a closer look at Ehrlich's defense of *The Population Bomb* later. What matters here is that the failure of Ehrlich's prediction is disputed, and untangling that dispute is complicated. That's typical because expert predictions are common and so are failed predictions. But experts who agree that their predictions failed are rare. As Paul Ehrlich did, they will often concede that they were off on some details here and there. But flat-out wrong? No. Never. Unless pinned down by circumstances as firmly as a butterfly in a display case, they will resolutely deny being wrong.

"I was *almost* right" is a standard dodge. Another is "It would have happened if I hadn't been blindsided by an unforeseeable event." And then there is the claim that the prediction was a "self-negating prophecy," that it caused others to act and it was those actions that prevented the predicted event from happening. Remember Y2K? The more excitable experts claimed the world's computers would crash on January 1, 2000, and take civilization with them. When nothing remotely like that happened, the doomsters boasted that their predictions had prompted massive remediation efforts that had saved humanity from certain doom: You're welcome.

Another mental maneuver is the wait-and-see twist. Many predictions have only vague time frames and so, when an observer thinks a forecast has failed, the expert can insist time isn't up yet: Wait and see. A variation on this is the off-on-timing gambit, which is used when a prediction comes with a clear time frame and the prediction clearly fails within the allotted time: The expert grudgingly concedes that the predicted event hasn't happened within the time frame but insists that's a minor detail. What matters is that the prediction *will* come to pass. Eventually. Someday. Paul Ehrlich, for example, acknowledges that the famines he predicted for the 1970s didn't happen, at least not to the extent he expected, but he insists that his analysis was sound and the disasters he foresaw are still coming. "The probability of a vast catastrophe looms steadily larger," he wrote in 2009, forty-one years after *The Population Bomb* warned of imminent peril. Similarly, when a journalist reminded Richard Perle in 2008 that five years earlier he had predicted a grand square in Baghdad would be named after George W. Bush within one year, Perle didn't respond with a forthright admission of error. Instead, he insisted Bush could still get his Baghdad square. It would just take a little longer than anticipated.

A third defense involves carefully parsing the language of the forecast so that a statement that was intended to be a rock-solid prediction that Event X would happen—and is taken that way by the media and the public—is shown to be much more elastic. "I didn't actually say Event X would *certainly* happen," the expert explains. "I said 'It *could* happen.'" And implicit in the phrase *could happen* is the possibility that the predicted event may *not* happen. Thus, the fact that the event did not happen does not mean the prediction was "wrong." This line of reasoning is often heard from liberal experts who claimed, in the early 1980s, that Ronald Reagan's policies put the world in danger. Very few said nuclear war was "inevitable." They only said Reagan's belligerence made war *more likely*. Does the fact that there was no war prove they were wrong? Not at all, they say. It's like a weather forecaster who says there is a 70 percent chance of rain. He can't be blamed if the sun shines because an implicit part of his forecast was "30 percent chance of sunshine." People should just be glad they got lucky.

Obviously, I'm being a little sarcastic here, because these arguments are often weak and self-serving. But not always. Sometimes there is real substance in them and they have to be taken seriously. Predictions about the damage a widening hole in the ozone layer would do, for example, did cause governments to make policy changes that would ensure the predictions did not come true: That's a genuine "self-negating prophecy." It is also undeniably true to say, as Paul Ehrlich does, that the failure of population growth to cause famines in the 1970s does not prove population growth will not cause famines sometime in the future. And the fact that there was no nuclear war in the 1980s really does not prove that Ronald Reagan's policies did not raise the risk of war.

Put all this together and it means there are substantial question marks over many of the failed predictions I presented. Did they really fail? I think so. But reasonable people can and do disagree. Sorting out who's right isn't easy. Different observers will come to different conclusions. In some cases, the truth may never be known.

And there's an even bigger objection that can be raised to my claim about the fallibility of expert predictions: Even if we accept that my examples of failed predictions really are failed predictions, they don't actually prove that expert predictions routinely fail. They only prove that *some* expert predictions have failed. Even if I were to stuff whole chapters with examples, all I would prove is that *many* expert predictions have failed. What would be missing is what's needed to prove my point: the *rate* of failure. If, say, ninety-nine out of one hundred predictions fail, we would probably be better off consulting fortune cookies. But if one in one hundred fails, expert predictions really should be treated with hushed reverence.

So how do we figure out the rate of failure? The first thing we would have to do is expand our inquiry beyond the misses to the hits. And there are hits. Here's one: In 1981, energy expert Amory Lovins predicted that sometime between 1995 and 2005 the world would see "the effective collapse of the Soviet Union from internal political stress." That's pretty impressive, and there are plenty of others like it in the pages of books, magazines, and journals.

But still I wouldn't be able to prove much. What's the total number of experts I would be examining? What's the total number of predictions they made? Over what period? Simply adding the hits and misses I collected wouldn't tell me any of that, and so I *still* wouldn't know the rate at which predictions fail.

And if that's not complicated enough, there's another frustrating problem to contend with: Imagine someone who throws a dart and—smack!—he hits the bull's-eye. Does that prove he is a great dart thrower? Maybe. But there's no way to be sure based on that one dart. If he throws a second, third, and fourth dart and they all hit the bull's-eye, it's increasingly reasonable to think we are witnessing skill, not luck. But what if he throws dozens more darts and not one hits the bull's-eye? What if he often misses the board entirely? What if this person leaves darts scattered around the room, even a few stuck in the ceiling? In that case, his bull's-eye is probably a fluke. Amory Lovins's amazing prediction about the Soviet Union is a case in point. It was only one of dozens of predictions Lovins made in the same forecast, and almost all the others completely missed the board. (By the end of the 1980s, Lovins predicted, nuclear power programs would "persist only in dictatorships," oil and gas would be scarce and fantastically expensive, unemployment would be high and persistent, the unreliability of food supplies in American cities would give rise to "urban farming and forestry" . . . and so on.) Once you know that, you know it probably wasn't keen geopolitical insight that produced Lovins's bull's-eye. It was luck.

By now, I suspect, your head is swimming. That's the point, I'm afraid. Figuring out how good experts are at predicting the future seems like a simple task, but if we take logic and evidence seriously, it's actually very difficult.

The media have occasionally taken a stab at sorting this out. In 1984, *The Economist* asked sixteen people to make ten-year forecasts of economic growth rates, inflation rates, exchange rates, oil prices, and other staples of economic prognostication. Four of the test subjects were former finance ministers, four were chairmen of multinational companies, four were economics students at Oxford University, and four were, to use the English vernacular, London dustmen. A decade later, *The Economist* reviewed the forecasts and discovered they were, on average, awful. But some were more awful than others: The dustmen tied the corporate chairmen for first place, while the finance ministers came last. Many other publications have conducted similar exercises over the years, with similarly humiliating results. The now-defunct magazine *Brill's Content,* for one, compared the predictions of famous American pundits with a chimpanzee named Chippy, who made his guesses by choosing among flash cards. Chippy consistently matched or beat the best in the business.

As suggestive and entertaining as these stunts are, they are not, to say the least, scientifically rigorous. Rising to that level requires much more: It requires an experiment that is elaborate, expensive, and exhausting.

THE EXPERIMENT

The first thing the experiment needs is a very large group of experts. The group should be as diverse as possible, with experts from different fields, different political leanings, different institutional affiliations, and different backgrounds. At the very beginning of the experiment, the experts should answer a battery of questions designed to test political orientation, worldview, personality, and thinking style.

The experts must be asked clear questions whose answers can later be shown to be indisputably true or false. That means vague pronouncements about "weakening state authority" or "growing public optimism" won't do. Even a question like "Will relations between India and Pakistan be increasingly strained?"—which is the standard language of TV pundits—isn't good enough. Questions have to be so precise that no reasonable person would argue about what actually happened—which means asking questions like "Will the official unemployment rate be higher, lower, or the same a year from now?" and "Will India and Pakistan go to war within the next five years?"

For each prediction, experts must state how likely they think it is to actually happen. If they are dead certain something will happen, that is a 100 percent probability. If they are sure it won't happen, it's a 0 percent probability. In between these extremes, experts will be required to attach precise percentages to guesses rather than use vague terms like *improbable* or *very likely.* There's no room for fudging when someone says, "There is a 30 percent chance India and Pakistan will go to war within the next five years."

The experiment must obtain a very large number of predictions from each expert in order to allow statistical analysis that can expose lucky hits for what they are. It also allows us to get past the problem of judging predictions in which the expert says the chance of something happening is, for example, "70 percent." If the expert is perfectly accurate, then a broad survey of his predictions will show that in 70 percent of the cases in which he said there was a 70 percent chance of something happening, it actually happened. Similarly, 60 percent of the outcomes said to have a 60 percent chance of happening should have happened. This measure of accuracy is called "calibration."

But there's more to the story than calibration. After all, someone who sat on the fence with every prediction—"Will it happen? I think the odds are 50/50"—would likely wind up with a modestly good calibration score. We can get predictions like that from a flipped coin. What we want in a forecaster, ideally, is someone with a godlike ability to predict the future. The gods don't bother with middling probabilities and they certainly don't say, "The odds are 50/50." The gods say, "This will certainly happen" or "This is impossible." So there must be a second measure of accuracy to go along with calibration. Experts should be scored by confidence. This means that an expert who said there is a 100 percent chance of something happening that actually did happen would score more points than another expert who had said there was only a 70 percent chance of it happening. This measure is called "discrimination."

A third measure must also be generated by answering the same questions that are put to the experts using a variety of simple and arbitrary rules. For example, there is the "no change" rule: No matter what the question is, always predict there will be no change. These results will create benchmarks against which the experts' results can be compared.

And finally, the experiment must continue over the course of many years. That will allow for questions involving time frames ranging from the short term—one to two years—to longer-term predictions covering five, ten, even twenty years, ensuring that the experiment will require experts to make predictions in times of stability and surprise, prosperity and recession, peace and war. When the passage of time has revealed the correct answers, they should show how well the experts did. And be given the opportunity to explain the results.

It's difficult to exaggerate how demanding this experiment would be. It would be expensive and complicated and would require the patience of Job. But most of all, it would require a skilled and devoted researcher prepared to give a big chunk of his life to answering one question: How accurate are expert predictions?

Fortunately, there is such a researcher. He is Philip Tetlock.

Today, Tetlock is a much-honored psychologist at the University of California's Haas School of Business. In 1984, he was a newly tenured academic who had just been appointed to a new committee of the National Research Council, a branch of the National Academy of Sciences, arguably the most prestigious scientific body in the world. The committee's remit was nothing less than figuring out how social scientists could help avoid nuclear war and the end of civilization.

"It's hard to re-create the tenor of the times," Tetlock recalls, "but there was a lot of uneasiness." It was the height of the "second" Cold War. The Reagan White House was stockpiling nuclear weapons, the Red Army was fighting CIA-backed guerrillas in Afghanistan, and the death of Leonid Brezhnev had put the Soviet regime into transition, though to what no one could be sure. Watching television in living rooms across the United States, Americans were shocked when the evening news reported a Soviet fighter jet had shot down a Korean Airlines passenger jet that had strayed into Soviet airspace; then they were terrified by a made-for-TV drama, *The Day After,* about the ash and tears of life following a nuclear exchange.

At this perilous moment, the committee brought together an array of renowned social scientists, along with one junior professor from the University of California. "I mostly sat at the table and listened very quietly to the arguments going back and forth," Tetlock says. "The liberals and conservatives in particular had very different assessments of the Soviet Union. The conservative view as of 1984 was not that they could bring the Soviet Union down, but that they could effectively contain and deter it. Whereas the liberal view of the Soviet Union was that the conservatives [in the White House] were increasing the influence of the hard-liners in the Kremlin and that they were going to trigger a neo-Stalinist retrenchment." Tetlock started tracking down and interviewing respected experts—in universities, governments, think tanks, and the media—about the current situation and where it was headed. With a good sense of the prevailing expert opinions, he waited to see what the future would bring.

He didn't have to wait long. In March 1985, Mikhail Gorbachev took control of the Soviet Union and dramatic liberalization followed. Neither liberals nor conservatives had expected that. But neither side took the surprise as evidence that their understanding of the situation was flawed or incomplete. Instead, they saw it as proof they had been right all along. "The conservatives argued that we forced the Soviets' hand, that we compelled these dramatic concessions in the late eighties," Tetlock says. "Whereas the liberal view is that the Soviet elite had learned from the failings of the economy [and that] if anything, Reagan had slowed down that process of learning and change."

It was hard to avoid the suspicion that what did or did not happen was almost irrelevant. The experts had their stories and they were sticking to them. "Each side was very well prepared to explain whatever happened," Tetlock says. "I found that puzzling and intriguing and worth pursuing."

And so Tetlock designed, prepared, and launched the massive experiment described above.

Scouring his multidisciplinary networks, Tetlock recruited 284 experts—political scientists, economists, and journalists—whose jobs involve commenting or giving advice on political or economic trends. All were guaranteed anonymity because Tetlock didn't want anyone feeling pressure to conform or worrying about what their predictions would do to their reputations. With names unknown, all were free to judge as best they could.

Then the predictions began. Over many years, Tetlock and his team peppered the experts with questions. In all, they collected an astonishing 27,450 judgments about the future. It was by far the biggest exercise of its kind ever, and the results were startlingly clear.

On "calibration," the experts would have been better off making random guesses. Tetlock puts it a little more acidly: The experts would have been beaten by "a dart-throwing chimpanzee," he says. On "discrimination," however, the experts did a little better. They were still terrible, but not quite so terrible. When the scores for "calibration" and "discrimination" were combined, the experts beat the chimp by a whisker. Technically, at least. In practical terms, that whisker is irrelevant. The simple and disturbing truth is that the experts' predictions were no more accurate than random guesses.

Astrologers and psychics can make random guesses as well as Harvard professors, so it's hard not to look at these results and conclude that those who seek forecasts of the future would be well-advised to consult fortune cookies or the Mysterious Madam Zelda. They're cheaper. And you can eat a fortune cookie.

But that's not Philip Tetlock's conclusion. Serious skepticism about the ability of experts to predict the future is called for, he says. But just as important as the dismal collective showing of experts in his experiment is the wide variation among individual experts. "There's quite a range. Some experts are so out of touch with reality, they're borderline delusional. Other experts are only slightly out of touch. And a few experts are surprisingly nuanced and well-calibrated."

What distinguishes the impressive few from the borderline delusional is not whether they're liberal or conservative. Tetlock's data showed political beliefs made no difference to an expert's accuracy. The same was true of optimists and pessimists. It also made no difference if experts had a doctorate, extensive experience, or access to classified information. Nor did it make a difference if experts were political scientists, historians, journalists, or economists.

What made a big difference is *how* they think.

Experts who did particularly badly—meaning they would have improved their results if they had flipped a coin through the whole exercise—were not comfortable with complexity and uncertainty. They sought to "reduce the problem to some core theoretical theme," Tetlock says, and they used that theme over and over, like a template, to stamp out predictions. These experts were also more confident than others that their predictions were accurate. Why wouldn't they be? They were sure their One Big Idea was right and so the predictions they stamped out with that idea must be too.

Experts who did better than the average of the group—and better than random guessing—thought very differently. They had no template. Instead, they drew information and ideas from multiple sources and sought to synthesize it. They were self-critical, always questioning whether what they believed to be true really was. And when they were shown that they had made mistakes, they didn't try to minimize, hedge, or evade. They simply acknowledged they were wrong and adjusted their thinking accordingly. Most of all, these experts were comfortable seeing the world as complex and uncertain—so comfortable that they tended to doubt the ability of anyone to predict the future. That resulted in a paradox: The experts who were more accurate than others tended to be much less confident that they were right.

In a famous essay, the political philosopher Isaiah Berlin recalled a fragment of an ancient Greek poem. "The fox knows many things," the warrior-poet Archilochus wrote, "but the hedgehog knows one big thing." In Berlin's honor, Tetlock dubbed his experts "foxes" and "hedgehogs."

Foxes beat hedgehogs. Tetlock's data couldn't be more clear. On both calibration and discrimination, complex and cautious thinking trounced simple and confident. By cross-checking other factors in the data, Tetlock also found that hedgehogs who are ideologically extreme are worse forecasters than others of their kind. He even found that when hedgehogs made predictions involving their particular specialty, their accuracy *declined*. And it got worse still when the prediction was for the long term.

Put all that together and there's a very clear lesson: If you hear a hedgehog make a long-term prediction, it is almost certainly wrong. Treat it with great skepticism. That may seem like obscure advice, but take a look at the television panels, magazines, books, newspapers, and blogs where predictions flourish. The sort of expert typically found there is the sort who is confident, clear, and dramatic. The sort who delivers quality sound bites and compelling stories. The sort who doesn't bother with complications, caveats, and uncertainties. The sort who has One Big Idea. Yes, the sort of expert typically found in the media is precisely the sort of expert who is most likely to be wrong. This explains one of the most startling findings to emerge from Philip Tetlock's data: The bigger the media profile of an expert, the less accurate his predictions are.

Paul Ehrlich is a hedgehog. So are many of the other famous experts whose failed predictions I mentioned earlier. That's not a coincidence. "There is a serious problem with overconfidence in many experts," Tetlock concludes. "But with the proper interventions and proper encouragement, people can be induced to become more self-critical, thoughtful, and foxlike." And better able to see what's coming.

But only to a modest extent, I'm afraid. I wish it were otherwise, but reality is stubborn. As delightful as it would be to think we could train ourselves to predict the future with ease and accuracy, even the predictions of the wisest foxes in Tetlock's experiment were miles from perfect. In fact, predictions made by applying mindless rules such as "always predict no change" beat not only the hedgehogs in the experiment but the foxes as well. No matter how clever we are, no matter how sophisticated our thinking, the brain we use to make predictions is flawed and the world is fundamentally unpredictable.

In Dante Alighieri's vision of hell, fortune-tellers and diviners are condemned to spend eternity with their heads twisted backward, unable to see ahead, as they had tried to do in life. This seems a little harsh. We all want to see the future. It's human nature. But it is also within us to understand what we can and cannot do—and to know that although attempting to do what we cannot do may not be a mortal sin worthy of eternal damnation, it is folly.

2

The Unpredictable World

I can forecast confidently that it will vary.

—LORD JOHN BROWNE, FORMER CEO OF
BRITISH PETROLEUM, ON THE PRICE OF OIL

"Tonight, I want to have an unpleasant talk with you about a problem unprecedented in history. With the exception of preventing war, this is the greatest challenge our country will face during our lifetimes. The energy crisis has not yet overwhelmed us, but it will if we do not act quickly."

It was April 18, 1977. The man who intoned these grim words was Jimmy Carter, perhaps the only American president who would begin a speech by telling his audience it would be "unpleasant." And it *was* unpleasant. In shag-carpeted living rooms all across the United States, Americans learned that their country—indeed, all of civilization—was in peril. The coming years would be hard. They would demand sacrifice and struggle.

"The oil and gas we rely on for seventy-five percent of our energy are running out," Carter declared. "Unless profound changes are made to lower oil consumption, we now believe that in the early nineteen eighties, the world will be demanding more oil than it can produce." If demand outstripped supply, prices would soar, and since production would never again catch up with demand, prices would never come back down. And that was the *best* that could be hoped for. It was even possible that if world oil consumption continued to grow "by five percent a year, as it has in the past, we could use up all the proven reserves of oil in the entire world by the end of the next decade."

Nothing short of nuclear war could be more devastating to the United States. Cheap oil had fueled the great postwar boom of the 1950s and 1960s and the resulting prosperity that made the ordinary American the envy of the world. Cheap oil had created the vast new tracts of suburban housing, the interstate highway system, the freedom of ordinary people to get in an inexpensive, American-built car and drive to that far-off horizon. Cheap oil was the very breath and blood of the American way of life. The Arab oil embargo of 1973 had made this painfully clear, by inflicting shortages, rationing, and a deep economic recession. But that had been an artificial scarcity, and it was over. Most Americans had assumed that the end of the embargo meant the return of cheap oil and good times.

"I know that some of you may doubt that we face real energy shortages," Carter said. "The 1973 gasoline lines are gone, and our homes are warm again. But our energy problem is worse tonight than it was in 1973 or a few weeks ago in the dead of winter. It is worse because more waste has occurred, and more time has passed by without our planning for the future. And it will get worse every day until we act." Petroleum must cease to be the foundation of the American economy.

Conservation was the top priority. There must also be huge increases in solar energy and coal production. And "we must start now to develop the new, unconventional sources of energy we will rely on in the next century." It was a huge effort, Carter warned—the "moral equivalent of war." It would require sacrifices. But it had to be done. "The alternative may be national catastrophe."

To the extent that it is remembered at all today, Carter's speech is known for two things. First, in using the stirring phrase "the moral equivalent of war" (cribbed from a 1906 essay by William James), Carter handed his opponents one of the most unfortunate acronyms in the history of modern politics: MEOW. Second, the president's forecast was wrong. It didn't seem wrong in the first few years that followed. But it was. In fact, it was spectacularly wrong.

At the time of Jimmy Carter's "unpleasant" talk, the world price of crude oil was more than double what it had been in the 1950s and '60s. In the three years following, it remained high. Then, in 1979, the Iranian revolution slowed the flow of oil from the Persian Gulf and the price shot up 70 percent. Shortages and long queues at the pumps returned. In California, agitated motorists pulled guns on queue-jumpers. A pregnant woman was beaten. Civilization's foundations suddenly seemed frighteningly fragile. A low budget Australian movie called *Mad Max* carried the trend into the near future and became a surprise worldwide smash with its depiction of a world where oil has dried up, civilization has collapsed, and all that remains is to drive fast and kill. "The world was powered by the black fuel and the deserts sprouted great cities of pipe and steel," intones the narrator of *The Road Warrior*, the blockbuster 1981 sequel. "Gone now, swept away."

But the disruption caused by the Iranian revolution didn't last. Exploration spurred by the earlier surge in prices delivered new production and the price drifted down. Then, in November 1985, the price of crude fell off a cliff, dropping 70 percent in just a few months. Oil that cheap hadn't been seen since the happy days before the 1973 embargo. And it stayed cheap. It would be another twenty years before oil was again as expensive as it was on the day Jimmy Carter warned oil would soon run out.

The mistake was not Carter's, however. On that grim day in 1977, he was just repeating what his advisers told him. And they were just passing along the views of oil experts. "All available evidence points to a serious risk of a serious energy crisis in the middle or late 1980s," warned Ulf Lantzke, executive director of the International Energy Agency, in

1978. "Putting it simply, there is a very great likelihood of a major world-wide depression." Of course, the experts were aware that new sources—in Mexico, Alaska, and the North Sea—would start producing in the 1980s. But they were sure this would do little but postpone the day of reckoning. Some thought the squeeze would start in the early 1980s. Others thought it would be a little later in the decade. But almost none doubted the storm was coming, and soon. "Though variations were to be found among the forecasts," wrote Daniel Yergin in *The Prize,* the definitive history of oil, "there was considerable unanimity on the central themes, whether the source was the major oil companies, the CIA, Western governments, international agencies, distinguished independent experts, or OPEC itself."

By itself, the failure of the oil consensus of the 1970s is a magnificent demonstration of the fallibility of expert predictions. But it shouldn't be seen by itself, because it is actually only one item on a very long list whose first entry actually precedes the oil era. "Coal stands not beside but entirely above all other commodities," wrote William Stanley Jevons in 1865. "It is the material energy of the country—the universal aid—the factor in everything we do. With coal almost any feat is possible or easy; without it we are thrown back into the laborious poverty of early times." Jevons was the leading British economist of his era, and he saw trouble ahead for the British Empire because its wealth and power were fueled by rapid economic growth, in turn fueled by an abundance of cheap coal that could not last. Jevons examined other energy sources but he saw little hope there. Oil could not substitute for coal, he concluded.

But oil did substitute for coal, beginning in the late nineteenth century. And not long after came the first warnings that the new fuel would soon run out. "Within the next two to five years," warned the director of the United States Bureau of Mines, "the oil fields of this country will reach their maximum production, and from that time on we will face an ever-increasing decline." That was 1919. The director's prediction was all the more alarming because, at the time, the United States was by far the world's largest oil producer, and a decline in American production meant worldwide shortages.

He was wrong, of course. American oil production didn't peak for another half century. But the director reflected the prevailing view among informed observers. "The position of the United States in regard to oil can best be characterized as precarious," an official of the U.S. Geological Survey told *The New York Times* in 1920. The same year, another Geological Survey official warned that "within perhaps three years, our domestic production will begin to fall off with increasing rapidity, due to the exhausting of our reserves." When a retiring official wrote President Woodrow Wilson in 1919 to say that securing foreign oil supplies was the toughest problem faced by the United States, Wilson glumly replied he could see "no method by which we could assure ourselves of the necessary supply at home or abroad." There was talk of producing synthetic oil from wheat, and a senator even urged the U.S. Navy to immediately restore coal-fired engines in its ships lest the coming oil shortage render America's shores defenseless.

The end of the Second World War brought another scare. "Sufficient oil cannot be found in the United States," declared the chief of the State Department's Petroleum Division in 1947. Two years later, Secretary of the Interior Julius Krug warned the "end of the United States' oil supply is almost in sight." In 1967, the oil giant Shell came to the even gloomier conclusion that global oil production would peak in twenty-eight years. This forecast lent itself to a nifty slogan of "95 in '95": 95 million barrels a day at $95 a barrel in 1995.

As extraordinary as this record of failed pessimistic forecasts is, we should also remember that oil analysts have also erred on the side of optimism. In February 1970, President Richard Nixon's Task Force on Oil Imports reported that the United States would remain essentially self-sufficient in oil for at least another decade and the international price of oil would remain low. The report was barely out of the news when American oil imports started to climb. Three years later, oil prices rocketed up, and four years after that, the president of the United States was on television warning Americans that oil was running out and without drastic action the 1980s would be the era of Mad Max.

"Oil experts, economists, and government officials who have attempted in recent years to predict the future demand and prices of oil have had only marginally better success than those who foretell the advent of earthquakes or the second coming of the Messiah," wrote James Akins, a U.S. foreign service officer. Akins penned that acid assessment in 1973, but it could as easily be written today. In fact, simply by removing the phrase *in recent years,* it could be chiseled on the tombstone of almost every oil analyst since oil became an industrial commodity in the nineteenth century. In 2007, economists Ron Alquist and Lutz Kilian published a paper in which they examined all the sophisticated methods one could use to determine the price of oil one month, one quarter, or one year in the future. They looked at fancy econometric models. They looked at oil prices in futures and spot markets. They looked at the consensus opinion of oil analysts. And they found that anyone could do better than all these crystal balls, sometimes far better, by applying a mindless rule: Always predict that the price in the future will be whatever the price is now. True, this technique is far from accurate. In fact, it's pretty awful. But the others are worse.

This simple truth was brutally underscored during the Carter years, when all the smart people agreed with *New York Times* columnist Tom Wicker that the energy crisis was "real, growing, and a grave threat to modern civilization." Ordinary Americans didn't buy it. Poll after poll showed most Americans thought rising prices at the pumps were nothing more than a scam of the oil companies. There was no real shortage. Wait a little while, the whole thing will blow over, they thought, and oil will be as cheap as ever. This attitude drove the smart people crazy. "There should be no such thing as optimism about energy for the foreseeable future," *The New York Times* lectured in 1980, when prices were at their peak. "What is certain is that the price will go up and up, at home as well as abroad." Americans who thought otherwise simply didn't know the facts, the smart people believed. And for good reason. A *New York Times*/CBS poll taken in 1977 found that more than half of college-educated Americans believed there was an oil shortage, but only one-quarter of those with a high school education or less agreed. "Moreover," *The New York Times* reported, Americans "were surprisingly ignorant of some basic energy facts. Despite all the publicity over the past four years about rising oil imports, which currently account for almost half the country's total needs . . . only 48 percent knew the United States must import oil." For Jimmy Carter, it was all too frustrating. "The American people have absolutely refused to accept a simple fact. We have an energy crisis. We have shortages of oil. The shortages are going to get worse in future," the president complained in 1979.

Six years later, the world was awash in cheap oil. Experts were surprised. The ignorant masses were not. It's a funny old world.

Basic economics tells us that the price of oil is driven by supply and demand. Two factors. That's it. So why can't sophisticated analysts predict the price of oil? We can predict solar eclipses years, decades, even centuries in advance. We know where Jupiter will be in thirty-seven years, three months, and twelve days. We can determine precisely when tomorrow's tide will peak in the Bay of Fundy, the Firth of Forth, and the southeast coast of Madagascar. So why can't experts put supply and demand together and come up with accurate predictions about the price of oil?

ABOUT THAT FUNNY OLD WORLD

It was Sir Isaac Newton who gave scientists the power to predict heavenly events. His great work, *Mathematical Principles of Natural Philosophy*, better known as the *Principia*, specified laws of motion that allowed the movements of the planets to be described with mathematical equations—and predicted with startling precision.

This thunderous development shaped scientific thinking for centuries. If even the heavens could be studied, understood, and predicted, surely lesser matters—earthly matters—could be as well. The only barrier was ignorance. Thus, as science advanced, our ability to predict would advance along with it. "If man can predict, almost with certainty, those appearances of which he understands the laws; if, even when the laws are unknown to him, experience of the past enables him to foresee, with considerable probability, future appearances, why should we suppose it a chimerical undertaking to delineate with some degree of truth, the picture of the future destiny of mankind from the results of history?" wrote the eighteenth-century philosopher marquis de Condorcet with the confidence and optimism typical of Enlightenment thinkers. But bold as de Condorcet was, he did not draw the ultimate conclusion of this sort of thinking. It was Pierre-Simon Laplace, "the Newton of France," who provided that, in 1814. "The present state of nature is evidently a consequence of what it was in the preceding moment," he wrote, "and if we conceive of an intelligence which at any given instant comprehends all the relations of the entities in this universe, it could state the respective position, motions, and general affects of all these entities at any time in the past or future." The universe is like a clock. A very complicated clock, of course. But still, a clock. If we identified and understood every piece of machinery in the clock, and if we knew precisely where each piece was at a particular moment, we could then calculate everything that happened in the past and everything that would happen in the future.

More than three centuries have passed since Newton published the *Principia,* and we have indeed learned a great deal and can predict much that we once could not, but the smooth equation between growing knowledge and advancing predictive ability has not been borne out. One problem is simply that the world is far more complicated than early scientists ever imagined. "The most important product of science is knowledge," the physicist and Nobel laureate David Gross likes to say. "However, the most important product of knowledge is ignorance." The more we learn, the more we reveal what we do not know.

This is reason enough to be humble about humanity's ability to predict, but there are far more fundamental problems as well. The French mathematician Henri Poincaré hinted at one in 1903. It is true, at least in theory, Poincaré wrote, that if we had perfect knowledge about all matter in the universe, we could calculate what that matter would do next. But if there was even a tiny problem with our knowledge about anything, anywhere— the smallest oversight, the slightest misunderstanding—that flaw would quickly magnify as the machinery of the universe ground on. Soon, it would be enormous and our forecasts would be completely wrong. In this way, "prediction becomes impossible," Poincaré concluded.

Poincare's observation remained little more than a theoretical insight until a meteorologist named Edward Lorenz made one of the accidental discoveries that are the stuff of scientific legend. In the winter of 1961, Lorenz, an MIT researcher, was testing weather forecasting models on what were then advanced computers. Among scientists, it was a giddy time. The new computing technology made it possible to run vast numbers of calculations, and complex modeling exercises became practical for the first time. Scientists were confident their ability to peer into the future would explode as a result: Soon they would predict earthquakes, the weather, and much else just as precisely as they did eclipses and tides.

One day, as Lorenz's computer ground out calculations, he stopped it midway through a modeling exercise. Later, he wanted the computer to resume, so he entered data the computer had produced on the first run and left it to its work. But Lorenz was startled to find the computer spitting out results that were dramatically different from the first time around. Something was wrong. It wasn't a programming error. And the computer was working fine. So what was the problem? Lorenz was stumped until he realized that he had programmed the computer to use data that extended to six decimal places. But when the computer delivered its results, it rounded numbers to three decimal places. It was the rounded numbers that Lorenz had reentered in the computer, not the actual results. The difference between the two was almost invisible, but even this slight deviation was enough to produce dramatically different forecasts. "This was exciting," Lorenz recalled. "If the real atmosphere behaved in the same manner as the model, long-range weather prediction would be impossible."

Actually, weather prediction was the least of it. Lorenz's discovery came to be known as "chaos," and it effectively made prediction impossible in all sorts of systems subject to change. An illustration developed by physicists showed the point vividly: Imagine a game of billiards played on a table that is frictionless, so the balls, once set in motion, will continue to bounce off the banks and each other forever. You rack up the balls, set the cue ball in place, and shoot. If you had perfect control over your shot—if it went exactly where you wanted at exactly the desired speed—for how long would you be able to predict the cue ball's path? Well, if you happened to know the precise placement of essentially everything in the universe, and if you were capable of factoring all that information into your unimaginably spectacular calculations, you could keep it up indefinitely. But if you were even slightly less than godlike, you would soon be in trouble. "If the player ignored an effect even as minuscule as the gravitational attraction of an electron at the edge of the galaxy, the prediction would become wrong after one minute!" Lorenz himself came up with a slightly more down-to-earth image to capture the idea of minuscule changes making a big difference to outcomes: The flutter of a butterfly's wings in Brazil, he said, could ultimately cause a tornado in Texas. The label "Butterfly Effect" has stuck ever since.

Strictly speaking, chaos theory doesn't make prediction impossible, as Lorenz's own field illustrates. Much as we like to complain about the errors of weather forecasters, they're actually pretty good—a day in advance. Two-day forecasts are generally less accurate. Three days less so again. And so on. But beyond a certain point—between five and seven days is the limit now—weather forecasts really aren't much use. Further advances in our understanding of weather and how to model it with computers may push that limit back some more, but everyone agrees that there is a point beyond which our predictions will never advance. No matter how much we learn, no matter how brilliant our models, no matter how powerful our computers, the Butterfly Effect simply will not allow us to peer farther into the future.

So why are tides and eclipses predictable when predictions about so much else can be blown away by the flap of a butterfly's wings? Because tides and eclipses are caused by the motions of the moon and the planets, which are governed by laws. And as grand as those motions and laws may be, they are relatively simple. In a word, they are linear. A linear system is the sum of its parts. Gravity, for example, is linear in mass. Double the mass and you get twice the gravity. Linearity allows for clear equations that produce unvarying conclusions, and that permits predictions: Simply by doing the math, we can know with great confidence precisely when a solar eclipse will next cast Rio de Janeiro into shadow at midday. Many things are linear, or so close to it that they can be treated as if they were—how much a bridge will bend under weight isn't precisely linear, for example, but engineers treat it as if it were because that works well enough. In this sense, tides and eclipses are much like bridges. "They are clockwork-like," notes David Orrell, an applied mathematician. "They are governed by the motion of the sun, the moon, and the planets and these things are all going around following Newton's law of gravity, which is very well determined. You get a tiny amount of chaotic wobble but it's insignificant, so it's basically a giant clock."

But linearity isn't the norm in the world around us, nonlinearity is. "Just about any system that you're really interested in predicting is characterized by nonlinearity," says Orrell, author of a book about science and prediction called *The Future of Everything*. To see a nonlinear system at work, look up. "The formation of clouds happens when you have particles of dust or pollen or other substances in the atmosphere and you get water vapor forming droplets around these particles." It sounds simple, but the growth of the cloud depends on the bewilderingly complex interactions within the vapor that cannot be reduced to an equation that produces unvarying results. And that makes it literally impossible to predict. "You can know all you want about particles. And you can know all you want about the H_2O molecule. But you still can't predict what a cloud will look like." You can only wait and see.

The study of nonlinear systems is a burgeoning field in modern science, but the challenges are enormous. Feedback is one that Orrell believes is an even bigger problem than chaos. A common component of nonlinear systems, feedback involves some element of the system looping back on itself and either driving the effect up (a microphone held close to a speaker producing escalating screech) or dampening it down (the flyball governor on steam engines, which is designed to let steam off when pressure grows beyond a certain point). "If you get the feedback even slightly wrong, your answer goes way off," Orrell says. And that's just feedback from one source. Often, multiple sources of feedback exist, and when these interact with each other, complexity soars. So does the potential for surprising results. "Quite often, it looks like systems are stable," Orrell says, "but actually they're in a state of internal tension through these feedback loops, which are acting in opposition to one another." If the balance tips even slightly, stability may suddenly be replaced by explosive change—a phenomenon seen in landslides, avalanches, volcanic explosions, and earthquakes.

This is not randomness, however. There is order in all of it. It's just not the sort of order that allows us to predict what happens next. Earthquakes are a classic example. As late as the 1970s, researchers were confident that as their understanding of the causes of earthquakes improved, so would their ability to predict them. One source of optimism was the discovery that variation in the strength of earthquakes is quite regular. The weakest earthquakes—the sort that usually go unnoticed—are very common. In California, there are hundreds each day. Somewhat stronger earthquakes are considerably rarer. And up the Richter scale it goes. It's so regular, it produces an equation: Double the energy released by an earthquake and it becomes four times rarer. And if there's an equation, scientists once believed, there must be predictability. But advances in understanding nonlinear systems have led most scientists to conclude that the possibility of earthquake prediction is strictly limited: Scientists can determine the *probability* of an earthquake of a certain size in a certain place, but it's impossible to say when the next earthquake of a certain magnitude will actually strike. "We all want to know when something is going to happen," notes Boston University physicist Eugene Stanley. "But there is no way of knowing when." Stanley likens it to life insurance: Using vast amounts of data, insurance companies may be able to determine that I have a 73 percent chance of living to the age of eighty—but there's still a 27 percent chance I won't and I may be hit by a bus tomorrow.

These insights have fundamentally changed how science views reality. "The old certainties of the Newtonian world machine, with its impressive capability of predicting and retrodicting the motions of sun, moon, planets, and even comets, unexpectedly dissolved into an evolving, historical, and occasionally chaotic universe," wrote historian William H. McNeill. In this new universe, some things are predictable, but many are not and never will be. Uncertainty is an ineradicable fact of existence.

BILLIARD BALLS WITH EYES

Note that all of this involves *physical* systems—molecules, grains of sand, snowflakes, and clouds. Mere objects. But people are not objects. Imagine how much more difficult it would be to predict trajectories on a billiard table if the balls had eyes, self-awareness, and complicated psychological motivations. And further imagine that each of the billiard balls knows the other billiard balls are also self-aware. All on its own, self-awareness can make prediction futile, a fact the economist Oskar Morgenstern illustrated with a simple story: Sherlock Holmes gets on a train bound for Dover. Midway, the train stops at a station. Holmes sees his murderous nemesis, Dr. Moriarty, on the platform. Moriarty sees Holmes. Holmes quickly calculates that Moriarty now knows

Holmes is bound for Dover on a non-express train and will therefore take the next express train to Dover and get there first. In order to elude Moriarty, Holmes decides to get off the train at the next intermediate stop. But then Holmes realizes there is a flaw in his plan: Moriarty is aware that Holmes is aware of him, and so he will anticipate Holmes's plan and also get off at the next intermediate stop. Ah, but Holmes is aware that Moriarity is aware! And so he calculates that he *should* carry on to Dover. But wait! Moriarity is aware that Holmes is aware that . . . "Always, there is exhibited an endless chain of reciprocally conjectural reactions and counter-reactions," Morgenstern wrote in 1935. The task is impossible. Holmes cannot predict what Moriarty will do. He might as well take one of those big Victorian pennies from his pocket and flip it.

With natural science increasingly aware of the limits of prediction, and with prediction even more difficult when people are involved, it would seem obvious that social science—the study of people—would follow the lead of natural science and accept that much of what we would like to predict will forever be unpredictable. But that hasn't happened, at least not to the extent it should. In fact, as the Yale University historian John Lewis Gaddis describes in *The Landscape of History,* "social scientists during the twentieth century embraced a Newtonian vision of linear and therefore predictable phenomena even as the natural sciences were abandoning it." Hence, economists issue wonky forecasts, criminologists predict crime trends that don't materialize, and political scientists foresee events that don't happen. And they keep doing it no matter how often they fail. Or how spectacularly. In a 1992 paper, Gaddis, an expert on the Cold War, surveyed the theories scholars erected in the belief they could be used to peer into the geopolitical future, as Newton had looked through his telescope into the night sky. The Soviet Union had just fallen and the Cold War was over. Had these prognosticators successfully foreseen one of the biggest events of the last century? Not by a long shot. "The efforts theorists have made to create a 'science' of politics that would forecast the future course of world events have produced strikingly unimpressive results," Gaddis concluded. "None of the three general approaches to theory that have evolved since 1945 came anywhere close to anticipating how the Cold War would end."

This is at the macro level in human affairs. Scale down from nations and teeming multitudes and ask this question: What makes one person tick? Her brain, of course. And how predictable is the operation of that brain? Not very. And for good reason. Its output is the result of electrical impulses leaping between the cells—neurons—that constitute the brain. In each brain, there are approximately twenty-three billion neurons, a number so immense that the level of complexity resulting from their interaction is literally unfathomable. And if that's not daunting enough, consider that there is significant scientific evidence indicating that those twenty-three billion neurons function much like earthquakes and other nonlinear systems that alternate between stability and bursts of change whose timing and outcome cannot be known in advance. "Networks of brain cells alternate between periods of calm and periods of instability—'avalanches' of electrical activity that cascade through the brain," writes science journalist David Robson "Like real avalanches, exactly how these occur and the resulting state of the brain are unpredictable."

This puts an interesting gloss on an argument made by the philosopher Karl Popper decades before the development of chaos and complexity theory. "The course of human history is strongly influenced by the growth of human knowledge," Popper wrote. But it's impossible to "predict, by rational or scientific methods, the future growth of our scientific knowledge" because doing so would require us to know that future knowledge, and, if we did, it would be present knowledge, not future knowledge. "We cannot, therefore, predict the future course of human history." Popper's case was strong when he first made it in the 1930s, and the decades since have produced an abundance of failed predictions to bolster it. And now that we know that the individual human brain is nonlinear and literally unpredictable, Popper is looking better than ever. This may seem a terribly abstract and theoretical point, but it's not. It has big, practical implications. Consider the case of the

Anaconda Copper Mining Company. All but forgotten today, Anaconda was once one of the largest companies in the world thanks to its dominance of the expanding market for copper telephone wires. "This company will still be going strong one hundred or even five hundred years from now," boasted Anaconda's president in 1968. There was likely a touch of fear in his bravado. Three years earlier, the brains of two British scientists had figured out how fiber optics could theoretically be a medium of communication. And two years after his boast, three scientists were able to make fiber optics a practical technology vastly superior to copper wires. The price of copper plummeted. Facing liquidation, Anaconda sold itself in 1977.

It's hard to imagine a better demonstration of Popper's argument and the critical role played by the unpredictable brain. As Sir Isaac Newton himself observed—after losing a bundle in one of history's first stock bubbles—"I can calculate the movement of the stars but not the madness of men." Centuries later, that's still true.

MONKEYS AND CHAOS

Most of us are familiar with the old proverb about a lost nail:

For want of a nail, the shoe was lost.
For want of a shoe, the horse was lost.
For want of a horse, the rider was lost.
For want of a rider, the battle was lost.
For want of a battle, the kingdom was lost.

It's intended to illustrate the importance of diligence in doing small things because they can magnify quickly and unpredictably. It is, in other words, chaos theory in human affairs—a theoretical application we might call the "monkey-bite factor" in honor of a seemingly trivial incident that had enormous consequences.

There were actually two monkeys involved. The first attacked a man's dog. The man intervened. The second monkey leapt in and bit the man. That's all there was to the incident. But the bite became infected, and since this was 1920, there were no antibiotics and the man died. This was certainly a tragedy but it was hardly a matter of great importance to anyone but the man and his family. Not even the fact that the man was King Alexander of Greece elevated the importance of the event, because the king was only the nominal ruler of Greece. His power was more symbolic than real. And so, by any reasonable measure, his surprising death was political trivia.

But like the flap of a butterfly's wings, this trivial event set in motion a series of escalating events: the surprise electoral defeat of the Greek government, a plebiscite, the return of the previously exiled king, and, ultimately, a military campaign in Turkey that went badly. Some 250,000 people were killed. "A quarter of a million persons died of that monkey's bite," Winston Churchill later wrote. He was exaggerating, of course. Vastly more lay behind the conflict than the demise of the king. But it was true that the war would not have unfolded as it did if the king had not died, and the king would almost certainly not have died—he was young and healthy at the time—if he had not been bitten by the monkey. And yet we can be sure that no one who saw the monkey bite the king thought it would lead to war and disaster. How could they? It would take godlike omniscience to foresee the chain of causation between a monkey's bite and the deaths of a quarter of a million people, just as it would take that same omniscience to predict the path of billiard balls even a minute into the future. And for the same reason.

History is riddled with "monkey bite" moments. On November 9, 1989, the Berlin Wall fell. Why? There were many reasons and some are the grand stuff of history. But one reason it happened is that an East German spokesman who was to announce President Egon Krenz's new policy permitting East Germans to travel to West Germany—under strict controls—bungled a question at a press conference. When will the new policy come into effect? he was asked. The correct answer was the next day, November 10, but the spokesman didn't say that. Instead, he looked through some papers, fiddled with his glasses, and finally replied with a shrug. "Immediately," he said. Maybe he intended that to mean "tomorrow." But East Germans took *immediately* to mean "right now" and they went to the wall en masse. Besieged by tens of thousands of people and having heard from an official that travel would be permitted "immediately," border guards opened the gates and the strict conditions the government had intended to impose came to nothing. Whether things would have turned out differently if the spokesman had said "tomorrow" instead of "immediately" is debatable. But he said what he said. "History turned on the misuse of a single word, pure human accident," noted journalist Michael Meyer.

One way to spot monkey-bite moments is to use what historians call "counterfactuals," which are scenarios in which minor changes are made to what actually happened. In 1923, for example, a fringe political figure by the name of Adolf Hitler led an armed coup attempt in the streets of Munich. In a brief gunfight, sixteen people were killed. Hitler was injured, but survived, and was imprisoned. History tells us Hitler spent his incarceration writing *Mein Kampf* and plotting his future, which would see him take power in 1933 and launch a catastrophic war in 1939. But what if one of the soldiers who took aim at Hitler that day in 1923 had spent just a little more time at the firing range? What if he had coughed and his bullet's trajectory had been oh-so-slightly different? It is unlikely the Nazis ever would have come to power, and there might not have been a Second World War. Or a Holocaust.

Trivia and accident routinely push history in this or that direction. The historian may be able to discern their role by looking backward and carefully tracing the loss of the kingdom to the battle, the rider, the horse, the shoe, and finally the missing nail. But looking forward into the future? No one can foresee the consequences of trivia and accident, and for that reason alone, the future will forever be filled with surprises.

THE DEMOGRAPHY OF UNCERTAINTY

Many of us, I think, can accept the idea that we will be blindsided by politics or technology. It's happened before and it will happen again. But we resist the suggestion that unpredictability is typical of human affairs. Much of it is regular and perfectly predictable, we insist. The standard example is demography. How many people there are, their sex, their age, their distribution, how many babies they have: These things are locked in far in advance, and so we can use them to forecast. If a population has a large cohort of ten-year-old boys, for example, we can be quite confident that in twenty years it will have a large cohort of thirty-year-old men. And other things are predictable too. Most men entering their thirties are married for the first time, or will be soon. They will get their first house; they will have their first child. So if we know there will be lots of thirty-year-old men in twenty years, we will also have a pretty good idea what goods and services will be in high demand. It's all predictable.

Demography is a staple for futurists, pundits, and others who make expert predictions. In many cases, it is the foundation of the entire forecast. A typical example is *The Next 100 Years,* a 2009 book written by George Friedman, the CEO of the private forecasting firm Stratfor. "The single most important fact of the twenty-first century," Friedman writes, will be "the end of the population explosion. By 2050, advanced industrial countries will be losing population at a dramatic rate. By 2100, even the most underdeveloped countries will have birthrates that will stabilize their populations." For Friedman, these changes are certain. They *will* happen. All that remains is to explore their implications. But it's only partly true that demography can be used to make accurate forecasts. Yes, demographic changes are slower than many others, and that does produce an unusual degree of predictability. "Among human social, economic, and political trends, projections of demographic change do offer some of the longest-term foresight available," wrote demographer Michael Teitelbaum. But even in demography, nothing is certain. Surprises abound. And long-term demographic forecasts like Friedman's are a bull moose walking on thin ice.

Take that cohort of ten-year-old boys I mentioned. It seems obvious that they will become an equally large cohort of thirty-year-old men in twenty years. And they probably will. But what if those boys are British, French, or German? And what if the year is 1906? Eight years later, the First World War erupts—to the surprise of most experts—and these boys are sent into the bloody mud of Verdun and the Somme. By the time their cohort is thirty years old, it is a fraction of the size it was at the age of ten. And no one predicted it. This is, of course, a unique and extreme example, but the history of demography is stuffed with surprises on an even bigger scale.

In Western countries, fertility rates—the number of babies the average woman has in her lifetime—started a steady, substantial, and sustained decline in the mid- to late nineteenth century. The drop came earlier to some countries than others, and the different fertility rates that resulted led to a spate of predictions. "To look into the future is not always an idle fancy or a wasteful foolishness," wrote Robert Sencourt in 1925. A nation's power is based on the robustness of its population—in demography "the parchment of fate unrolls"—and so, by looking at fertility rates, it is possible to forecast which countries would be the dominant powers of Europe in 1950. The future belonged to Italy and Spain, Sencourt concluded. In 1922, the American political scientist and journalist Lothrop Stoddard cast a wider gaze and came to a more frightening conclusion. "Ours is a solemn moment," he wrote in his widely read and influential book *The Rising Tide of Color Against White World-Supremacy.* "There is no immediate danger of the world being swamped by black blood. But there is a very imminent danger that the white stocks may be swamped by Asiatic blood." This would mean the end of civilization, apparently.

In the 1930s, as fertility rates continued to decline, experts increasingly worried that fertility would slip below the level needed simply to replace populations. Growth would stop, then populations would shrink. A 1934 projection showed Britain's population falling from forty-four million to thirty-three million by 1976. Fear that the West's political and economic fortunes would follow the population's trajectory became widespread. This was one of the "most critical epochs" in all of human history, wrote Aldous Huxley, author of *Brave New World*, in a British magazine. "Will the depopulation of Western Europe and North America proceed to the point of extinction or military annihilation?"

When the Second World War ended, fertility rates shot up. The experts were surprised but they quickly adjusted to the new landscape. By the late 1950s, Paul Ehrlich and countless others worried that high fertility rates, in combination with low death rates, would keep Western populations spiraling upward to disaster. They needn't have worried. Starting around 1965, fertility rates reversed again across the Western world. Even the global rate of population growth slowed for the first time ever, a critical turning point that was not foreseen. By the 1970s, Western fertility rates had slipped below the level needed to maintain the population. In the 1980s, they rose modestly in the United States but not in other rich countries. By the late 1990s, pundits had started warning once again of imminent population decline and the end of the developed world.

In the developing world, demographic changes have been even more startling. Iran's fertility rate in 1975 was a sky-high 6.4 babies per woman. Then came the 1979 revolution and Iran became a theocracy. The authorities abolished the family-planning system, and by 1984, fertility was seven babies per woman. At that point, any reasonable person would expect the rate to stay high, or even rise more. But it didn't. In fact, it crashed and, by 2006, it was 1.9. No one predicted this, and why it happened isn't even fully understood in hindsight. Similar changes in many other countries have left experts amazed and puzzled.

This long record of forecasting failure has convinced most demographers to be cautious. When they issue projections based on current trends, they emphasize that they are *only* projections: If the trends change, they will be wrong. And trends *do* change, they emphasize. All the time. This is why demographers are constantly revising their projections. Even basic demographic facts about the present or the past aren't entirely reliable. Consider the population of the world in 1951. That's a pretty basic fact. Of course, it would have been hard to predict it in, say, 1901. But one would think that in 1952, it was much easier to determine: All you have to do is look in the United Nations' *Demographic Yearbook* and there it is. But demographic facts like this are based on available research, and when new research suggests the established "fact" isn't accurate, it has to be changed. Between 1951 and 1996, the official estimate of the world's population in 1951 changed seventeen times.

"The social sciences have little ability to predict the aggregate course of the fundamental demographic processes of birth, death, and migration," noted demographer Joel Cohen. At best—assuming reliable numbers, steady trends, and no surprises—forecasts "are usefully accurate for less than a generation (up to twenty or twenty-five years)." Beyond that, forget it. Demographic trends a century out are "unknowable, and quite literally so," wrote Michael Teitelbaum. Will fertility rates rise or fall? Don't know. Will disease throw a spanner into the works? Don't know. Will changes in technology make a difference? Don't know. How will people and governments respond to trends? "We cannot know what collective reactions might be embraced if fertility rates in a given country were to remain well below replacement for many decades," Teitelbaum wrote. "We cannot anticipate the size, rates, or even direction of international migrations. Nor can we predict if current national boundaries will be roughly comparable to those of today, very different from today's, or even totally absent."

The first and most famous demographic forecast was that made by Thomas Robert Malthus in 1798. Population would outstrip available food in the nineteenth century, Malthus concluded. Starvation and disease would sweep the land; the population would collapse, and the economy with it. An intense debate ensued because Malthus was not some wild-eyed prophet. His conclusions were based on careful observation of past centuries, and his logic was sound. But the dire future he forecast never arrived. In fact, what happened was pretty much the opposite of what Malthus expected, as population, food production, and economies all grew rapidly—thanks to advances in science and technology Malthus did not foresee. One might reasonably have predicted that a century or two after Malthus, people would have learned from his example to be much more cautious about using demography to predict the future. But that prediction would have been wrong. As they usually are.

WHITHER OIL?

Fine, the reader may say. The world may be too big and complicated to predict in important ways. Even something as seemingly reliable as demography may be shot through with uncertainty. But we were talking about the price of oil. It's not complicated. It's the product of two factors: supply and demand. There's nothing else to it. Surely it can be determined by one of those linear equations scientists use to predict the movements of the planets, eclipses, and the tides?

Alas, no. As the dismal record of oil forecasts shows, there is no equation. And there never will be, as a quick tour of the Niger Delta reveals.

The Niger is one of Africa's great rivers. Where it enters the Atlantic Ocean, it has formed a fan-shaped delta spanning some seventy thousand square kilometers. The human diversity on the delta is almost as complex as the river's pathways, and the region is home to some thirty million people drawn from forty different ethnic groups speaking 250 dialects. The poverty on the delta is staggering, as is the volume of oil buried beneath it and the surrounding ocean—a combination that goes some way to explaining why the Niger Delta is one of the most unstable major sources of oil on the world market. Criminal gangs and rebels routinely blow up pipelines, kidnap oil workers, and assault offshore drilling platforms. Significant attacks have immediate effects on world oil prices, particularly when the margin between supply and demand is thin. The instability is a major drag on production, and analysts constantly worry that the violence could mount, further curtailing production. It has happened before: In 1967, the attempted secession of the delta and surrounding regions from Nigeria led to a civil war that killed more than one million people.

No one can be sure how the future will unfold in the Niger Delta. And the supply of oil—and therefore the price—may depend on that future. The implication is obvious. And it becomes even clearer when we consider that oil is found in dozens of other unstable sources subject to sudden and unpredictable change. The fearsome price surge in 1979, remember, was the result of revolution in Iran. Who predicted that? Not the Central Intelligence Agency. Five months before the shah was driven from power, the CIA's senior political analyst on Iran—who spoke Farsi and had twenty years' experience tracking Iranian affairs—wrote that the country was "not in a revolutionary or even a 'prerevolutionary' situation." That opinion was shared by most experts, including the Iranian opposition leader Mehdi Bazargan. In his examination of the causes of the Iranian revolution, sociologist Charles Kurzman concluded that the revolution was just as confusing and uncertain for participants as it was for observers, and so it was, quite literally, unpredictable: Just as one cannot know the shape a cloud will take until it takes it, the course of events in Iran could only be known after they had happened.

Clearly, the supply of oil is nothing like the movement of Jupiter around the sun. Yet politics is just one factor complicating supply forecasts. Much also depends on the technology used to discover and extract oil, which in turn depends on scientific knowledge. But as Karl Popper noted, it's impossible to predict the progress of scientific knowledge. And the long, sorry history of predictions about technology provides ample evidence that the course of technology is little more predictable than the course of Iranian politics.

The demand side of the oil-price equation is, if anything, even more bewildering. Demand depends in part on advances in science and technology, and in part on social changes, like the move to the suburbs in the 1950s and 1960s that did so much to make the gas-powered car an essential feature of daily life in the developed world. Politics also plays a key role, because the laws and regulations enacted by politicians can make a big difference: In Europe, the high taxes levied on gasoline during the 1980s and 1990s did much to dampen demand; in the United States, low gas taxes allowed demand to rise far more. For demand to be predictable, politics, social change, and the advance of science and technology would all have to be predictable. They aren't, of course, and so forecasts of demand routinely fail.

One afternoon in the lobby of a London hotel, Peter Schwartz let me in on a little secret. "The truth is," he said, "in the oil industry today, the most senior executives don't even try to pretend they can predict the price of oil." As a former strategic planner for Shell whose work preparing the oil giant for the price collapse of the mid-1980s is famous in the industry, Schwartz knows oil. As a consultant to the biggest corporations at the highest levels, Schwartz also knows corporate executives, and he underscores his point by waving over a friend of his. Lord John Browne, the legendary former chief executive officer of British Petroleum, worked all his life in the oil business, and he is convinced the price of oil is fundamentally unpredictable. "I can forecast confidently that it will vary. After that, I can gossip with you. But that's all it is, because there are too many factors which go into the dynamics of the pricing of oil."

Still, the oil forecasting industry keeps growing because lots of people are prepared to pay for something top oil executives consider worthless. "There's a demand for the forecasts, so people generate them," Schwartz says with a shrug.

BUT WHAT ABOUT THE PREDICTABLE PEAK?

Anyone familiar with the history of oil forecasts will object. What about peak oil? Yes, predictions about prices have failed over and over. But one oil forecaster made an important prediction that proved exactly right.

That forecaster was M. King Hubbert, a geophysicist who worked with Shell and, later, the U.S. Geological Survey. Hubbert wrote a paper in 1957 that predicted overall petroleum production in the United States would peak sometime between the late 1960s and early 1970s, after which it would irreversibly decline. Experts scoffed. They stopped scoffing when American oil production peaked fourteen years later.

Hubbert's methods were relatively simple. When an oil field is discovered, its production rises steadily until it peaks and starts to fall as smoothly as it rose. Although the field may never run completely dry, what matters is that more drilling and pumping will not significantly change the downward slope of production. Eventually, a chart of the field's production will look like a classic bell curve. If this happens to a single field, Hubbert reasoned, it can happen to a group of fields, or a whole oil-producing region. Or a nation. By examining reserves and production rates, Hubbert calculated the moment when the chart of American oil production would hit its peak and begin its long, slow decline. And he was right.

If American production can peak and decline, so can the world's, and that is the sense in which the term *peak oil* is generally used today. No one disputes that peak oil will come. Oil is a finite resource and so a peak in production is inevitable. What matters is the timing. Some analysts think we've already reached the peak. Many others see it coming within a few years, or perhaps in a decade or two. Some insist peak oil lies in a future far too distant to worry about, but the ranks of these optimists have thinned in recent years. This is a debate with enormous ramifications. Hitting peak oil in a world of expanding economies whose expansion depends on oil would shake the foundations of the global economy.

"Peak oil" advocates are convinced that we are at, or near, the top of the bell curve, but it's important to understand that Hubbert's prediction for American production was based on a linear equation and some big assumptions. For one thing, it took as a given that demand growth wouldn't change in a big way. Nor would technology. And of course it assumed that Hubbert's estimate of total reserves in the ground was right. These assumptions turned out to be right, in that case. But will they always be? We can answer that question by noting that Hubbert applied his methods to global oil production. It would peak in 1995, he predicted. The decline that followed would be rapid. By 2010, it would be down a terrifying 17 percent. "The end of the Oil Age is in sight," Hubbert proclaimed in 1974.

The fault was not Hubbert's. A very long list of experts got the same call wrong. An international group of analysts brought together by MIT, for example, concluded two and a half years of work in 1977 with a declaration that global oil production would peak around 1990 "at the latest," although the group thought it more likely that the peak would be reached in the early 1980s. No wonder Jimmy Carter was gloomy.

Lord John Browne only chuckles when I mention the latest panic over peak oil. "In my career this must be about number seven," he says.

ASKING THE RIGHT QUESTION

So why can't we predict the price of oil? That's the wrong question. What we should ask is, in a nonlinear world, why would we think oil prices can be predicted? Practically since the dawn of the oil industry in the nineteenth century, experts have been forecasting the price of oil. They've been wrong ever since. And yet this dismal record hasn't caused us to give up on the enterprise of forecasting oil prices.

Vast numbers of intelligent people continue to spend their days analyzing data and crafting forecasts that are no more likely to be right than all those that came before. Nassim Taleb, author of *The Black Swan*, recalled giving a lecture to employees of the U.S. government about the futility of forecasting. Afterward, he was approached by someone who worked for an agency doomed, like Sisyphus, to do the impossible. "In January, 2004, his department was forecasting the price of oil for 25 years later at $27 a barrel, slightly higher than what it was at the time. Six months later, around June 2004, after oil doubled in price, they had to revise their estimate to $54," Taleb wrote. "It did not dawn on them that it was ludicrous to forecast a second time given that their forecast was off so early and so markedly, that this business of forecasting had to be somehow questioned. And they were looking *25 years* ahead!" That twenty-five-year prediction was actually modest, believe it or not. The International Energy Agency routinely issues thirty-year forecasts.

We never learn. When the terrifying forecasts of the 1970s were followed by the return of cheap oil in the 1980s, it wasn't the concept of forecasting that was humiliated and discarded. It was only those particular forecasts. New forecasts sprang up. When prices stayed low year after year, the consensus of the late 1990s was that any price increases would quickly be offset by conservation and stepped-up production. Thus, the era of cheap oil would last far into the future.

It lasted until 2004.

In 2005, as oil prices climbed steadily and sharply, Steve Forbes, publisher of *Forbes* magazine, said it was a bubble that would soon pop. "I'll make a bold prediction," he said. "In 12 months, you're going to see oil down to $35 to $40 a barrel." The price kept rising. By 2007, a new consensus had emerged: Oil was going higher. And it did. In the first half of 2008, oil pushed above the previously unimaginable level of $140 a barrel. "The Age of Oil is at an end," declared environmental writer Timothy Egan in *The New York Times,* echoing, whether he knew it or not, M. King Hubbert's declaration of thirty-five years earlier. Experts who had led in forecasting the rising trend became media stars, quoted everywhere, and what they had to say was not good: The price would continue to climb. It will break the $200 mark soon, predicted Arjun Murti at Goldman Sachs. Jeff Rubin, the chief economist at CIBC World Markets, agreed. "It's going to go higher. It might go way higher," investment banker and energy analyst Matthew Simmons said on CNBC. "It's not going to collapse." Simmons said that in July 2008, when oil was selling at $147 a barrel.

It didn't go higher. In September 2008, financial markets melted down, precipitating a dramatic slowing in the global economy. The experts hadn't foreseen that. The decline in growth drove down demand for oil and what Matthew Simmons said would not happen did. By December, oil traded at $33 a barrel. If any analyst had made that call six months earlier, when the price was more than four times higher, he would have found himself out of a job.

At the time I'm writing these words—early 2010—the price has risen, then fallen, then risen again. It's now a little more than $80 a barrel. Where will it go from here? I don't know. But plenty of other people have no doubt at all. "Petroleum is a finite resource that is going to $200 a barrel by 2012," wrote a business columnist with the confidence of someone predicting that trees will lose their leaves in the autumn. The British newspaper *The Independent* declared, "The era of cheap oil has come to an end," without mentioning that this was not cheap oil's first death notice. A poll conducted in June 2009 revealed that business executives are even more sure of themselves than journalists: Asked what the price of oil would be in five years, only 5 percent answered, "Don't know." Asked about the price in ten years, 10 percent answered, "Don't know." Even when they were asked about the price twenty years in the future, a mere one-third of business executives doubted their powers of divination.

Maybe the era of Mad Max really is coming, finally. Or maybe cheap oil will rise from the dead once again. Or maybe new technologies will surprise us all and create a future quite unlike anything we imagine. The simple truth is no one really knows, and no one will know until the future becomes the present. The only thing we can say with confidence is that when that time comes, there will be experts who are sure they know what the future holds and people who pay far too much attention to them.

3

In the Minds of Experts

*It is a singular fact that the Great Pyramid always predicts the
history of the world accurately up to the date of publication of the
book in question, but after that date it becomes less reliable.*

—BERTRAND RUSSELL

Arnold Toynbee was brilliant. About that, even his critics agreed.
The British historian's magnum opus, *A Study of History,* was
stuffed with so many historical details drawn from so many
times and places it seemed Toynbee knew more history than anyone on
the planet. Even more dazzling was the central revelation of *A Study of
History*: Toynbee claimed to have discovered an identical pattern of gen-
esis, growth, breakdown, and disintegration in the history of every civilization that had ever existed. The implication was obvious. If there is a
universal pattern in the past, it must be woven into the present. And the
future. In the late 1940s and the 1950s, as the United States and the world
entered a frightening new era of atom bombs and Cold War, *A Study of
History* became a massive best seller. Arnold Toynbee was celebrated
and revered as the man who could see far into the frightening mael-
strom ahead. He was no mere historian or public intellectual. He was a

prophet—"a modern St. Augustine," as a reviewer put it in *The New York Times* in 1949.

But for all Toynbee's brilliance, *A Study of History* never won the respect of historians. They didn't see the pattern Toynbee saw. Instead, what they saw was a man so obsessed with an idea—a hedgehog, to put it in this book's terms—that he had devoted his energy, knowledge, and decades of toil to the construction of a ten-volume illusion. In the blunt words of the Dutch historian Pieter Geyl, "The author is deceiving himself."

Arnold Joseph Toynbee was born April 14, 1889, to a proper Victorian family that valued education and religious piety above all else. Young Arnold did not disappoint. In 1902, he won a scholarship to the illustrious Winchester College, where he was immersed in the history, language, and literature of ancient Greece and Rome. The experience shaped him profoundly. The ancient world became as comfortable and familiar to him as the Britain of cricket pitches and Empire. It was his foundation, his universal frame of reference. He even dreamed in Latin.

In 1906, Toynbee landed a scholarship to Balliol College, Oxford, and proceeded to win awards at a satisfyingly brisk pace. An appointment to the faculty naturally followed graduation.

Toynbee's tidy world ended with the outbreak of the First World War. Rejected from military service on medical grounds, he conducted political analysis for the British government, an involvement with current affairs he maintained through the rest of his life. It was a natural fit. Tying together past, present, and future was something Toynbee did intuitively. "What set me off," he wrote decades later in an essay explaining where he got the idea to write *A Study of History,* "was a sudden realization, after the outbreak of the First World War, that our world was just then entering an experience that the Greek World had been through in the Peloponnesian War."

In the summer of 1920, a friend gave Toynbee a copy of *The Decline of the West* by the German Oswald Spengler. The book was a sensation in postwar Germany, where defeat had been followed by revolutionary turmoil and the sense that the world as people knew it was collapsing. Spengler captured the gloomy mood perfectly. All civilizations rise and fall as predictably and inescapably as the swing of a clock's pendulum, he wrote. The West was old and doomed to decay, senility, and death. There would be no more science and art. No creation, innovation, and joy. "The great masters are dead," Spengler proclaimed. The West could do nothing now but dig its grave.

"As I read those pages teeming with firefly flashes of historical insight," Toynbee later recalled, "I wondered at first whether my whole inquiry had been disposed of by Spengler before even the question, not to speak of the answers, had fully taken shape in my own mind." But Toynbee was appalled by the absence of concrete evidence in *The Decline of the West*. Spengler's argument consisted of nothing more than assertions, Toynbee realized. "You must take it on trust from the master. This arbitrary fiat seemed disappointingly unworthy of Spengler's brilliant genius; and here I became aware of a difference of national traditions. Where the German *a priori* method drew a blank, let us see what could be done by English empiricism. Let us see alternative possible explanations in the light of the evidence and see how they stood the ordeal." Toynbee would do what Spengler had done, but scientifically.

One evening in 1921, leaving Turkey aboard the fabled Orient Express, Toynbee took out a fountain pen and sketched an outline of what would become *A Study of History*. Although Toynbee had yet to study non-Western history seriously, his outline confidently stated that the course taken by all civilizations follows a pattern: Birth was followed by differentiation, expansion, breakdown, empire, universal religion, and finally, interregnum. Toynbee's terminology changed a little over the years, and the list of laws and regularities in history steadily expanded, adding layers of complexity, but the basic scheme never changed from the publication of the first three volumes in 1934 to the release of the final four in 1954.

With grand outline in hand, Toynbee set out to study Chinese, Japanese, Indian, Incan, and other non-Western histories. Over and over again, he found he was right: They did indeed follow the pattern. The parallels were most pronounced in the terminal stage of "disintegration," he found. In what he called the "Time of Troubles," a dispossessed minority founds a new religion, there are increasingly violent wars, and the civilization rallies to form a "universal state." This is followed by a brief respite—an "Indian Summer"—from the internal decline. But the clashes resume and decay worsens. Gradually, the universal state collapses, and the civilization with it. But that is not the end. For the new religion continues to grow, holding out the promise of renewal in some distant future.

It's not hard to see Greece, Rome, and the Christian church in Toynbee's allegedly universal pattern of history. But did the other twenty civilizations identified by Toynbee all follow the same course? He insisted they did. And his spectacular erudition—only Arnold Toynbee could write a sentence like "If Austerlitz was Austria's Cynosephalae, Wagram was her Pydna"—cowed the average reader. The man seemed to know everything about everywhere. He was Wikipedia made flesh. Who could doubt him?

But historians *did* doubt Arnold Toynbee. Pieter Geyl and others who took the trouble to carefully sift through Toynbee's vast heap of evidence found he routinely omitted inconvenient facts, twisted others, and even fabricated out of whole cloth. A blatant example was his handling of Mohammed and the Islamic explosion in the seventh century, in which a handful of peripheral tribes on the Arabian peninsula suddenly swept across much of North Africa and the Middle East. This was a problem for Toynbee's system because it created a single government— the Umayyad Caliphate—ruling over a vast swath of territory. That's a "universal state" in Toynbee's terms. But in Toynbee's scheme, universal states come about only when a civilization is old and on its way down. Yet here was a universal state that seemed to spring up out of the sand. Holding a square peg, Toynbee pounded it into his round hole: "He declared that the Arab conquerors, inspired by Mohammed's newly minted revelation, were 'unconscious and unintended champions' of a 'Syriac' civilization that had gone underground a thousand years before at the time of Alexander's conquest," wrote William H. McNeill. "No one before Toynbee had conceived of a Syriac civilization, and it seems safe to assume that he invented the entire concept in order to be able to treat the Ummayad Caliphate as a universal state with a civilization of its own."

With few exceptions, Toynbee's fellow historians thought his project was absurd. The criticisms began with the publication of the first works in *A Study of History*. They grew louder as more books appeared. "His methods, he never ceases to tell us, are empirical," wrote Hugh Trevor-Roper, one of the major historians of the twentieth century. "In fact, wherever we look, it is the same. Theories are stated—often interesting and suggestive theories; then facts are selected to illustrate them (for there is no theory which some chosen facts cannot illustrate); then the magician waves his wand, our minds are dazed with a mass of learned detail, and we are told that the theories are 'empirically' proved by the facts and we can now go on to the next stage in the argument. But in truth this is neither empiricism nor proof, nor even argument: it is a game anyone can play, a confusion of logic with speculation." Another eminent historian was even more cutting. "This is not history," declared A. J. P. Taylor.

To be fair to Toynbee, historians were a tough audience. Most were—and are—deeply skeptical of the notion that there are universal patterns and "laws" to be discovered in history. Some go further and argue that all events are unique and history is simply "one damned thing after another"—an idea H. A. L. Fisher put more elegantly when he wrote, "I can see only one emergence following upon another, as wave follows upon wave, only one great fact with respect to which, since it is unique, there can be no generalizations, only one safe rule for the historian, that he should recognize in the development of human destinies the play of the contingent and the unforeseen." (Although he wasn't aware of it, the very reason Toynbee was in Turkey on the night he drafted the outline of *A Study of History* supports Fisher's view that "the contingent and the unforeseen" played leading roles in history: As a correspondent for the *Guardian* newspaper, Toynbee had been reporting on the disastrous Greek military campaign whose origins lay, as we saw in the last chapter, in a monkey bite.)

The chorus of catcalls from historians, which reached a crescendo in the mid-1950s, shook Toynbee. But it didn't make the slightest difference to how the public received Toynbee and his work. When volumes one to three were released in 1934, and again following the release of volumes four to six in 1939, *A Study of History* was acclaimed, particularly in the United Kingdom. Sales were brisk. In the depths of the Depression, with British power waning, totalitarianism rising, and another horrific war increasingly likely, pessimism flourished. Like Spengler before him, Toynbee captured the mood perfectly. Although he explicitly dealt with the prospects of modern Western civilization in only one of the last volumes of *A Study of History*, his writing was covered in a pall of gloom and he left no doubt about where, in the grand pattern of civilizations, the West found itself. Breakdown was now long past and we were deep into disintegration. The end was approaching, as it had for Rome all those centuries before.

In 1942, when Toynbee traveled to the United States on behalf of the British government, he expounded on his theories, and what they meant for the coming postwar future, with American officials and notables. One was Henry Luce, the publisher of *Time*, *Life*, and *Fortune* magazines, whose circulation and influence were immense. Luce was deeply impressed. A devout Christian and a passionate advocate of American leadership in world affairs, Luce was thrilled by Toynbee's message because, gloomy as it was, it was not without hope. Western civilization had not yet brought forth a "universal state" and the "Indian Summer" that follows, Toynbee noted. So that must be what lies ahead. Who could bring about such a universal state? Britain was finished. The Nazis or the Soviets could, but that would be a horror. No, it must be done by the United States.

Luce asked Toynbee to speak to the editors of *Time* and they, in turn, made his views a fixture of the most important magazine in the United States. In March 1947, when a mercifully abridged version of *A Study of History* was released, Toynbee's somber face graced *Time*'s cover and an effusive story detailed his great work for the mass American audience. "The response has been overwhelming," *Time*'s editors wrote in the next edition. Academics, governors, congressmen, journalists, and "plain citizens" wrote in unprecedented numbers. The military asked for seventeen hundred reprints "for distribution to Armed Forces chaplains everywhere." The abridgement of *A Study of History* became a best seller and "Toynbee's name," a writer in *Time* recalled, "tinkled among the martini glasses of Brooklyn as well as Bloomsbury."

Once again, timing was everything. The prewar order was shattered, a terrifying new weapon had entered the world, and it seemed obvious that the United States could not go back to isolationism. But what should America do instead? Friction with the Soviet Union—which some had taken to calling a "Cold War"—was growing steadily. "Western man in the middle of the twentieth century is tense, uncertain, adrift," wrote Arthur Schlesinger Jr. in the famous opening to 1949's *The Vital Center*. "We look upon our epoch as a time of troubles, an age of anxiety. The grounds of our civilization, of our certitude, are breaking up under our feet, and familiar ideas and institutions vanish as we reach for them, like shadows in the falling dusk." Arnold Toynbee was the man for the moment.

For literary critics, philosophers, theologians, politicians, writers, journalists, and others interested in big ideas, Toynbee's vision was electrifying. "If our world civilization survives its threatened ordeals, *A Study of History* will stand out as a landmark, perhaps even a turning point," wrote the critic Lewis Mumford. Toynbee was hailed as "the most renowned scholar in the world" and "a universal sage." "There have been innumerable discussions of Toynbee's work in the press, in periodicals, over radio and television, not to mention countless lectures and seminars," marveled the anthropologist Ashley Montagu in 1956. "Through the agency of all these media Toynbee has himself actively assisted in the diffusion of his view." Toynbee loved his fame, not so much for the money and adoration that went with it—or at least, not only for that—but for the opportunities to expound on the state of the world and where it was headed.

Toynbee's vision of the future never wavered, as might be expected given his belief that there is a universal pattern woven into all civilizations. If there is such a pattern, after all, it suggests a deterministic process is at work: All civilizations must and will follow the same path, no exceptions. Oswald Spengler had no trouble with such determinism, and he bluntly concluded that an old civilization could no more avoid collapse than an old man could avoid death. But not Toynbee. It chafed against his Christian conception of free will, which insists that people are free to choose their actions, and so, even as he promoted the idea of a universal pattern in the life of civilizations and made predictions for the future based on that pattern, Toynbee insisted choices matter. And in the Atomic Age, the choice was between a universal state, followed by a profound religious revival or a war that would bring the violent end of humanity. One or the other. Nothing else was possible.

Toynbee repeated this general prognosis constantly. Occasionally, he was more specific. For a 1962 volume on the population explosion, he foresaw the creation, by the end of the century, of an international agency with unchecked power to control the production and distribution of food. It would be "the first genuine executive organ of world government that mankind will create for itself." Other iterations of his vision were more ambitious. In a 1952 lecture, Toynbee sketched the world of 2002. "The whole face of the planet will have been unified politically through the concentration of irresistible military power in some single set of hands," he declared. Those hands wouldn't inevitably be American but he thought that most likely. Nor was it clear whether the unification would come about by world war. But "if a modern westernizing world were to be unified peacefully, one could imagine, in 2002, a political map not unlike the Greco-Roman world in A.D. 102. . . ." Nominally, the universal state would be democratic but the public would no longer exercise real control over the government, and the government—faced with severe overcrowding and resource shortages—would regulate every aspect of its citizens' lives. People would accept this control as the price of order and prosperity, but the suppression of freedom "on the material plane" would generate an explosion of freedom "on the spiritual plane." Humanity "will turn back from technology to religion," Toynbee predicted. The leaders of the future would no longer be men of business and power; they would be spiritual guides. "There will be no more Fords and Napoleons, but there may still be St. Francises and John Wesleys." As for the origins of this religious revival, "it might not start in America or in any European or Western country, but in India. Conquered India will take her matter-of-fact American conqueror captive. . . . The center of power will ebb back from the shores of the Atlantic to the Middle East, where the earliest civilizations arose 5,000 or 6,000 years ago."

In his later years, Toynbee's support for American leadership faded but his belief that a universal state must come into being, and soon, was unshakable. In 1966, he mused about the possibility of a "Russo-American consortium" and suggested that if the Cold War antagonists couldn't get the job done, China would. In any event, freedom would certainly be extinguished, perhaps brutally. "I can imagine," he told a Japanese interviewer in 1970, "the world being held together and kept at peace in the year 2000 by an atrociously tyrannical dictatorship which did not hesitate to kill or torture anyone who, in its eyes, was a menace to the unquestioning acceptance of its absolute authority." As horrible as this version of the universal state sounded, Toynbee insisted it would be for the best. In an age of nuclear weapons and overpopulation, it is simply impossible to have freedom, peace, and national sovereignty at the same time. Humanity "has to choose between political unification and mass suicide."

In 1961, long after *A Study of History* had provoked the condemnation of historians and made Toynbee wealthy and famous, he published a final volume, simply entitled *Reconsiderations*. In it, Toynbee conceded much and failed to respond to more. "By the time Toynbee had agreed with some points made by his critics, met them halfway on others, and left questions unresolved in still other instances, little was left of the original, and no new vision of human history as a whole emerged from *Reconsiderations*," wrote his biographer, the historian William H. McNeill. Of course, Toynbee didn't consider this to be final proof that the pattern he saw in history was an illusion and his whole project a waste of a brilliant mind. But that's what it was.

The collapse of Toynbee's vision was not the end of his renown, because neither Toynbee nor his adoring public noticed that it had collapsed. Toynbee continued to publish books and commentary at a furious pace, and demand for his views about the present and future never flagged. He even won new acclaim in Japan, where "Toynbee societies" sprang up and the great man was invited to lecture the royal family. "No other historian, and few intellectuals of any stripe," concluded McNeill, "have even approached such a standing."

But when Toynbee died in 1975, his fame and influence were buried with him. The grand schema of *A Study of History* left no lasting mark on historical research and his visions of the future all came to naught. The "thick volumes of *A Study of History* sit undisturbed on the library shelves," Hugh Trevor-Roper wrote in 1989. "Who will ever read them? A few Ph.D. students, perhaps, desperate for a subject."

And so we are left with a riddle. Here was a man who probably knew more history than anyone alive. His knowledge of politics and current affairs was almost as vast. He brimmed with intelligence, energy, and imagination. And yet, his whole conception of the past and present was based on a mirage, and his supposed visions of the future were no more insightful than the ramblings of a man lost and wandering beneath a desert sun.

How could such a brilliant man have been so wrong?

ENTER THE KLUGE

The answer lies in Arnold Toynbee's brain. It was one of the finest of its kind, which is saying something because *any* human brain is a truly marvelous thing. But no brain is perfect, not even the brain of a genius like Toynbee.

The brain was not designed by a team of engineers. It was not beta-tested, reworked, and released with a big ad campaign; it *evolved*. When the ancestors of today's humans parted ways with the ancestors of today's chimpanzees some five to seven million years ago, the protohuman brain was much smaller than the modern brain's fourteen hundred cubic centimeters. Around 2.5 million years ago, and again 500,000 years ago, our ancestors' brains went through growth spurts. The final ballooning occurred some 150,000 to 200,000 years ago. Throughout all this vast stretch of time—and in the much longer years when the brains of our ancestors' ancestors were forming—evolutionary pressures shaped the brain's development.

Genes normally replicate and make exact copies of themselves, but occasionally they misfire and produce mutations. If a mutation makes the person who has it significantly less likely to survive and reproduce, it will die off along with the unlucky person who got it. But mutations that assist survival and reproduction spread. They may even, eventually, become universal features of the species. This is true of mutations involving muscles, bones, and organs. And it's true of mutations involving the brain.

So positive changes proliferate. Mistakes are removed. And we get smarter and smarter. It's all so simple, neat, and efficient.

And yet the human brain is anything but "simple, neat, and efficient." Borrowing a term from engineering, psychologist Gary Marcus has dubbed the brain a "kluge"—an inelegant but effective solution to a problem. When the carbon dioxide filters on board the *Apollo 13* capsule failed, engineers at mission control dreamed up a replacement made out of "a plastic bag, a cardboard box, some duct tape, and a sock." That's a kluge.

"Natural selection, the key mechanism of evolution, is only as good as the random mutations that arise," Marcus writes. "If a given mutation is beneficial, it may propagate but the most beneficial mutations imaginable, alas, never appear." As a result, an evolutionary solution to an environmental problem that is flawed or suboptimal but nonetheless does the job—a kluge, in other words—may spread and become standard operating equipment for the species. Once in place, the new equipment may be used to deal with other problems if, once again, it does the job adequately. And when new challenges arise, it may be the platform on which new less-than-perfect solutions will be built—thus multiplying the quirks and oddities. This is how we got spines that allow us to walk upright but are so flawed they routinely leave us bent over with back pain; vision marred by a built-in blind spot caused by the absurd design of our retina; and wisdom teeth that emerge to inflict pain for no particular reason. And then there is the brain. Imagine its mass, complexity, and general kluginess growing as our ancestors encountered one problem after another, across unfathomable spans of time, and it becomes obvious why the brain is anything but simple, neat, and efficient.

It's also critical to remember that natural selection operates in response to pressures in a *particular* environment. Change the environment and a solution may no longer be so helpful. Consider pale skin. It was a useful adaptation for human populations living at high latitudes, where sunlight is weaker, because it allowed the body to maximize production of vitamin D. But that advantage is strictly limited to the environment in which pale skin evolved. Not only is pale skin unnecessary at lower latitudes, where the sun's rays are stronger, it puts people at greater risk of skin cancer. The fact that evolutionary adaptations are specific to the environments in which they evolved didn't matter much throughout most of human history, for the simple reason that the environments in which we lived changed slowly. But as a result of the explosion of technology and productivity of the last several centuries, most people live in human-constructed environments that are dramatically different from the natural environments in which their ancestors lived— producing such novel sights as pasty-faced Englishmen clambering aboard airplanes for tropical destinations where the lucky vacationers will lie in the sun, sip fruity drinks, and boost their risk of skin cancer. From the perspective of one person, several centuries is a very long time, but in biological terms, it is a blink of a chimpanzee's eye. Human evolution doesn't move at anything like that speed and thus we are left with one of the defining facts of modern life: We live in the Information Age but our brains are Stone Age.

These two facts—the brain's kluginess and the radically changed environment in which we live—have a vast array of consequences. And almost all of us, almost always, are blissfully unaware of them.

Consider an experiment in which psychologists dropped 240 wallets on various Edinburgh streets. In each wallet, there was a personal photo, some ID, an old raffle ticket, a membership card or two, and a few other minor personal items. There was no cash. The only variation in the wallets was the photograph, which could be seen through a clear plastic window. In some, it showed a smiling baby. In others, there was a puppy, a family, or an elderly couple. A few of the wallets had no photo at all. The researchers wanted to know how many of the wallets would be dropped in mailboxes, taken to the police, or otherwise returned. More specifically, the researchers wanted to know if the content of the photograph in each wallet would make a difference. It shouldn't, of course. A lost wallet is important to whoever loses it and returning it is a bother no matter what's in it. In strictly rational terms, the nature of the photograph is irrelevant.

And yet psychologist Richard Wiseman discovered that the photograph made an enormous difference. Only 15 percent of those without one were returned. A little more than one-quarter of the wallets with a picture of an elderly couple were returned, while 48 percent of the wallets with a picture of a family, and 53 percent with the photo of a puppy, werc returned. But the baby walloped them all; an amazing 88 percent of wallets with pictures of infants were returned.

This doesn't make sense—until we consider the "two-system" model of decision making. Researchers have demonstrated that we have not one mind making decisions such as "Should I bother sending this wallet back to its owner?" We have two. One is the conscious mind, and since that mind is, by definition, aware only of itself, we think of it as being the single, unified, complete entity that is "me." Wrong. Quite wrong, in fact. Most of what the brain does happens without our having any conscious awareness of it, which means this "unconscious mind" is far more influential in our decision making than we realize.

The two minds work very differently. Whereas the conscious mind can slowly and carefully reason its way to a conclusion—"On the one hand, returning the wallet is the nice thing to do, but when I weigh that against the time and bother of returning it . . ."—the unconscious mind delivers instantaneous conclusions in the form of feeling, hunches, and intuitions. The difference in speed is critical to how the two systems work together. "One of psychology's fundamental insights," wrote psychologist Daniel Gilbert, "is that judgments are generally the products of nonconscious systems that operate quickly, on the basis of scant evidence, and in a routine manner, and then pass their hurried approximations to consciousness, which slowly and deliberately adjusts them." The unconscious mind is fast so it delivers first; the conscious mind then lumbers up and has a look at the unconscious mind's conclusion.

When someone spots a wallet on the streets of Edinburgh, picks it up, and decides to return it, she thinks that's all there is to the story. But far more happened. Even before her conscious thoughts got rolling, unconscious systems in her brain took a look at the situation and fired off a conclusion. That conclusion was the starting point for her conscious thoughts.

One unconscious mental system equates a photographed object with the real thing. That sounds mad—only a deranged person thinks a photo of a puppy is a puppy—until you recall that in the environment in which our brains evolved, there were no images of things that were not what they appeared to be. If something looked like a puppy, it was a puppy. Appearance equals reality. In the ancient environment in which our brains evolved, that was a good rule, which is why it became hardwired into the brain and remains there to this day. Of course, the reader will object that people do not routinely confuse photos of puppies with puppies. This is true, fortunately, but that's only because other brain systems intervene and correct this mistake. And a correction is not an erasure. Thus there remains a part of our brain that is convinced an image of something actually is that something. This quirk continues to have at least a little influence on our behavior, as jilted girlfriends reveal every time they tear up photos of the cad who hurt them or parents refuse to throw duplicate photos of their children in the trash. Still doubt this? Think of a lovely, tasty piece of fudge. But now imagine this fudge is shaped like a coil of dog poo. Still want to eat it? Right. That's exactly the reaction psychologists Paul Rozin and Carol Nemeroff got when they asked people to eat fudge shaped like dog poo, among other experiments involving a gap between image and reality. "In these studies, subjects realized that their negative feelings were unfounded but they felt and acknowledged them anyway."

We *really* like babies. The sight of a chubby little infant gurgling and grinning is enough to make even Scrooge smile. Babies are the best. And for good reason. In evolutionary terms, nothing is more important than reproducing. Among our ancestors, parents who didn't particularly care if their babies were well-fed, healthy, happy, and safe were much less likely to see those babies become adults with children of their own. So that attitude was going nowhere. But those who felt a surge of pleasure, compassion, and concern at the very sight of their darling little ones would take better care of them and be more likely to bounce grandchildren on their knees. Thus the automatic emotional response every normal person feels at the sight of a baby became hardwired, not only among humans but in every species that raises its young to maturity: Never come between a bear and her cubs.

But there's a problem here. Evolution is ruthless. It puts a priority on *your* reproduction, which means it cares about *your* offspring, not somebody else's. And yet that's not how we respond to babies. The sight of *any* gurgling and grinning infant makes us feel all warm and compassionate. Why is that? Our compassionate response to babies is a kluge. In prehistoric environments, we would seldom encounter a baby that was not our own, or that of our kin or our neighbor. Thus an automatic surge of compassion in response to the sight of *any* baby was not a perfect response—in ruthless reproduce-above-all terms—but it didn't cause us to do anything too foolish. So it did the job; it was good enough.

Now let's go back to those wallets on the streets of Edinburgh. Someone comes along, spots one, picks it up—and finds there is no picture. What does she do? Well, for her, there's not much more than rational calculation to go on. She knows the owner would probably like the wallet back, but there's no money in it so the loss wouldn't be too bad. And besides, returning it would be a hassle. Hence, only 15 percent of these wallets are returned. But another person picks up a different wallet, looks in it, and sees a photo of an elderly couple. This humanizes the problem—literally so, for the brain system that mistakes a photo of an elderly couple for the elderly couple themselves. An intuitive impulse is elicited, a feeling, a sense of compassion. Then the conscious brain steps in and thinks about the situation. Result: 25 percent of these wallets are returned, a significant increase.

The photo of a family generates a stronger unconscious response and a 48 percent return rate. And the baby, of course, produces an amazing 85 percent return rate. But what about the photo of the puppy? At 53 percent, its return rate is roughly equal to the photo of a family and double that of the elderly couple. And it's not even human! One might think that makes no sense from an evolutionary perspective, and yet, it does. The puppy and the baby may be different species but both have big eyes, a little mouth and chin, and soft features. Our automatic response to babies is triggered by these features, so anything or anyone that presents them can elicit a similar response. It's not a coincidence that all the animals and cartoon characters we find cute and adorable—from baby seals to Mickey Mouse—have the same features. Nor is it a coincidence that, as psychologists have shown, people often stereotype "baby-faced" adults as innocent, helpless, and needy. It's our kluge at work.

SEEING THINGS

It would be nice if feeling compassion for puppies and baby seals were the worst thing that happens when cognitive wires get crossed. Unfortunately, it's not. Thanks to the brain's evolutionary character, we often make mistakes about far more consequential matters.

In the last years of the Second World War, Germany pounded London with V-1 and V-2 rockets. These "flying bombs" were a horrible new weapon, unlike anything seen before. At first, Londoners didn't know what to make of the threat. All they knew was that, at any moment, with little or no warning, a massive explosion would erupt somewhere in the city. But gradually people began to realize that the rocket strikes were clustered in certain parts of the city, while others were spared. Rumors spread. Nazi spies were directing the missiles, some said. The spies must live in the parts of the city that weren't being hit. But what was the German strategy? The East End was being particularly hard hit and the East End is working class. Aha! The Germans must be trying to inflame class resentment in order to weaken the war effort.

It was a compelling explanation and yet it was wrong. As terrifying as the rockets were, they lacked precision guidance equipment and the best the Germans could do was point them at London and let them explode where they might. In 1946, statistician R. D. Clarke made a simple one-page calculation that compared the extent of clustering in the flying-bomb attacks to the clustering that could be expected if the bombs had been randomly distributed. There was a near-perfect match.

We have a hard time with randomness. If we try, we can understand it intellectually, but as countless experiments have shown, we don't get it intuitively. This is why someone who plunks one coin after another into a slot machine without winning will have a strong and growing sense— the "gambler's fallacy"—that a jackpot is "due," even though every result is random and therefore unconnected to what came before. Similarly, someone asked to put dots on a piece of paper in a way that mimics randomness will distribute them fairly evenly across the page, so there won't be any clusters of dots or large empty patches—an outcome that is actually very unlikely to happen in a true random distribution. And people believe that a sequence of random coin tosses that goes THTHHT is far more likely than the sequence THTHTH, even though they are equally likely.

Many people experienced this intuitive failure listening to an iPod. When it's set on "shuffle," it's supposed to choose and play songs randomly. But it often doesn't seem random. You may have heard six in a row from one artist and wondered if the program is biased in favor of that guy. Or maybe it gave top billing to your favorites and you suspected it's actually mimicking your nonrandom choices. Or perhaps— as some conspiracy-minded bloggers insisted—it seemed to favor songs from record companies that have a close relationship with Apple, the maker of the iPod. Peppered with complaints and accusations, Apple subsequently reprogrammed the shuffle feature: The idea was to make it "less random to make it feel more random," Steve Jobs said.

People are particularly disinclined to see randomness as the explanation for an outcome when their own actions are involved. Gamblers rolling dice tend to concentrate and throw harder for higher numbers, softer for lower. Psychologists call this the "illusion of control." We may know intellectually that the outcome is random and there's nothing we can do to control it, but that's seldom how we feel and behave. Psychologist Ellen Langer revealed the pervasive effect of the illusion of control in a stunning series of experiments. In one, people were asked to cut cards with another person to see who would draw the higher card and to make bets on the outcome. The outcome is obviously random. But the competitor people faced was in on the experiment, and his demeanor was carefully manipulated. Sometimes he was confident and calm; sometimes he was nervous. Those who faced a nervous competitor placed bigger bets than those who squared off against a confident opponent. Langer got the same result in five other experiments testing the "illusion of control"—including an experiment in which people put a higher value on a lottery ticket they chose at random than a ticket they were given, and another in which people rated their chances of winning a random-outcome game to be higher if they were given a chance to practice than if they had not played the game before.

Disturbing as these findings were, it was another of Langer's experiments that fully revealed how deluded the brain can be. Yale students were asked to watch someone flip a coin thirty times. Before each flip, the students were asked to predict whether the flip would come up heads or tails; after each, they were told whether they had "won" or "lost." In reality, the results were rigged so there would always be fifteen wins and fifteen losses, but some of the students would get a string of wins near the beginning while others first encountered a string of losses. At the end of the thirty flips, students were asked how many wins they thought they got in total, how good they thought they were at predicting coin tosses, and how many wins they thought they would get if they did the test again with a hundred flips in total. Langer discovered a clear tendency: Students who got a string of wins at the beginning thought they did better than those who didn't; they said their ability to predict was higher; and they said they would score significantly more wins in a future round of coin flipping. So the string of early wins had triggered the illusion of control. Students then focused on subsequent wins and paid little attention to losses, which led them to the false conclusion that they had notched more wins than losses and that they could do it again.

Langer's results are particularly startling when we consider the full context of the experiment. These are top-tier students at one of the world's best universities. They're in a clinical environment in which they believe their intelligence is being tested in some way. Under the circumstances, Langer noted, they "are likely to be 'superrational.'" And this is hardly a tricky task. A flipped coin is the very symbol of randomness and any educated person knows it is absurd to think skill has anything to do with calling "heads" or "tails." And yet Langer's test subjects still managed to fool themselves.

Langer's research inspired dozens more studies like it. Psychologists Paul Presson and Victor Benassi of the University of New Hampshire brought it all together and noticed that although psychologists use the term *illusion of control,* much of the research wasn't about "controlling" an outcome. As in Langer's coin-flipping experiment, it was really about *predicting* outcomes. They also found the illusion is stronger when it involves prediction. In a sense, the "illusion of control" should be renamed the "illusion of prediction."

This illusion is a key reason experts routinely make the mistake of seeing random hits as proof of predictive ability. Money manager and *Forbes* columnist Kenneth Fisher recalled attending a conference at which audience members were invited to predict how the Dow would do the next day. At the time, the index hovered around 800, so Fisher guessed it would drop 5.39 points. "Then I noticed the gent next to me jotting down a 35-point plunge," Fisher recalled in 1987. "He said he hadn't the foggiest idea what might happen," but he certainly had a strategy. "If you win," the man told Fisher, "the crowd will think you were lucky to beat everyone else who bets on minor moves. But if my extreme call wins, they'll be dazzled." The next day the Dow dropped 29 points. "That afternoon, folks bombarded the winner for details on how he had foreseen the crash. He obliged them all, embellishing his 'analysis' more with each telling. That night, when I saw him alone, he had convinced himself that he had known all along, and became indignant when I reminded him that his call was based on showmanship."

Blame evolution. In the Stone Age environment in which our brains evolved, there were no casinos, no lotteries, and no iPods. A caveman with a good intuitive grasp of randomness couldn't have used it to get rich and marry the best-looking woman in the tribe. It wouldn't have made him healthier or longer-lived, and it wouldn't have increased his chances of having children. In evolutionary terms, it would be a dud. And so an intuitive sense of randomness didn't become hardwired into the human brain and randomness continues to elude us to this day.

The ability to spot patterns and causal connections is something else entirely. Recognizing that the moon waxes and wanes at regular intervals improved the measurement of time, which was quite handy when someone figured out that a certain patch of berries is ripe at a particular period every summer. It was also good to know that gazelles come to the watering hole when the rains stop, that people who wander in the long grass tend to be eaten by lions, and a thousand other useful regularities. Pattern recognition was literally a matter of life and death, so natural selection got involved and it became a hardwired feature of the human brain.

And not only the human brain. Birds and animals also benefit from spotting patterns, and thus their cognitive wiring makes them adept at seeing connections. Sometimes they are too good at it. When B. F. Skinner put pigeons in his famous "Skinner box" and gave them food at randomly selected moments, the pigeons quickly connected the appearance of the food to whatever they happened to be doing when it appeared. A pigeon that happened to be thrusting its head into a corner, for example, ate the food, then went back to the lucky corner and resumed thrusting its head, over and over, expecting more food to drop. It would be nice to blame this behavior on the limited intelligence of pigeons, but they are far from the only species that draws false connections between unrelated events. Humans do it all the time. Skinner believed it was a root cause of superstition. "The birds behaved as if they thought that their habitual movement had a causal influence on the reward mechanism, which it didn't," wrote biologist Richard Dawkins. "It was the pigeon equivalent of a rain dance."

Rain dances are ineffective, but they aren't harmful. Someone who does a dance, gets rained on, and concludes that dancing causes rain has made a serious mistake, but he won't increase his chances of an early death if he dances when he wants rain. That's typical of false positives.

Seeing patterns that aren't there isn't likely to make a big difference to a person's chances of surviving and reproducing—unlike *failing* to see patterns that *do* exist. This profound imbalance is embedded in our cognitive wiring. We consistently overlook randomness but we see patterns everywhere, whether they are there or not. The stars may be scattered randomly across the night sky, but people see bears, swans, warriors, and the countless other patterns we call constellations. We see faces in clouds, rocks, and the moon. We see canals on Mars and the Virgin Mary on burnt toast. Of course, we also see a great many patterns that really are there, often with astonishing speed and accuracy. But the cost of this ability is a tendency to see things that don't exist.

Although humans may share this tendency with other animals, at least to some extent, there is something quite different about the human quest to spot patterns. In a classic experiment that has been conducted with many variations, people sit before a red light and a green light. The researchers ask them to guess which of the two lights will come on next. At first, there isn't much to go on. There seems to be no pattern. And indeed, there isn't a pattern. The flashing of the lights is random, although the test subjects aren't told this. But as lights continue to flash and time passes, it becomes apparent that there is one regularity: The red light is coming on much more often than the green. In fact, the distribution is 80 percent red, 20 percent green. Faced with this situation, people will tilt their guesses to match the frequency with which the lights are coming on—so they'll guess red about 80 percent of the time and green 20 percent. In effect, they are trying to match the "pattern" of the flashes. But that's impossible because it's random. Needless to say, people don't do very well on this test.

But pigeons do. So do rats and other animals. Put to the same test, they follow a different strategy. Since there are more red flashes than green, they simply choose red over and over. That yields far better results. You might say it's the rational thing to do. But we rational humans don't do it.

Why not? That's the question University of California neuroscientist

Michael Gazzaniga explored in a fascinating experiment. For decades, Gazzaniga has worked with people who have had the connection between the right and left hemispheres of their brain severed, usually as a form of treatment for severe epilepsy. These "split-brain patients" function surprisingly well under most circumstances. But because the hemispheres control different aspects of perception, thought, and action, severing the two does produce some startling results. Most important for researchers is the fact that it is possible to communicate with one hemisphere of the brain—by revealing information to one eyeball but not the other, for example—while keeping the other in the dark.

When Gazzaniga and his colleagues put the left hemispheres of split-brain patients to the red-green test, he got the usual results: They tried to figure out the pattern and ended up doing poorly. But right hemispheres did something startling: Like rats and other animals, they guessed red over and over again and thus got much better results. For Gazzaniga, this was important proof of an idea he has pursued for many years. In the left hemisphere of the brain—and only the left hemisphere—is a neural network he calls "the Interpreter." The Interpreter makes sense of things. After the brain experiences perceptions, emotions, and all the other processes that operate at lightning speed, the Interpreter comes along and explains everything. "The left hemisphere's capacity of continual interpretation means it is always looking for order and reason," Gazzaniga wrote, "even when they don't exist."

The Interpreter is ingenious. And relentless. It never wants to give up and say, "This doesn't make sense," or "I don't know." There is *always* an explanation. In one experiment, Gazzaniga showed an image to the left hemisphere of a split-brain patient and another to the right hemisphere. An array of photos was spread out on a table. The patient was asked to pick the photo that was connected to the image they had seen. In one trial, the left hemisphere of the patient was shown an image of a chicken claw; on the table was a photo of a chicken. The right hemisphere was shown a snow scene; on the table was a photo of a snow shovel. When the patient's left hand—which is controlled by the right hemisphere—pointed to the shovel, Gazzaniga asked the left hemisphere why. It had no idea, of course. But it didn't say that. "Oh, that's simple," the patient answered confidently. "The chicken claw goes with the chicken and you need a shovel to clean out the chicken shed."

For humans, inventing stories that make the world sensible and orderly is as natural as breathing. That capacity serves us well, for the most part, but when we are faced with something that *isn't* sensible and orderly, it's a problem. The spurious stories that result can seriously lead us astray, and, unfortunately, more information may not help us. In fact, more information makes more explanations possible, so having lots of data available can actually empower our tendency to see things that aren't there. Add a computer and things only get worse. "Data mining" is now a big problem for precisely this reason: Statisticians know that with plenty of numbers and a powerful computer, statistical correlations can always be found. These correlations will often be meaningless, but if the human capacity for inventing explanatory stories is not restrained by constant critical scrutiny, they won't *appear* meaningless. They will look like hard evidence of a compelling hypothesis—just as the apparent clustering of rocket strikes in London looked like evidence that the Nazis were targeting certain neighborhoods in order to advance their cunning strategy.

We can all fall victim to this trap, but it's particularly dangerous for experts. By definition, experts know far more about their field of expertise than nonexperts. They have read all the books, and they have masses of facts at their fingertips. This knowledge can be the basis of real insight, but it also allows experts to see order that isn't there and to explain it with stories that are compelling, insightful, and false. In a PBS interview, Jeff Greenfield, an American journalist, recalled how he and other pundits were tripped up during the presidential election of 1988. Vice President George H. W. Bush wouldn't win, they believed. The reason was an obscure fact known only to political experts: "No sitting vice-president has been elected since Martin Van Buren." Aha! A meaning-ful pattern! Or so it seemed. But as it turned out, Bush didn't lose and the pundits would have been better off if they had never heard of Martin Van Buren.

This is the quicksand that consumed Arnold Toynbee. His lifelong project began with an intuition—a "flash of perception," he called it—that the trajectory of Western history was following that of ancient Greece and Rome. After spotting that pattern, Toynbee elaborated on it and committed it to paper in 1921. When, in the course of writing *A Study of History*, Toynbee was confronted with information that didn't fit his tidy scheme—such as the sudden appearance of the Islamic "universal state"—he was in the position of the hapless split-brain patient whose hand was pointed at a photo of a shovel for some reason. It didn't make sense; it didn't fit the pattern. So Toynbee's left hemisphere got busy. Drawing on his intelligence and his vast store of knowledge, Toynbee created ingenious stories that explained the seemingly inexpli-cable and maintained order in his mental universe.

Arnold Toynbee wasn't deluded *despite* his brilliance. He was deluded *because* of it.

ALWAYS CONFIDENT, ALWAYS RIGHT

Is absinthe a precious stone or a liquor? You probably know the right answer. But how *certain* are you that your answer is right? If you are 100 percent certain, you are dead sure. There's *no way* you can be wrong. Ninety percent certainty is a little lower but still quite confident. Eighty percent a little lower still. But if you only give yourself a 50 percent chance of being right, it's a toss-up, a random guess, and you're not con-fident at all. In 1977, psychologists Paul Slovic, Sarah Lichtenstein, and Baruch Fischhoff used a series of questions and a rating system like this one in order to test the confidence people have in their own judgments. What they were looking for was not how many questions people got right or wrong. They were interested in calibration: When people said they were 100 percent confident, were they right 100 percent of the time? Were they right in 70 percent of the cases in which they gave a 70 percent confidence rating? That's perfect calibration—proof that they are exactly as confident as they should be.

The researchers found that no one was perfectly calibrated. In fact, their confidence was consistently skewed. When the questions were easy, people were a little underconfident. But as the questions got harder, they became more sure of themselves and underconfidence turned into overconfidence. Incredibly, when people said they were 100 percent sure they were right, they were actually right only 70 to 80 percent of the time.

This pattern has turned up in a long list of studies over the years. And, no, it's not just undergrads lacking in knowledge and experience. Philip Tetlock discovered the same pattern in his work with expert predictions. Other researchers have found it in economists, demographers, intelligence analysts, doctors, and physicists. One study that directly compared experts with laypeople found that both expected experts to be "much less overconfident"—but both were, in fact, equally overconfident. Piling on information doesn't seem to help, either. In fact, knowing more can make things worse. One study found that as clinical psychologists were given more information about a patient, their confidence in their diagnosis rose faster than their accuracy, resulting in a level of certainty about their decisions that "became entirely out of proportion to the actual correctness of those decisions." Other studies with different test subjects got similar results.

Overconfidence is a universal human trait closely related to an equally widespread phenomenon known as "optimism bias." Ask smokers about the risk of getting lung cancer from smoking and they'll say it's high. But *their* risk? Not so high. Starting a new business? Most fail, but mine won't. Getting married? Other people should have a prenuptial agreement. But not me, my love is forever. The evolutionary advantage of this bias is obvious: It encourages people to take action and makes them more resilient in the face of setbacks. Overconfidence contributes to this, since feeling good about a judgment is a prerequisite to acting on it.

And thanks to yet another bias, excessive certainty is only too likely to grow.

After coming to a conclusion, Sir Francis Bacon wrote, "the human understanding . . . draws all things else to support and agree with it. And though there be a greater number and weight of instances to be found on the other side, yet these it either neglects or despises, or else by some distinction sets aside and rejects; in order that by this great and pernicious predetermination the authority of its former conclusions may remain inviolate." Heaps of research conducted in the twentieth and twenty-first centuries have only confirmed Bacon's wisdom. Dubbed "confirmation bias" by psychologist Peter Wason, it is as simple as it is dangerous: Once we form a belief, for any reason, good or bad, rational or bonkers, we will eagerly seek out and accept information that supports it while not bothering to look for information that does not—and if we are unavoidably confronted with information that doesn't fit, we will be hypercritical of it, looking for any excuse to dismiss it as worthless.

One famous experiment was conducted in 1979, when capital punishment was a hot issue in the United States. Researchers assembled a group of people who already had an opinion about whether the death penalty was an effective way to deter crime. Half the group believed it was; half did not. They were then asked to read a study that concluded capital punishment does deter crime. This was followed by an information sheet that detailed the methods used in the study and its findings. They were also asked to read criticisms of the study that had been made by others and the responses of the studies' authors to those criticisms. Finally, they were asked to judge the quality of the study. Was it solid? Did it strengthen the case for capital punishment? The whole procedure was then repeated with a study that concluded the death penalty does *not* deter crime. (The order of presentation was varied to avoid bias.) At the end, people were asked if their views about capital punishment had changed.

The studies were not real. The psychologists wrote them with the intention of producing two pieces of evidence that were mirror images of each other, identical in every way except for their conclusions. If people process information rationally, this whole experience should have been a wash. People would see a study of a certain quality on one side, a study of the same quality on the other, and they would shrug, with little or no change in their views. But that's not what happened. Instead, people judged the two studies—which were methodologically identical, remember—very differently. The study that supported their belief was deemed to be high-quality work that got to the facts of the matter. But the other study? Oh, it was flawed. Very poor stuff. And so it was dismissed. Having processed the information in a blatantly biased fashion, the final outcome was inevitable: People left the experiment more strongly convinced than when they came in that they were right and those who disagreed were wrong.

"If one were to attempt to identify a single problematic aspect of human reasoning that deserves attention above all others," wrote psychologist Raymond Nickerson, "the confirmation bias would have to be among the candidates for consideration." In Peter Wason's seminal experiment, he provided people with feedback so that when they sought out confirming evidence and came to a false conclusion, they were told, clearly and unmistakably, that it was incorrect. Then they were asked to try again. Incredibly, half of those who had been told their belief was false continued to search for confirmation that it was right: Admitting a mistake and moving on does not come easily to *Homo sapiens*.

Like everyone else, experts are susceptible to confirmation bias. One study asked seventy-five social scientists to examine a paper that had been submitted for publication in an academic journal. This sort of peer review is routine and is intended to weed out work that is uninformative or methodologically weak. What it's *not* supposed to do is screen papers based on their conclusions. Research is either solid or not. Whether it happens to confirm the reviewer's beliefs is irrelevant. At least, it's supposed to be irrelevant. But it's not, as this study demonstrated. One version of the paper sent out for peer review came to conclusions that were in line with the commonly held view in the field; a second version of the paper was methodologically identical but its conclusions contradicted the conventional wisdom. Reviewers who got the paper that supported their views typically judged it to be relevant work of sound quality and they recommended it be published; those who got the paper that contradicted their views tended to think it was irrelevant and unsound and they said it should be rejected. "Reviewers were strongly biased," the researcher concluded. Not that they were *aware* of their bias, mind you. In fact, they would have been offended at the very suggestion.

Perhaps we should call this the "Toynbee phenomenon," because there is no more spectacular example than Arnold Toynbee's *A Study of History*. By 1921, Toynbee's vision was locked in. He was certain there was a pattern in classical and Western histories. That pattern became the outline of *A Study of History*. Then Toynbee started rummaging through the histories of other civilizations and found that they, too, followed the same pattern—not because the pattern was real but because Toynbee's information processing was profoundly biased. To paraphrase Sir Francis Bacon, Toynbee energetically searched for and collected information that supported his convictions while "neglecting or despising" information that did not—and when contrary evidence was too big to dismiss or ignore, he cobbled together ingenious stories that transformed contradiction into confirmation. "His whole scheme is really a scheme of pigeon-holes elaborately arranged and labelled, into which ready-made historical facts can be put," wrote the philosopher and historian R. G. Collingwood. A. J. P. Taylor's judgment was even more severe. "The events of the past can be made to prove anything if they are arranged in a suitable pattern, and Professor Toynbee has succeeded in forcing them into a scheme that was in his head from the beginning."

BETTER A FOX THAN A HEDGEHOG

It is a heartening fact that many experts saw through the delusions of Arnold Toynbee. In a phrase, they showed better judgment. That's worth emphasizing because it's tempting to become cynical about experts and their opinions. We should resist that temptation, for all experts are not alike.

In Philip Tetlock's research, he was careful to have experts make predictions on matters both within and beyond their particular specialty. Only when they were operating within their specialty were experts really predicting as capital-*E* Experts. Otherwise, they were more like smart, informed laypeople. Analyzing the numbers, Tetlock found some experts making predictions as Experts were more accurate than when they made them as laypeople. No surprise, they know more. They *should* be more accurate. More surprising is that others were actually *less* accurate.

As the reader should be able to guess by now, the experts who were more accurate when they made predictions within their specialty were foxes; those who were less accurate were hedgehogs. Hedgehogs are bad at predicting the future under any circumstances, but it seems the more they know about what they're predicting, the *worse* they get. The explanation for this important and bizarre result lies, at least in part, in the psychological mechanisms discussed here.

Expertise means more knowledge, and more knowledge produces more detail and complication. More detail and complication make it harder to come to a clear and confident answer. At least it *should* make it harder. Say the question is "How will the economy do next year?" Someone who has only a few facts to go by may find they all point in one direction. But someone who has masses of information available—facts about economic history and theory, about finance, bonds and stocks, production and consumption trends, interest rates, international trade, and so on—won't find *all* the facts neatly lined up and pointing like an arrow in one direction. It's far more likely the facts will point to boom, and bust, and lots of places in between, and it will be a struggle to bring even modest clarity to the whole chaotic picture.

Foxes are okay with that. They like complexity and uncertainty, even if that means they can only draw cautious conclusions and they have to admit they could be wrong. "Maybe" is fine with them.

But not hedgehogs. They find complexity and uncertainty unacceptable. They want simple and certain answers. And they are sure they can get them using the One Big Idea that drives their thinking. With this mindset, the hedgehog's greater knowledge doesn't challenge the psychological biases we're all prone to. Instead, it supercharges them. As Arnold Toynbee demonstrated so well, expertise boosts the hedgehog's ability to see patterns that aren't there and to deal with contradictory evidence by rationalizing it away or twisting it so it supports what the hedgehog believes. In this way, the hedgehog gets an answer that will almost certainly be—to quote H. L. Mencken—clear, simple, and wrong. Of course the hedgehog isn't likely to accept that he may be wrong. Confidence is a defining feature of the species: Not only are hedgehogs more overconfident than foxes, they are far more likely to declare outcomes "certain" or "impossible." Could they be wrong? Never!

In his classic 1952 examination of pseudoscience, *Fads and Fallacies in the Name of Science,* Martin Gardner took a fascinating look at the work of late nineteenth- and early twentieth-century "pyramidologists." These obsessive investigators measured every nook and cranny of the pyramids, inside and out, using every imaginable unit and method. They then tried to prove "mathematically" that the pyramid's dimensions were encoded with a vast trove of knowledge, including a complete record of all the great events of the past and future. With masses of data at hand, and an unrestrained desire to prove what they were certain was right, they succeeded. In a sense. And only up to a point. "Many great books have been written on this subject, some of which have been presented to me by their authors," Bertrand Russell dryly observed. "It is a singular fact that the Great Pyramid always predicts the history of the world accurately up to the date of publication of the book in question, but after that date it becomes less reliable." As Gardner demonstrated, the pyramidologists were filled with passionate belief. Almost without exception, they were devout Christians, and by picking the numbers that fit, while ignoring the rest, they made the pyramid's dimensions align with past events. Projecting forward, they then "discovered" that the events described in the Book of Revelation would soon unfold. One of the earliest pyramidologists claimed 1882 would mark the beginning of the end. Later investigators predicted it would come in 1911, 1914, 1920, or 1925. When those predictions failed to pan out, claims were made for 1933 and 1936. As one prediction after another passed without Jesus descending from the clouds, interest in this first wave of pyramidology slowly faded.

By the time Gardner wrote his book in 1952, most people had forgotten pyramidology. Or they thought it was silly. In 1952, smart people knew the future was written in the pages of Toynbee.

Gardner wasn't so sure. The same tendency to fit data to belief can be seen, he wrote, "in the great cyclical theories of history—the works of men like Hegel, Spengler, Marx, and perhaps, though one must say it in hushed tones, the works of Toynbee. The ability of the mind to fool itself by unconscious 'fudging' on the facts—an overemphasis here and an underemphasis there—is far greater than most people realize. The literature of Pyramidology stands as a permanent and pathetic tribute to that ability. Will the work of the prophetic historians mentioned above seem to readers of the year 2000 as artificial in their constructions as the predictions of the Pyramidologists?"

It's fitting that Gardner made his point by asking a question about the future rather than making a bold and certain claim. Martin Gardner was a classic fox. So were the historians who scoffed when so many other smart people were venerating Toynbee as a prophet. History is immensely complex, they insisted, and each event is unique. Only the delusional see a simple pattern rolling smoothly through the past, present, and future. "He dwells in a world of his own imagining," wrote Pieter Geyl in one of his final attacks on Arnold Toynbee, "where the challenges of rationally thinking mortals cannot reach him."

The foxes were right. About history. And about Arnold Toynbee. That brilliant hedgehog never understood how badly he deceived himself and the world, which makes his life story, for all the man's fame and wealth, a tragedy.

4

The Experts Agree: Expect Much More of the Same

[Against the menace of Japanese economic power] there is now
only one way out. The time has come for the United States to
make common cause with the Soviet Union.

—GORE VIDAL, 1986

"We are definitely at war with Japan," says the American
hero of *Rising Sun,* Michael Crichton's 1992 suspense
novel. Americans may not know it; they may even deny
it. But the war rages on because, to the Japanese, business is war by other
means. And Japan is rolling from victory to victory. "Sooner or later,
Americans must come to grips with the fact that Japan has become the
leading industrial nation in the world," Crichton writes in an afterword.
"The Japanese have the longest lifespan. They have the highest employ-
ment, the highest literacy, the smallest gap between rich and poor. Their
manufactured goods have the highest quality. They have the best food.
The fact is that a country the size of Montana, with half our population,
will soon have an economy equal to ours."

More op-ed than potboiler—not many thrillers come with
bibliographies—*Rising Sun* was the culmination of a long line of Amer-

ican jeremiads about the danger in the East. Japan "threatens our way of life and ultimately our freedoms as much as past dangers from Nazi Germany and the Soviet Union," wrote Robert Zielinski and Nigel Holloway in the 1991 book *Unequal Equities.* A year earlier, in *Agents of Influence,* Pat Choate warned that Japan had achieved "effective political domination over the United States." In 1988, the former American trade representative Clyde Prestowitz worried that the United States and Japan were "trading places," as the title of his book put it. "The power of the United States and the quality of American life is [*sic*] diminishing in every respect," Prestowitz wrote. In 1992, Robert Reich— economist and future secretary of labor—put together a list of all the books he could find in this alarming subgenre. It came to a total of thirty-five, all with titles like *The Coming War with Japan, The Silent War,* and *Trade Wars.*

Japan blocked American companies from selling in its domestic market, these books complained, while it ruthlessly exploited the openness of the American market. Japan planned and plotted; it saved, invested, and researched; it elevated productivity. And it got stronger by the day. Its banks were giants, its stock markets rich, its real estate more valuable than any on earth. Japan swallowed whole industries, starting with televisions, then cars. Now, with Japan's growing control of the semiconductor and computer markets, it was high tech. In Crichton's novel, the plot revolves around a videotape of a murder that has been doctored by Japanese villains who are sure the American detectives— using "inferior American video technology"—will never spot the fake. Meanwhile, American debt was piling up as fast as predictions of American economic decline; in 1992, a terrifying book called *Bankruptcy 1995* spent nine months on the *New York Times* best-seller list. American growth was slow, employment and productivity were down, and investment and research were stagnant.

Put it all together and the trend lines revealed the future—the Japanese economy would pass the American, and the victors of the Second World War would be defeated in the economic war. "November, 2004," begins the bleak opening of Daniel Burstein's *Yen!*, a 1988 best seller. "America, battered by astronomical debts and reeling from prolonged economic decline, is gripped by a new and grave economic crisis." Japanese banks hold America's debt. Japanese corporations have bought out American corporations and assets. Japanese manufacturers look on American workers as cheap overseas labor. And then things get really bad. By the finish of Burstein's dramatic opening, the United States is feeble and ragged while Japan is no longer "simply the richest country in the word." It is the strongest.

Less excitable thinkers didn't see Japan's rise in quite such martial terms but they did agree that Japan was a giant rapidly becoming a titan. In the 1990 book *Millennium,* Jacques Attali, the former adviser to French president François Mitterrand, described an early twenty-first century in which both the Soviet Union and the United States ceased to be superpowers, leaving Japan contending with Europe for the economic leadership of the world. Moscow would fall into orbit around Brussels, Attali predicted. Washington, DC, would revolve around Tokyo. Lester Thurow sketched a similar vision in his influential best seller *Head to Head,* published in 1992. The recent collapse of the Soviet Union meant the coming years would see a global economic war between Japan, Europe, and the United States, wrote Thurow, a famous economist and former dean of the MIT Sloan School of Management. Thurow examined each of the "three relatively equal contenders" like a punter at the races. "If one looks at the last 20 years, Japan would have to be considered the betting favorite to win the economic honors of owning the 21st century," Thurow wrote. But Europe was also expanding smartly, and Thurow decided it had the edge. "Future historians will record that the 21st century belonged to the House of Europa!" And the United States? It's the weakest of the three, Thurow wrote. Americans should learn to speak Japanese or German.

The details varied somewhat from forecast to forecast, but the views of Thurow and Attali were received wisdom among big thinkers. "Just how powerful, economically, will Japan be in the early 21st-century?"

asked the historian Paul Kennedy in his much-discussed 1987 best seller *The Rise and Fall of the Great Powers*. "Barring large-scale war, or ecological disaster, or a return to a 1930s-style world slump and protectionism, the consensus answer seems to be: *much* more powerful." As they peered nervously into the future, the feelings of many Americans were perfectly expressed by an ailing President George H. W. Bush when he keeled over and vomited in the lap of the Japanese prime minister.

They needn't have worried. The experts were wrong.

By the time the Hollywood adaptation of *Rising Sun* was released in 1993, Japan was in big trouble. Real estate had tanked, stocks had plunged, and Japan's mammoth banks staggered under a stupendous load of bad debt. What followed would be known as "the lost decade," a period of economic stagnation that surprised experts and made a hash of forecasts the world over.

Europe did better in the 1990s but it, too, failed to fulfill the forecasts of Lester Thurow and so many others. The United States also surprised the experts, but in quite a different way. The decade that was so widely expected to see the decline, if not the fall, of the American giant, turned into a golden age as technology-driven gains in productivity produced strong growth, surging stocks, rock-bottom unemployment, a slew of social indicators trending positive, and—miracle of miracles—a federal budget churning out huge surpluses. By the turn of the millennium, the United States had become a "hyperpower" that dominated "the world as no empire has ever done before in the entire history of humankind," in the purple words of one French observer. The first decade of the twenty-first century was much less delightful for the United States—it featured a mild recession, two wars, slow growth, the crash of 2008, a brutal recession, and soaring deficits—but Europe and Japan still got smaller in Uncle Sam's rearview mirror. Between 1991 and 2009, the American economy grew 63 percent, compared to 16 percent for Japan, 22 percent for Germany, and 35 percent for France. In 2008, the gross national income of the United States was greater than that of Germany, the

United Kingdom, France, Italy, and Spain combined. And it was more than three times that of Japan.

How could so many experts have been so wrong? A complete answer would be a book in itself. But a crucial component of the answer lies in psychology. For all the statistics and reasoning involved, the experts derived their judgments, to one degree or another, from what they felt to be true. And in doing so, they were fooled by a common bias.

In psychology and behavioral economics, *status quo bias* is a term applied in many different contexts, but it usually boils down to the fact that people are conservative: We stick with the status quo unless something compels us otherwise. In the realm of prediction, this manifests itself in the tendency to see tomorrow as being like today. Of course, this doesn't mean we expect nothing to change. Change is what made today what it is. But the change we expect is more of the same. If crime, stocks, gas prices, or anything else goes up today, we will tend to expect it to go up tomorrow. And so tomorrow won't be *identical* to today. It will be *like* today. Only more so.

This tendency to take current trends and project them into the future is the starting point of most attempts to predict. Very often, it's also the end point. That's not necessarily a bad thing. After all, tomorrow typically *is* like today. Current trends *do* tend to continue. But not always. Change happens. And the farther we look into the future, the more opportunity there is for current trends to be modified, bent, or reversed. Predicting the future by projecting the present is like driving with no hands. It works while you are on a long stretch of straight road, but even a gentle curve is trouble, and a sharp turn always ends in a flaming wreck.

In 1977, researchers inadvertently demonstrated this basic truth when they asked eight hundred experts in international affairs to predict what the world would look like five and twenty-five years out. "The experts typically predicted little or no change in events or trends, rather than predicting major change," the researchers noted. That paid off in the many cases where there actually was little or no change. But the experts went off the road at every curve, and there were some spectacular crashes. Asked about Communist governments in 2002, for example, almost one-quarter of the experts predicted there would be the same number as in 1977, while 45 percent predicted there would be more. As a straight-line projection from the world of 1977, that's reasonable. As insight into the world as it actually was in 2002—more than a decade after most Communist governments had been swept away—it was about as helpful as a randomly selected passage from Nostradamus.

Similar wrecks can be found in almost any record of expert predictions. In his 1968 book *The End of the American Era,* for example, the political scientist Andrew Hacker insisted race relations in the United States would get much, much worse. There will be "dynamiting of bridges and water mains, firing of buildings, assassination of public officials and private luminaries," Hacker wrote. "And of course there will be occasional rampages." Hacker also stated with perfect certainty that "as the white birth rate declines," blacks will "start to approach 20 or perhaps 25 percent of the population." Hacker would have been bang on if the trends of 1968 had continued. But they didn't, so he wasn't. The renowned sociologist Daniel Bell made the same mistake in his landmark 1976 book *The Cultural Contradictions of Capitalism.* Inflation is here to stay, he wrote, which is certainly how it felt in 1976. And Bell's belief was widely shared. In *The Book of Predictions*—a compilation of forecasts published in 1981—every one of the fourteen predictions about inflation in the United States saw it rising rapidly for at least another decade. Some claimed it would keep growing until 2030. A few even explained why it was simply impossible to whip inflation. And yet, seven years after the publication of Bell's book, and two years after *The Book of Predictions,* inflation was whipped.

Some especially breathtaking examples of hands-free driving can be found in *The World in 2030 A.D.,* a fascinating book written by F. E. Smith in 1930. Smith, also known as the earl of Birkenhead, was a senior British politician and a close friend of Winston Churchill. Intellectually curious, scientifically informed, well-read, and imaginative, Smith expected the coming century to produce astonishing change. "The child of 2030, looking back on 1930, will consider it as primitive and quaint as the conditions of 1830 seem to the children of today," he wrote. But not even Smith's adventurous frame of mind could save him from the trap of status quo bias. In discussing the future of labor, Smith noted that the number of hours worked by the average person had fallen in recent decades and so, he confidently concluded, "by 2030 it is probable that the average 'week' of the factory hand will consist of 16 or perhaps 24 hours." He was no better on military matters. "The whole question of future strategy and tactics pivots on the development of the tank," he wrote. That was cutting-edge thinking in 1930, and it proved exactly right when the Second World War began in 1939, but Smith wasn't content to look ahead a mere nine years. "The military mind of 2030 will be formed by what engineers accomplish in this direction during the next 60 or 70 years. And, in view of what has been accomplished since 1918, I see no limits to the evolution of mobile fortresses." Smith was even worse on politics, his specialty. "Economic and political pressure may make it imperative that the heart of the [British] Empire should migrate from London to Canada or even to Australia at some date in the next century or in the ages which are to follow," he wrote. But no matter. "The integrity of the Empire will survive this transplantation without shock or disaster." And India would still be the jewel in the crown. "British rule in India will endure. By 2030, whatever means of self-government India has achieved, she will still remain a loyal and integral part of the British Empire."

Among literary theorists and historians, it is a truism that novels set in the future say a great deal about the time they were written and little or nothing about the future. Thanks to status quo bias, the same is often true of expert predictions, a fact that becomes steadily more apparent as time passes and predictions grow musty with age. *The World in 2030* is a perfect demonstration. Read today, it's a fascinating book full of marvelous insights that have absolutely nothing to do with the subject of its title. In fact, as a guide to the early twenty-first century, it is completely worthless. Its value lies entirely in what it tells us about the British political class, and one British politician, in 1930. The same is true of *Rising Sun* and so many of the other books written during the panic about Japan Inc. They drew on the information and feelings available to the authors at the time they were written, and they faithfully reflect that moment, but the factors that actually made the difference in the years that followed seldom appear in these books. The Internet explosion was a surprise to most, as was the rise of Silicon Valley, abetted by the shift in high-tech development from hardware to software. The turnaround in the American budget and the decline of Japan's banks were dramatically contrary to current trends. A few observers may have spotted some of these developments coming but not one foresaw them all, much less understood their cumulative effect. And perhaps most telling of all, these books say little or nothing about one of the biggest economic developments of the 1990s and the first decade of the twenty-first century: the emergence of China and India as global economic powers. In Clyde Prestowitz's *Trading Places,* the Asian giants are ignored. In Jacques Attali's *Millennium,* the existence of China and India was at least acknowledged, which is something, but Attali was sure both would remain poor and backward. Their role in the twenty-first century, he wrote, would be to serve as spoils in the economic war waged by the mighty Japanese and European blocs; or, if they resisted foreign domination, they could instigate war. Attali did concede that his forecast would be completely upended if China and India "were to be integrated into the global economy and market"—but "that miracle is most unlikely." Lester Thurow did even worse. In *Head to Head,* he never mentioned India, and China was dismissed in two short pages. "While China will always be important politically and militarily," Thurow wrote, "it will not have a big impact on the world economy in the first half of the 21st century. . . ."

Why didn't the experts and pundits see a problem with what they were doing? Trends end, surprises happen—everyone knows that. And the danger of running a straight-line projection of current trends into the future is notorious. "Long-term growth forecasts are complicated by the fact that the top performers of the last ten years may not necessarily be the top performers of the next ten years," noted a 2005 Deutsche Bank report. "Who could have imagined in 1991 that a decade of stagnation would beset Japan? Who would have forecast in the same year that an impressive rebound of the U.S. economy was to follow? Simply extrapolating the past cannot provide reliable forecasts." Wise words. Curiously, though, the report they are found in predicts that the developed countries whose economies will grow most between 2005 and 2020 are, in order, Ireland, the United States, and Spain. That looks a lot like a straight-line projection of the trend in 2005, when those three countries were doing wonderfully. But three years later—when Ireland, the United States, and Spain led the world in the great cliff-plunge of 2008—it looked like yet another demonstration that "simply extrapolating the past cannot provide reliable forecasts."

Daniel Burstein's *Yen!* has a chart showing Japanese stock market levels steadily rising for the previous twenty years under the headline "Tokyo's One Way Stock Market: Up." That's the sort of hubris that offends the gods, which may explain why, three years later, Japanese stocks crashed and the market spent the next twenty years going anywhere but up. One would think it's obvious that a stock market cannot go up forever, no matter how long it has been going that way, but the desire to extend the trend line is powerful. It's as if people can't help themselves, as if it's an addiction. And to understand an addiction, it's back to the brain we must go.

PICK A NUMBER

You are in a university lab where a psychologist is talking. Already you are on high alert. There's a trick question coming because that's what they do, those psychologists. But you're ready.

The psychologist shows you a wheel of fortune. He gives it a spin. The wheel whips around and around, slows, and finally the marker comes to rest on a number. That number is randomly selected. You know that. It means nothing. You know that too.

Now, the psychologist says, What percentage of African countries are members of the United Nations?

This strange little experiment was devised by Daniel Kahneman and Amos Tversky, two psychologists whose work on decision making has been enormously influential in a wide array of fields. It even launched a whole field of economics known as "behavioral economics," which is essentially a merger of economics and psychology. In 2002, Kahneman was awarded the Nobel Prize in economics—Tversky died in 1996— which is particularly impressive for a man who had never taken so much as a single class in the subject.

The wheel-of-fortune experiment was typical of the work of Kahneman and Tversky. It appeared trivial, even silly. But it revealed something profoundly important. When the wheel landed on the number 65, the median estimate on the question about African countries in the UN was 45 percent (this was at a time when UN membership was lower than it is today). When the wheel stopped at the number 10, however, the median guess was 25 percent. With this experiment, and many others like it, Kahneman and Tversky showed that when people try to come up with a number, they do not simply look at the facts available and rationally calculate the number. Instead, they grab on to the nearest available number—dubbed the "anchor"—and they adjust in whichever direction seems reasonable. Thus, a high anchor skews the final estimate high; a low anchor skews it low.

This result is so bizarre it may be hard to accept, but Kahneman and Tversky's experiment has been repeated many times, with many variations, and the result is always the same. Sometimes, people are asked to make a number out of the digits of their telephone number. In others, the anchor is constructed from the respondent's Social Security number. Different versions slip a number in surreptitiously. In one experiment, people were asked whether Gandhi was older or younger than nine when he died. It's a silly question, of course. But when people were subsequently asked, "How old was Gandhi when he died?" the number nine influenced their answer. We know that because when others were first asked whether Gandhi was older or younger than 140 and then asked how old Gandhi was when he died, their average answer was very different: In the first case, the average was 50; in the second, 67. Researchers have even found that when they tell people that the first number they are exposed to is irrelevant and should not have any bearing on their estimate, it still does. The "anchoring and adjustment heuristic," as it is called, is unconscious. The conscious mind does not control it. It cannot turn it off. It's not even aware of it: When people are asked if the anchor number influenced their decision, they insist it did not.

When experts try to forecast numbers, they don't begin by spinning a wheel of fortune, so the number that acts as the unconscious anchor isn't likely to be so arbitrary. On the contrary. If an expert is predicting, say, the unemployment rate in three years, he will likely begin by recalling the unemployment rate today. If another tries to anticipate how many countries will have nuclear weapons a decade in the future, she will start by calling to mind the number with nuclear weapons now. In each case, the current number serves as the anchor, which is generally a reasonable way of coming up with an estimate. But it does mean the prediction starts with a built-in bias toward the status quo. And bear in mind that sometimes the current number is *not* a reasonable starting point. Consider that in 2006, plenty of people in the United States, the United Kingdom, Ireland, and elsewhere were estimating how much their houses would be worth in 2009 or 2010 because house prices had been rising rapidly and they wanted to know if refinancing their mortgages made sense, or if they should buy another property or make some other investment in real estate. Many factors weighed on their judgment, naturally, but one that certainly did is the anchoring and adjustment heuristic. How much will my house be worth in a few years? Ask that question and you inevitably bring to mind how much it's worth now. And then you adjust—up. But by 2006, a real estate bubble had grossly inflated house prices and so the anchor value people used was unrealistic, and they paid the price when the bubble burst. The very same process undoubtedly went on in the brains of the bankers and financial wizards who bundled mortgage debt into arcane products for sale on global markets, setting in place the explosives that detonated in 2008. In every case, a number that should not have been the starting point very likely was.

This anchoring and adjustment heuristic is one source of status quo bias. But it's a minor one, admittedly. A much bigger contributor is another discovery of Kahneman and Tversky.

THINK OF AN EXAMPLE

In one of their earliest experiments, Kahneman and Tversky had people read a list of names. Some were men, some were women, but all were famous to some degree. The researchers then asked people to judge whether the list had more men or women. In reality, there were equal numbers of men and women, but that's not how people saw it. They consistently said there were more women. Why?

When people attempt to judge how common something is—or how likely it is to happen in the future—they attempt to think of an example of that thing. If an example is recalled easily, it must be common. If it's harder to recall, it must be less common. Kahneman and Tversky called this "the availability heuristic"—a simple rule of thumb that uses how "available" something is in memory as the basis for judging how common it is. In Kahneman and Tversky's experiment, the women on the list were more famous than the men, and this made their names more memorable. After reading the list, it was easier to recall examples of women and so, using the availability heuristic, people concluded there must be more women than men on the list. Kahneman and Tversky confirmed these results with different trials in which the men on the list were more famous than the women, and, predictably, people concluded there were more men than women.

Again, this is not a conscious calculation. The "availability heuristic" is a tool of the unconscious mind. It churns out conclusions automatically, without conscious effort. We experience these conclusions as intuitions. We don't know where they come from and we don't know how they are produced, they just feel right. Whether they *are* right is another matter. Like the other hardwired processes of the unconscious mind, the availability heuristic is the product of the ancient environment in which our brains evolved. It worked well there. When your ancestor approached the watering hole, he may have thought, "Should I worry about crocodiles?" Without any conscious effort, he would search his memory for examples of crocodiles eating people. If one came to mind easily, it made sense to conclude that, yes, he should watch out for crocodiles, for two reasons: One, the only information available in that environment was personal experience or the experience of the other members of your ancestor's little band; two, memories fade, so recent memories tend to be easier to recall. Thus, if your ancestor could easily recall an example of a crocodile eating someone, chances are it happened recently and somewhere in the neighborhood. Conclusion: Beware crocodiles.

Needless to say, that world is not ours, and one of the biggest differences between that environment and the one we live in is information. We are awash in images, stories, and data. Sitting here in my Ottawa office, I Googled the words *Rome, live, feed* and now I'm looking at real time pictures of Palatine Hill in the Eternal City. The whole process took about six seconds. Of course, no one is impressed by this, as the Internet, cell phones, satellites, television, and all our other information technologies are old hat for most people living in developed countries. But they're only old hat from the perspective of an individual living today. From the perspective of our species, and biology, they are startlingly new innovations that have created an information environment completely unlike anything that has ever existed. And we are processing information in this dazzling new world of information superabundance with a brain that evolved in an environment of extreme information scarcity.

To see how profound the implications of this mismatch can be, look at the reactions to the terrorist attacks of September 11, 2001.

Almost everyone on the planet remembers the attacks. We saw the second plane hit live, on television, and we stared as the towers crumbled. It was as if we watched the whole thing through the living room window, and those images—so surprising and horrific—were seared into memory. In the weeks and months after, we talked about nothing but terrorism. Will there be another attack? When? How? Polls found the overwhelming majority of Americans were certain terrorists would strike again and it would be catastrophic. Most thought they and their families were in physical danger. These perceptions were shaped by many factors, but the availability heuristic was certainly one. How easy is it to think of an example of a terrorist attack? After 9/11, that question would have sounded absurd. It was hard *not* to think of an example. Nothing was fresher, more vivid, more *available* to our minds than that. The unconscious mind shouted its conclusion: This is going to happen again!

And yet it did not. Years later, this was considered proof that the government had successfully stopped the attacks that would certainly have come. The absence of attacks was "contrary to every expectation and prediction," wrote conservative pundit Charles Krauthammer in 2004. "Anybody—any one of these security experts, including myself— would have told you on September 11, 2001, we're looking at dozens and dozens and multiyears of attacks like this," former New York mayor Rudy Giuliani said in 2005. Both Krauthammer and Giuliani concluded that the Bush administration deserved the credit. And maybe it did. After all, it's impossible to know conclusively what would have happened if the administration had taken different actions. But we do know the government did not smash "dozens and dozens" of sophisticated terrorist plots. We also know that the most recent Islamist terrorist attack in the United States prior to 9/11 was the bombing of the World Trade Center in 1993, so the fact that the United States went years without another attack was actually in line with experience. "Occam's razor" is the rule of logic that says a simpler explanation should be preferred over a more complex explanation, and here there is a very simple explanation: After 9/11, our perception of the threat was blown completely out of proportion. And for that we can thank, in part, the Stone Age wiring of our brains.

Bear in mind this fits perfectly with how people routinely think. When something big happens, we expect more of the same, but when that thing hasn't happened in ages, or never has, we expect it won't. Earthquakes illustrate the point perfectly. When tectonic plates push against each other, pressure builds and builds, until the plates suddenly shudder forward in the spasm of brief, violent motion that ends when the built-up energy is dissipated. Then the whole process begins again. This means that the probability of a serious earthquake is generally lowest after an earthquake and it grows as time passes. If people assessed the risk of earthquake rationally, sales of earthquake insurance should follow the same pattern—lowest after an earthquake but steadily growing as time passes. Instead, the opposite happens. There is typically a surge in sales after an earthquake, which is followed by a long, slow drop-off as time passes and memories fade. That's the availability heuristic at work.

The mental rut of the status quo is often bemoaned, particularly after there's a disaster and people ask, "Why didn't anyone see it coming?" It was a "failure of imagination" that blinded the U.S. government to the terrorist attacks of 9/11, concluded a national commission. "A failure of the collective imagination" prevented economists from foreseeing the credit crisis of 2008, a group of eminent British economists wrote in an open letter to Queen Elizabeth. The solution to this dearth of imagination seems obvious. After 9/11, the U.S. government assembled science fiction authors, Hollywood screenwriters, futurists, novelists, and a wide array of other creative people to dream up ways terrorists could strike. After the crash of 2008, people again wanted to understand what had gone wrong, and what would go wrong next, and, obligingly, the shelves of bookstores overflowed with imaginative descriptions of how the crash would be followed by catastrophic depression or worse.

But notice what's really happening here. Shocking terrorist attack? Didn't see it coming? Let's imagine more shocking terrorist attacks. Economic disaster? Big surprise, wasn't it? So let's imagine more economic disasters. This sort of reaction doesn't actually get us out of the mental rut of the status quo. It merely creates a *new* rut. And all that imagining carves it deep. In a 1976 experiment, psychologists asked Americans to imagine either Jimmy Carter or Gerald Ford winning that year's presidential election, and then they were asked to rate each man's chances. The researchers discovered that those who had imagined Jimmy Carter winning tended to give him a better shot at winning, while those who imagined Ford winning did the same for Ford. What this and similar experiments showed is that when we imagine an event, we create a vivid image that is easily recalled from memory. If we later try to judge how likely it is that the event will actually happen, that memory will drive up our estimate via the availability heuristic. And of course we will be unaware that our judgment was biased by the imagining we did earlier. Our conclusion will simply feel right.

So all that imagining we do after getting walloped by a surprise may not prepare us for the next surprise. In fact, it is likely to make us all the more convinced that tomorrow will be like today, only more so—setting us up for another shock if it's not.

EVERYONE KNOWS THAT!

So far I've been discussing judgment as if it's something done locked away in a dark, lonely corner of the basement. It's not, of course. People are connected. They talk, they swap information, and they listen very carefully to what everyone's saying because people are profoundly social animals. And experts are people too.

One of those experts is Robert Shiller. An economist at Yale University, Shiller is a leading scholar, a tenured professor, an innovator, and the author of the 2000 book *Irrational Exuberance,* which warned that the boom in tech stocks was really a bubble set to burst. Shortly after *Irrational Exuberance* was published, the tech bubble burst and the book became a best seller. Only a few years later, Shiller worried that another bubble was inflating, this time in real estate. If regulators didn't act, it would keep growing, and the inevitable pop would be devastating. There could be "a substantial increase in the rate of personal bankruptcies, which could lead to a secondary string of bankruptcies of financial institutions as well," he wrote in a 2005 edition of *Irrational Exuberance*. A recession would follow, perhaps even "worldwide." Thus, Robert Shiller can reasonably claim to be one of the very few economists who predicted the disaster of 2008. Unlike anyone else, however, Shiller was in a position to do something about the disaster he foresaw because, from 1990 until 2004, he was a member of a panel that advises the president of the Federal Reserve Bank of New York. And the president of the Federal Reserve Bank of New York is the vice chairman of the committee that sets interest rates. If interest rates had been raised in 2002 or 2003, the housing bubble likely would have stopped inflating and the disaster of 2008 might have been averted or at least greatly reduced in scale.

But when the advisory panel met in 2002 and 2003, Shiller didn't shout and jump up and down on the table. "I felt the need to use restraint," he recalled. The consensus in the group was that there was no bubble and no need to raise interest rates. To suggest otherwise was distinctly uncomfortable. Shiller did make his point, but "I did so very gently, and felt vulnerable expressing such quirky views. Deviating too far from consensus leaves one feeling potentially ostracized from the group, with the risk that one may be terminated." Don't be misled by the reference to "termination," which suggests that Shiller's reluctance to speak out was solely the product of a conscious calculation of self-interest. There's much more to it than that, as Shiller knows better than most. He's a pioneer of behavioral economics, the field that merges economics and psychology, and one thing psychology has demonstrated beyond dispute is that the opinions of those around us—peers, colleagues, co-workers, neighbors—subtly and profoundly influence our judgments.

In the 1950s, Solomon Asch, Richard Crutchfield, and other psychologists conducted an extensive series of experiments that revealed an unmistakable tendency to abandon our own judgments in the face of a group consensus—even when the consensus is blatantly wrong. In Asch's experiments, three-quarters of test subjects did this at least once. Overall, people ignored what they could see with their own eyes and adopted the group answer in one-third of all trials. They did this even though there were no jobs, promotions, or appointments at stake. They even did it when they were anonymous and there was no risk of embarrassment. But the very fact that there was nothing at stake in these experiments may suggest that people didn't take them seriously. If there are no consequences to their judgment, why not shrug and go with the group? Another experiment, conducted in 1996, put that possibility to the test. This time, people were led to believe that their judgments would have important consequences for the justice system. Did this raising of the stakes reduce the rate of conformity? When the task was easy, yes, it did, although conformity did not disappear entirely. But when the task was hard and the stakes high, conformity shot up—and those who conformed were more certain their group-influenced judgment was right.

It's tempting to think only ordinary people are vulnerable to conformity, that esteemed experts could not be so easily swayed. Tempting, but wrong. As Shiller demonstrated, "groupthink" is very much a disease that can strike experts. In fact, psychologist Irving Janis coined the term *groupthink* to describe *expert* behavior. In his 1972 classic, *Victims of Groupthink,* Janis investigated four high-level disasters—the defense of Pearl Harbor, the Bay of Pigs invasion, and escalation of the wars in Korea and Vietnam—and demonstrated that conformity among highly educated, skilled, and successful people working in their fields of expertise was a root cause in each case.

In the mid-1980s, the Japanese future looked dazzling. After two decades of blistering growth, Japan was a bullet train racing up the rankings of developed nations. Extend the trend lines forward and Japan took the lead. The argument was compelling. Not only did it make sense rationally, it *felt* right. More and more experts agreed, and that fact helped persuade others. An "information cascade" developed, as the growing numbers of persuaded experts persuaded still more experts. By 1988, there was, as Paul Kennedy wrote, an expert "consensus" about Japan's shiny future. In that environment, those who might not have been entirely convinced, or were worried about factors that might derail the bullet train, found themselves in the same position as Robert Shiller sitting down with colleagues who all agreed there was no real estate bubble. It was worse for private economists and consultants. Tell clients what they and all informed people believe to be true and they will be pleased. We all enjoy having our beliefs confirmed, after all. And it shows that we, too, are informed people. But dispute that belief and the same psychology works against you. You risk saying good-bye to your client and your reputation. Following the herd is usually the safer bet.

Of course, people don't always bow to the consensus. In fact, when a strong expert consensus forms, critics inevitably pop up. Often, they do not express their disagreement "very gently," as Robert Shiller did, but are loud and vehement, even extreme. As the housing bubble was building in the early years of this century, Peter Schiff was one such critic. In many TV appearances, Schiff, a money manager, insisted that there was a bubble, that it would soon burst, and the result would be catastrophic. "The United States economy is like the *Titanic*," he said in 2006. Contrarians like Schiff are almost always outsiders, which is not a coincidence. They don't have a seat at the table and so they aren't subject to the social pressures identified by Asch and other psychologists. Which is not to say that the group consensus doesn't influence them. The frustration of having critical views shut out or, worse, ignored altogether can drive critics to turn up the volume. Calculation may also be involved. An outsider who wants the attention of insiders won't get it if he agrees with the group consensus or politely expresses mild disagreement. He must take great exception to the consensus and express his objection with strong language—and hope that subsequent events demonstrate his genius and make his name.

Thus, in a very real sense, the group opinion also influences the views of outsider-critics: It drives them in the opposite direction.

IT'S 2023 AND AN ASTEROID WIPES OUT AUSTRALIA. . . .

So are we forever doomed to be trapped inside the mental universe of the status quo? Futurists would say no, but there's plenty of evidence futurists are as stuck in the present as the rest of us. One analyst looked at articles published in *Futures,* an academic journal, to see what sort of relationship there was between the articles appearing in the journal and real-world events over the four decades *Futures* has been published. "One might hope for a causal correlation showing that a surge of articles about the economy precedes any significant change of the world economy," he wrote. If that were so, it would show that futurists are anticipating developments and not merely reflecting the status quo. Alas, it was not to be. "Statistical correlation suggests the reverse since changes in the number of articles lag changes in economic growth rates." That's a polite way of saying the futurists consistently failed to see change coming, but when it arrived, they wrote about it.

Still, we keep trying. One popular method of getting out of the trap of the status quo is scenario planning.

As they were originally devised by Herman Kahn in the 1950s, scenarios were intended to deal with uncertainty by dropping the futile effort to predict. "Scenarios are not predictions," emphasizes Peter Schwartz, the guru of scenario planning. "They are tools for testing choices." The idea is to have a clever person dream up a number of very different futures, usually three or four. One may involve outcomes that seem likely to happen; another may be somewhat more unlikely; and there's usually a scenario or two that seem a little loopy. Managers then consider the implications of each, forcing them out of the rut of the status quo, and thinking about what they would do if confronted with real change. The ultimate goal is to make decisions that would stand up well in a wide variety of contexts.

No one denies there may be some value in such exercises. But how much value? What can they do? The consultants who offer scenario-planning services are understandably bullish, but ask them for evidence and they typically point to examples of scenarios that accurately foreshadowed the future. That is silly, frankly. For one thing, it contradicts their claim that scenarios are not predictions and shouldn't be judged as predictions. Judge them as predictions and all the misses would have to be considered, and the misses vastly outnumber the hits. It's also absurd because, given the number of scenarios churned out in a planning exercise, it is inevitable that some scenarios will "predict" the future for no reason other than chance.

Consultants also cite the enormous popularity of scenario planning as proof of its enormous value, as Peter Schwartz did when I asked him for evidence. "There's the number of companies using it," he said. "Most surveys indicate that something like 70 percent do scenario planning." That's interesting, but it's weak evidence. In 1991, most companies thought the Japanese were taking over; in 1999, most were sure Y2K was a major threat; in 2006, most thought real estate and mortgage-backed securities were low-risk investments. Sometimes all the smart people are wrong.

Lack of evidence aside, there are more disturbing reasons to be wary of scenarios. Remember that what drives the availability heuristic is not how many examples the mind can recall but how easily they are recalled. Even one example easily recalled will lead to the intuitive conclusion that, yes, this thing is likely to happen in the future. And remember that the example that is recalled doesn't have to be real. An imagined event does the trick too. And what are scenarios? Vivid, colorful, dramatic stories. Nothing could be easier to remember or recall. And so being exposed to a dramatic scenario about terrorists unleashing smallpox—

or the global economy collapsing or whatever—will make the depicted events feel much more likely to happen. If that brings the subjective perception into alignment with reality, that's good. But scenarios are not chosen and presented on the basis that they are likely. They're done to shake up people's thinking. As a result, the inflated perceptions raised by scenario planning may be completely unrealistic, leading people to make bad judgments.

And that's only *one* psychological button pushed by scenarios. There is another. Discovered by Kahneman and Tversky, it goes by the clunky name of "the representativeness heuristic."

In 1982, the Cold War was growing increasingly frosty, as a result of the Soviet invasion of Afghanistan, the declaration of martial law in Poland, and the harder line taken by U.S. president Ronald Reagan. In this chilly atmosphere, Kahneman and Tversky attended the Second International Congress on Forecasting and put the assembled experts to the test. One group of experts was asked how likely it was that in 1983 there would be "a complete suspension of diplomatic relations between the USA and the Soviet Union." Another group was asked how likely it was that there would be a Soviet invasion of Poland that would cause "a complete suspension of diplomatic relations between the USA and the Soviet Union." Logically, the first scenario *has* to be more likely than the second because the second requires that the breakdown in diplomatic relations happens as a result of a Soviet invasion of Poland, whereas the first covers a breakdown of diplomatic relations *for any reason*. And yet the experts judged the second scenario to be more likely than the first.

What Kahneman and Tversky demonstrated, in this experiment and many others, is the operation of a mental shortcut using "representativeness," which is simply the presence of something typical of the category as a whole. Collectively, basketball players are very tall, so a representative basketball player is very tall. Just the words *basketball player* are enough to conjure an image of a tall man. And chances are the tall man you are imagining is black, at least if you are an American, because that's another feature of the representative basketball player in American culture. If that sounds like stereotyping, you get the idea. For better *and* worse, the brain is a relentless stereotyper, automatically and incessantly constructing categories with defining characteristics. These categories and characteristics are the basis of the representativeness heuristic.

In 1953, the Soviet Union put down a worker's uprising in Communist East Germany. In 1956, it crushed opposition in Communist Hungary. In 1968, it sent tanks into Communist Czechoslovakia. In the Western mind, invading satellite countries was typical Soviet behavior: It was "representative." And so, when the experts quizzed by Kahneman and Tversky read about a Soviet invasion of Poland, it made intuitive sense. Yes, the brain concluded, that sounds like something the Soviets would do. That feeling then boosted the experts' assessment of the likelihood of the whole scenario. But experts who were asked to judge a scenario that didn't mention a Soviet invasion of Poland did not get the same charge of recognition and the boost that came with it—and so they rated the scenario to be less likely.

Simple logic tells us that a complicated sequence of events like "A will happen, which will cause B, which will lead to C, which will culminate in D" is less likely to unfold as predicted than a simple forecast of "D will happen." After all, in the complicated scenario, a whole chain of events has to unfold as predicted or D won't happen. But in the simple forecast, there's only one link—D either will happen or won't—and only one chance of failure. So the simple forecast *has* to be more likely. But thanks to the representativeness heuristic, it's unlikely to feel that way. If any of the events in the complicated forecast seem "typical" or "representative," we will have a feeling—"That's right! That fits!"—and that feeling will influence our judgment of the whole scenario. It will seem more likely than it should. "This effect contributes to the appeal of scenarios and the illusory insight they often provide," Kahneman and Tversky wrote. And it's so easy to do. Just add details, color, and drama. And pile on the predictions. The actual accuracy will plummet but the feeling of plausibility will soar.

So there's the danger. Scenario planning—and any other sort of imaginative speculation about the future—can indeed push us out of the rut of the status quo. But it can also shove us right over to the other extreme, where we greatly *overestimate* the likelihood of change. The more sophisticated advocates of scenario planning argue that it's a matter of counterbalancing one set of psychological biases that blind us to change with another set that make us overestimate it: Get the balance right and you'll get a realistic appraisal of the future and solid decision making. It's an interesting theory, but there's little evidence on the matter, and what there is provides scant encouragement.

In the early 1990s, at a time when Quebecers increasingly supported the drive to separate their province from Canada, Philip Tetlock ran a scenario exercise with some of his experts. First, he asked them to judge the likelihood of outcomes ranging from the continuation of the status quo to the crumbling of Canada. Then the experts read scenarios describing each outcome in dramatic detail and they were asked again to judge how likely it was that they would happen. Tetlock found the scenarios were effective, in that they boosted the experts' estimates across the board. In fact, they were *too* effective. After reading the scenarios, the experts' estimates tended to be so high they didn't make sense: After all, it's not possible that there is a 75 percent chance that Quebec will break away *and* a 75 percent chance that it will not! Tetlock also discovered that scenarios of change tended to cause the biggest jump in estimated likelihood, and that the more flexible cognitive style of foxes caused them to get more carried away than hedgehogs—the one and only example of foxes falling into a trap hedgehogs avoided.

Tetlock confirmed these results with more experiments and although he still thinks scenarios may provide value in contingency planning, he is wary. Scenarios aren't likely to pry open the closed minds of hedgehogs, he says, but they may befuddle foxes. Unless and until contrary evidence arises, there doesn't seem to be a solution here.

FORGET WHAT WE SAID ABOUT THAT OTHER ASIAN COUNTRY AND LISTEN TO THIS. . . .

So we are left where we began. People who try to peer into the future—both experts and laypeople—are very likely to start with an unreasonable bias in favor of the status quo. Today's trends will continue, and tomorrow will be like today, only more so. With that belief in place, the confirmation bias that so misled Arnold Toynbee kicks in. Evidence that supports the belief is embraced without question; evidence that contradicts the belief is treated with extreme suspicion or, more often, ignored. Steadily, the belief that tomorrow will be like today grows into a strong conviction. Occasionally, a surprise—the decline of Japan, the terrorist attacks of 9/11, the crash of 2008—slaps us in the face and we are reminded that tomorrow may *not* be like today. Suitably chastened, we get imaginative and think of all the ways the surprise that just happened could happen again . . . and we are right back in the mental rut of the status quo. Genuinely imaginative attempts to portray change—including scenario planning—may help pull us out of that rut, but they may also cause us to develop an unrealistic sense of how likely those imaginative futures really are. And all the while, no matter what happens, we are convinced we are right.

The fundamental result of this deeply entrenched bias toward the status quo is that predictions are most likely to be right when current trends continue and least likely to be right when there is drastic change. That's most unfortunate, because when the road is straight, anyone can see where it is going. It's the curves and corners that cause crashes. And so, in general, predictions are most likely to be right when they are least needed and least likely to be right when they are essential.

Almost two decades have passed since the peak of the "Rising Sun" hysteria. Japan is still struggling and almost nobody expects it to return to its former prominence. Today, the future is China. After years of spectacular growth, the Chinese economy is on the verge of passing Japan's to become the second-largest in the world. Meanwhile, the American economy is sickly and the American government is running record deficits—financed in large part by China—that threaten to bankrupt the country. Extend those trend lines forward and it's obvious that China will soon tower over the twenty-first century like the Colossus of Rhodes. "In 2040, the Chinese economy will reach $123 trillion, or nearly three times the output of the entire globe in 2000," writes the Nobel Prize–winning economist Robert Fogel. "China's per capita income will hit $85,000, more than double the forecast for the European Union, and also much higher than that of India and Japan. . . . China's share of global GDP—40 percent—will dwarf that of the United States (14 percent) and the European Union (five percent) thirty years from now. This is what economic hegemony will look like." As one author summed it up in the title of his book, this will be the era *When China Rules the World.*

All that may come to pass. In the early 1960s, when the Japanese economy started to surge, Herman Kahn extended the trend line forward and predicted Japan would be a leading member of the developed world by the 1980s. He was right. But then the line curved and the experts driving with their hands in the air went straight off the road. Today, it is perhaps noteworthy that one of the experts writing books about the coming era of Chinese dominance is Clyde Prestowitz—the same Clyde Prestowitz who didn't mention China in his 1988 best seller *Trading Places,* about the coming era of Japanese dominance.

It's also a little sobering to recall that in the 1950s and 1960s it was widely believed that the economy of the Soviet Union was expanding far more quickly than that of the United States, and that the USSR would catch up with and pass the United States. In the most widely used economics textbook of the era—*Economics: An Introductory Analysis* by the renowned economist Paul Samuelson—the moment of truth was forecast for sometime between 1984 and 1997. As time passed and the two economies failed to follow the trajectories expected, Samuelson didn't acknowledge that he had been off. Instead, he pushed the goalposts forward. In the 1980 edition of his textbook, students were told the Soviet economy would take the lead sometime between 2002 and 2012.

So twice in modern times, lots of experts have agreed that the United States would lose the economic leadership of the world. And twice they have been wrong. But who knows? Maybe the third time is the charm. Maybe China really will pass the United States. Or maybe it won't. Want to settle it? Take a coin from your pocket. Flip it. You'll have a 50 percent chance of being right, which is as good as that of the experts.

5

Unsettled by Uncertainty

During the Great Plague of London, in 1665, the people listened with avidity to the predictions of quacks and fanatics. Defoe says that at that time the people were more addicted to prophecies and astronomical conjurations, dreams, and old wives' tales than ever they were before or since.

—CHARLES MACKAY, *EXTRAORDINARY POPULAR DELUSIONS AND THE MADNESS OF CROWDS, 1841*

Two years and three months after President Jimmy Carter had his "unpleasant talk" with the American people, he did it again. Except this time he was *really* grim.

"I had planned to speak to you about an important topic—energy," Carter said solemnly to a television camera. It was July 15, 1979. The president sat at the big desk in the Oval Office. "For the fifth time, I would have described the urgency of the problem and laid out a series of legislative recommendations to the Congress. But as I was preparing to speak, I began to ask myself the same question that I now know has been troubling many of you. Why have we not been able to get together as a nation to solve our serious energy problems? It's clear that the true problems of our nation are much deeper—deeper than gasoline lines or energy shortages, deeper even than inflation or recession."

It had been a rotten year. Inflation was rising and the economy was stumbling into recession. Carter's greatest triumph—the signing of a peace treaty between Egypt and Israel at the White House—was forgotten days later when an accident at Three Mile Island in Pennsylvania seemed to confirm Americans' worst fears about nuclear power. Meanwhile, revolution in Iran had produced a militant government and uncertain oil supplies, a tenuous situation that OPEC exploited by jacking up prices.

The gas shortages started in California and spread east. Lineups were massive. It could take hours to get to the pumps. Frustration and exhaustion spawned fistfights—even shootings and stabbings. In one infamous incident, a pregnant woman was beaten. The shortages were especially tough on truck drivers, so a national strike was called. Most truckers stopped work, leaving food rotting in fields and store shelves growing increasingly bare. The minority who kept driving suffered vandalism and assaults so widespread that the National Guard was called out to provide armed escorts in at least nine states. In one incident, a trucker who refused to join the strike was told via CB radio that he was losing a tire; when he pulled over to check, he was shot. "If someone shoots at you, threatens you, then you can use full force against them," advised Alabama governor Fob James after a trucker was murdered on State Highway 72. In June, truckers and teenagers in Levittown, Pennsylvania, set fires and fought running battles with police in the first full-scale gas riot. "This country is getting ugly," a White House staffer declared.

It seemed as if everything was coming unglued. Three days before Carter took to the airwaves, at a "Disco Demolition Night" promotion held at Comiskey Park, home of the Chicago White Sox, stoned fans shouting "Disco sucks!" raced onto the field and tore the place apart. The president's approval rating sank lower than Richard Nixon's in the blackest days of the Watergate scandal.

Things were no better elsewhere. In Britain, a massive public-sector strike crippled the country, making 1979 "the Winter of Discontent." The gloom was punctuated by occasional terrorist attacks. When Prime Minister James Callaghan tried to calm the nation with confident words, he was walloped with the instantly famous headline "Crisis? What Crisis?" and promptly lost office to Margaret Thatcher.

All this was before Carter delivered his July address. Still to come in 1979 was the Soviet invasion of Afghanistan, the disturbingly symbolic crash of the American space station Skylab, and the taking of hostages in Tehran. "Hardly more than a quarter-century after Henry Luce proclaimed 'the American century,' American confidence has fallen to a low ebb," wrote social critic Christopher Lasch in his 1979 best seller *The Culture of Narcissism.* "Those who recently dreamed of world power now despair of governing the city of New York. Defeat in Vietnam, economic stagnation, and the impending exhaustion of natural resources have produced a mood of pessimism in higher circles, which spreads through the rest of society as people lose faith in their leaders. The same crisis of confidence grips other capitalist countries as well. In Europe, the growing strength of communist parties, the revival of fascist movements, and a wave of terrorism all testify, in different ways, to the weakness of established regimes and to the exhaustion of established tradition. Even Canada, long a bastion of stolid bourgeois dependability, now faces in the separatist movement in Quebec a threat to its very existence as a nation." Who could the public look to for salvation? Trust in government had waned, especially after Watergate. Science and technology had been revered in the 1950s and 1960s but that faith, too, had suffered in the 1970s. More than one observer was reminded of William Butler Yeats's famous line "Things fall apart; the center cannot hold."

Other leaders might have put on a brave smile and promised better days ahead, as James Callaghan did. But not Jimmy Carter. After canceling his planned speech on energy, he retreated to Camp David and asked a wide array of guests to come and tell him what they thought of his presidency and the state of the nation. For ten days, academics, labor leaders, businesspeople, preachers, governors, and congressmen sat down with the polite and humble man from Plains, Georgia, and told him they didn't think much of his presidency and the state of the nation was awful. Carter listened stoically to every word. He even went looking for more, with visits to the homes of two middle-class families who got over the shock of having the president in their living room and told him that, well, they didn't think much of his presidency and they thought the state of the nation was awful. They did think President Carter was very nice, however.

For one of Carter's advisers, it was a bittersweet vindication. Pollster Pat Caddell had long been arguing that a profound loss of faith—in government, in the military, in science and technology, in society and each other—was at the root of America's woes. Only by tackling that could the president hope to make a difference. Carter's other advisers were wary of this tack. They wanted him to stick to gas lines, inflation—the usual stuff of government. But by the time Carter decided to retreat to Camp David, Caddell had the edge. When Carter invited the three prominent cultural critics whose books formed the foundation of Caddell's case—Christopher Lasch, Daniel Bell, and Robert Bellah—he won. The result was Jimmy Carter's address of July 15, which would have a massive audience and, the White House knew, would define Carter's presidency. Officially, it was known as the "crisis of confidence" speech, but the media immediately dubbed it the "malaise" speech, even though Carter never used that word.

"I invited to Camp David people from every segment of society," Carter said from the Oval Office. "I got a lot of advice. Let me quote a few of the typical comments that I wrote down." Picking up a piece of paper, Carter carefully recited a long list of comments like "You don't see the people enough anymore" and "Mr. President, you are not leading this nation—you're just managing the government." Carter looked pained. "This kind of summarized a lot of other statements: 'Mr. President, we are confronted with a moral and spiritual crisis.'"

Of course, this was Carter's point. While the threats of energy shortages and inflation were serious, the "crisis of confidence" threatens "the very heart and soul and spirit of our national will," he said. "The erosion of our confidence in the future is threatening to destroy the social and the political fabric of America."

The signs were all around. "For the first time in the history of our country a majority of our people believe that the next five years will be worse than the past five years. Two-thirds of our people do not even vote. The productivity of American workers is actually dropping, and the willingness of Americans to save for the future has fallen below that of all other people in the Western world. As you know, there is a growing disrespect for government and for churches and for schools, the news media, and other institutions. This is not a message of happiness or reassurance, but it is the truth and it is a warning." He was right. It was not a happy message. And Carter insisted that solutions would not be found in mere economic fixes. More money would just buy more things and consumerism was another symptom of the disease. "Too many of us now tend to worship self-indulgence and consumption. Human identity is no longer defined by what one does, but by what one owns. But we've discovered that owning things and consuming things does not satisfy our longing for meaning. We've learned that piling up material goods cannot fill the emptiness of lives which have no confidence or purpose."

At last, in the final section of the speech, Carter returned to the usual talk of policies and legislation. But by then, political observers were numb. The president had told Americans there was something wrong with them. And him. No president had ever said anything remotely like it before. Network news anchors looked slightly stunned. Then came another surprise: The White House's telephone operators were overwhelmed by thousands upon thousands of phone calls, 84 percent of which expressed support for the president. A poll taken the following day found the president's approval rating had shot up an astonishing 11 percent. In the days and weeks that followed, the White House was snowed under with letters—85 percent of which praised Carter for saying what had to be said. The speech may have been critical and depressing, but for much of the population it was also urgent and true.

This isn't how "the malaise speech" is remembered, however, thanks to Carter's decision to fire his entire cabinet a few days after the speech. The move was intended to make the president appear decisive, but instead he looked desperate. As historian Kevin Mattson has demonstrated, the proximity of the speech to the firing resulted in the two events being jumbled together in the public mind. The speech was further tainted when Carter's opponents used his talk of "malaise"—it didn't matter that he had never used the word—as proof that the president was defeatist. And so a triumph was redefined in memory as a debacle.

But that evening in July 1979, Americans *did* respond to Jimmy Carter's grim prognosis of a "crisis of confidence." It rang true. As Caddell's polls showed, Americans had fallen into a funk. Their famous optimism had faltered. After more than a decade of bad news and frightening predictions, the country had come to believe the present was awful and the future would be much worse.

We can think of "the seventies" as the years sandwiched between 1969 and 1980, but historian Bruce Schulman considers the real beginning of the era to be 1968. It was the year of the rupture—the violent moment when assassins' bullets cut down 1960s idealism (Robert Kennedy, Martin Luther King Jr.), and setbacks abroad (the Tet offensive in Vietnam, the Soviet invasion of Czechoslovakia) hinted that America's might was waning. It was also a cultural watershed, as social changes that started at the fringes in the 1960s began to spread into the mainstream. Schulman notes that a high school yearbook from 1966, "or even 1967 or 1968, shows clean-cut faces, ties, and demure dresses; they resemble stereotyped images of the 1950s. But the 1972 or 1974 yearbook reveals shaggy hair, beads, granny glasses."

The defining feature of the era was change—a tidal wave of young people, women's lib, black consciousness, gay pride, the sexual revolution, legal abortion. Many basic assumptions about right and wrong crumbled with startling speed. In 1968, three-quarters of Americans told pollsters they disapproved of marriage between whites and non-whites; ten years later, that had fallen to one-half. In 1969, only 57 percent of Americans said they would vote for a qualified woman to be president; a mere six years later, 76 percent said they would. In 1970, Yale law professor Charles Reich argued in *The Greening of America,* which first appeared as an essay in *The New Yorker,* then as a book, that the counterculture was rapidly replacing a consumerist and obedient mindset with a new egalitarian and spiritual way of looking at the world, which Reich called Consciousness III. It would be nothing less than a revolution without violence and everything would change. Many were thrilled by Reich's vision; many more were frightened and appalled. *The New Yorker* received more mail in response to Reich's essay than to anything it had ever published, and Reich's book was an instant smash, dominating best-seller charts for months and generating passionate debates for years.

All this ferment suggested promise *and* peril, and no change better represented the dual-edged nature of the fast-moving reality than no-fault divorce, a legal innovation that swept the Western world in the 1960s. It made splitting up easy, and the "Me Generation"—Tom Wolfe's coinage—did it with abandon. At first, this was widely believed to be to everyone's benefit because ex-spouses would be happier, and happier mothers and fathers would make for happier children, but it didn't take long for people to realize this was naïve. The reality of divorce was captured in *Kramer vs. Kramer,* the painfully sad story of a couple's battle for custody of a frightened child that won the Academy Award for best picture of 1979 and was the year's top box-office draw.

Another big change was unambiguously bad. Crime and disorder soared, especially in the rapidly decaying inner cities, and municipal governments seemed powerless to stop it. New York was in the worst shape—City Hall teetered on the edge of bankruptcy, the subways were a filthy no-man's-land, and Central Park was reduced to a punch line: "The city of New York is importing a temple from Egypt to be placed in Central Park," Johnny Carson told his *Tonight Show* audience in 1970.

"That's what we need is a temple. We can go in there and pray to get out of the park alive." No one saw anything good in New York's future, a sentiment reflected in *Taxi Driver*, *The Warriors*, *Escape from New York*, and other movies and novels that imagined the city becoming an urban ruin populated by the feral, the psychotic, and the terrified. And the plague wasn't confined to the United States or to garden-variety criminals. Terrorism surged around the world. Even Canada suffered bombings and kidnappings. "From countries as disparate as Britain and Nigeria and the Soviet Union," wrote *New York Times* columnist Anthony Lewis, "there are reports of increasing criminal violence and of official inability to cope with it. Is there some universal desperation, some loss of social glue?"

The use of illicit drugs rose even more rapidly than crime. In 1969, a mere 4 percent of Americans had ever smoked marijuana; eight years later, one-quarter had. When Richard Nixon became the first American president to declare a "war on drugs" in 1969, heroin could be found only in a few major American cities, while cocaine was restricted to the elite circles of the "jet set"; a decade later both drugs had spread across the country, and cocaine was so popular that *Time* magazine ran a cover featuring a martini glass filled with white powder—the new cocktail of the upper-middle class. The story was the same in every other Western country, but nowhere was the change more dramatic than in Britain. For decades, the British government had allowed doctors to prescribe maintenance doses of heroin and other drugs to addicts. Addiction rates were extremely low and there was literally no black market in drugs anywhere in the country. But in the late 1960s, that program was scrapped and things started to change. Cindy Fazey, an expert on drug use, was working in the Home Office in 1969 when the head of the drugs branch "called me into his office and said, hey, look at this. He opened his drawer and there's this little plastic bag. And that was the first time we'd seen illegal heroin." Within a decade, British addicts numbered in the tens of thousands and a previously unimaginable subculture of addiction, disease, squalor, and crime was growing like mold on old bread.

Then there was the economy. Since the end of the late 1960s, the long postwar boom had slowed—stock markets would be stuck in the mud for more than a decade—but it was the Arab oil embargo of 1973 that finished it off. As oil prices soared, country after country plunged into recession. Unemployment rose. Inflation exploded. Economists were dismayed because, according to standard economic theory, the horrible combination of stagnation and rising prices—"stagflation"—wasn't possible. And yet, there it was. "Inflation, our public enemy number one, will, unless whipped, destroy our country, our homes, our liberty, our property . . . as surely as any well-armed wartime enemy," President Gerald Ford told Congress in 1974. Watergate made everything worse because government could no longer be trusted; like a crippled boat in a hurricane, the United States was adrift at the worst possible moment. A Gallup survey released in June 1974 revealed "a profound sense of disillusionment, even despondency, over Watergate and economic conditions." Things went reasonably well between 1976 and 1978, but for the most part the ills that befell developed economies in 1973 continued to worsen as a long-term decline in manufacturing in the United States, Britain, Canada, and many other Western countries left millions of low-skilled blue-collar workers without jobs or prospects. The fear was intense. In 1968, the Conference Board's Consumer Confidence Index hovered in the 130 range: By the end of 1974, it was a miserable 43. Pessimism like that wouldn't be seen again until the crash of 2008. In *The New York Review of Books,* the historian Geoffrey Barraclough cited a long list of authors who foresaw either depression or the rise of fascism before delivering his own verdict: "The odds, it seems to me, are that we shall get both."

"What is in your future?" asked Howard Ruff in his 1978 book *How to Prosper During the Coming Bad Years.* "A grisly list of unpleasant events—exploding inflation, price controls, erosion of your savings (eventually to nothing), a collapse of private as well as government pension programs (including Social Security), vastly more government regulation to control your life, and eventually an international monetary holocaust which will sweep all paper currencies down the drain and turn the world upside down." Ruff told his readers to move to a small town, buy gold, and store a large quantity of food to protect themselves against shortages. *How to Prosper During the Coming Bad Years* was praised by everyone from corporate executives to senators. Former CIA director and future president of the United States George H. W. Bush called it "sound advice." Even Ronald Reagan was a fan of Ruff's. Some 2.6 million copies of *How to Prosper During the Coming Bad Years* were sold, making it one of the best-selling financial advice books of all time.

Abroad, things looked just as bad for the United States and other Western countries. Maybe worse. In 1968, as the last bits of the British Empire crumbled away, Britain announced that after more than a century and a half in the Persian Gulf, it could no longer afford to patrol the region and all forces would be removed by 1971. The worsening situation in Vietnam made many Americans wonder if the United States had begun the long decline suffered by the British Empire; when the last helicopter lifted off the roof of the American embassy in Saigon, many were certain it had. In *The End of the American Era*, an influential book in the early 1970s, political scientist Andrew Hacker interwove fears of declining American power abroad with worries about consumerist rot at home. "America is the first nation in history to have succeeded in bestowing material comfort and moral equality throughout the majority of a population," Hacker wrote. That triumph had the unfortunate effect of making people selfish. Wanting only private pleasures, Americans had no collective goals and would not sacrifice for the common good. This was why the United States was failing in Vietnam and why any future wars would be fought without support at home. "Americans will no longer possess that spirit which transforms a people into a citizenry and turns territory into a nation," Hacker wrote. "America's terminal hour has arrived at a time when most Americans still see their nation as vigorous in potential and youthful in spirit. Few are prepared to consider the possibility that their country will never again experience the stature it has so recently known." Hacker wrote those words in 1968. Five years later, they weren't accurate: By then, lots of Americans were prepared to consider the United States a fading power. The sting of wounded pride was sharp. In 1973, when the crusty old Canadian newspaper columnist Gordon Sinclair broadcast a table-pounding defense of Americans—"I am one Canadian who is damned tired of hearing them kicked around!"—radio announcer Byron MacGregor set it to the strains of "America the Beautiful" and released it as a single. It got to number four on *Billboard*'s Top 100.

As if all this weren't enough, the growing environmental consciousness of the 1960s turned frighteningly dark in the decade that followed. "I do not wish to seem overdramatic," cautioned U Thant, the secretary general of the United Nations in 1969, "but I can only conclude from the information that is available to me as Secretary General, that the members of the United Nations have perhaps ten years left in which to subordinate their ancient quarrels and launch a global partnership to curb the arms race, to improve the human environment, to defuse the population explosion, and to supply the required momentum to development efforts. If such a global partnership is not forged within the next decade, then I very much fear that the problems I have mentioned will have reached such staggering proportions that they will be beyond our capacity to control." Chilling as it was, Thant's warning was mild compared to many others. "If current trends are allowed to persist," a statement by leading British scientists began, "the breakdown of society and the irreversible disruption of the life-support systems on this planet—possibly by the end of the century, certainly within the lifetimes of our children—are inevitable." Published by *The Ecologist* magazine in 1972, *The Blueprint for Survival* called on the British government to tax resources, end all construction of new roads, and draft a plan that would ultimately cut Britain's population—fifty-five million at the time—by one-half.

A similar call for an end to escalating populations and consumption became one of the most famous and influential documents of the era. *The Limits to Growth* was a report prepared for the Club of Rome, a group of industrialists, economists, scientists, and others concerned about environmental and social problems. Using computer modeling techniques developed by MIT professor Jay Forrester, researchers examined population, industrialization, resource consumption, food production, and pollution and attempted to forecast how each would play out in the decades ahead. It was a monumental task. Not only was each of the issues huge and complex, they combined to form intricate feedback loops. Forrester's techniques were supposed to model these dynamics and deliver accurate forecasts, and that, combined with the fact that the number crunching was done by a powerful new computer, gave the impression of cutting-edge science. The report's reception among academics was decidedly mixed. Some were impressed; many others thought it was nonsense— decades later, Paul Krugman, the economist and Nobel laureate, called it "a mess." But with economic and environmental worries on the rise, *The Limits to Growth* was a popular sensation even before the oil embargo of 1973 produced shortages of gas and products either made from petroleum or otherwise dependent on cheap oil. Americans became nervous. Would the shortages spread? In late 1973, a congressman commented that the government was having trouble getting supplies of cheap toilet paper, which inspired jokes on Johnny Carson's *Tonight Show*, which led, in turn, to panic buying that stripped the shelves bare for almost two months. It seemed the "age of scarcity"— a phrase that got a lot of use over the decade —had arrived.

"Will this be the world that your grandchildren will thank you for? A world where industrial production has sunk to zero. Where population has suffered a catastrophic decline. Where the air, sea, and land are polluted beyond redemption. Where civilization is a distant memory. *This is the world that the computer forecasts. What is even more alarming, the collapse will come not gradually, but with awesome suddenness, with no way of stopping it.*" This terrifying summary, appearing on the first page of the 1972 edition of *The Limits to Growth*, was written by the publisher, not the researchers. The report itself is mostly dry and technocratic, which added to its aura of scientific authority. In the report's own words: "If the present trends in world population, industrialization, pollution, food production, and resource depletion continue unchanged, the limits to growth on this planet will be reached some-time within the next 100 years. The most probable result will be a rather sudden and uncontrollable decline in population and industrial capac-ity." That distant time frame makes it impossible—even four decades later—to definitively judge the report's accuracy. It is also a little mis-leading. Although formally a forecast for a century out, the whole tone and focus of *The Limits to Growth*—particularly the projections that showed that radical changes implemented immediately would stop the disaster but the same changes introduced in the year 2000 would not—was on the very near future. The authors were also quick to claim vindi-cation when things got ugly in 1973. "If I had stood up in March 1972 and said that within two years we would see beef on the black market in this country, and retail food prices up 20 percent or more, and fami-lies going cold for lack of heating oil, I'd have got very long odds," Den-nis Meadows, the lead author, said in *The New York Times*. "But those things have happened, and they will continue happening."

Fears of overpopulation and starvation mounted steadily. "Next to the pursuit of peace, the greatest challenge to the human family is the race between food supply and population increase," warned President Lyndon Johnson in the 1967 State of the Union address. The same year, William and Paul Paddock published *Famine—1975!*, which said the most terrible famines in history were "foredoomed." In 1968, Paul Ehrlich became an intellectual celebrity when he made the same case in *The Population Bomb*. Even the "father of the Green Revolution," the scientist Norman Borlaug, was terrified of what was coming. "Most people still fail to comprehend the magnitude and menace of the 'Popu-lation Monster,'" Borlaug declared in a speech accepting the 1970 Nobel Peace Prize. "Currently, with each second, or tick of the clock, about 2.2 additional people are added to the world population. The rhythm of the increase will accelerate to 2.7, 3.3, 4.0, for each tick of the clock by 1980, 1990, and 2000, respectively, unless man becomes more realistic and preoccupied about this impending doom." Increased agricultural yields were important, but, Borlaug insisted, "there can be no permanent progress in the battle against hunger until the agencies that fight for increased food production and those that fight for population control unite in a common effort." The situation became critical in 1973. In 1974, at a World Food Congress in Rome, delegates listened somberly to dire forecasts by the likes of Philip Handler, a nutritionist and president of the United States National Academy of Sciences, who concluded that the worst pessimists—the Paddocks and Paul Ehrlich—had been on the mark. In a new introduction to the 1976 edition of *Famine—1975!* (suitably renamed *Time of Famines*), the Paddocks crowed that "this volume demonstrates that it is possible to predict the course of at least some human events."

Paul Ehrlich was also emboldened by the way things were going, and he published a string of jeremiads, each more certain of worse disasters than the last. "In the early 1970s, the leading edge of the age of scarcity arrived," he wrote in 1974's *The End of Affluence*. "With it came a clearer look at the future, revealing more of the nature of the dark age to come." Of course there would be mass starvation in the 1970s—"or, at the latest, the 1980s." Shortages "will become more frequent and more severe," he wrote. "We are facing, within the next three decades, the disintegration of nation-states infected with growthmania." Only the abandonment of growth-based economics and other radical changes offered any hope of survival. And some countries were doomed no matter what they did. India was among the walking dead, Ehrlich was sure. "A run of miraculously good weather might delay it—perhaps for a decade, maybe even to the end of the century—but the train of events leading to the dissolution of India as a viable nation is already in motion." Japan is almost certainly "a dying giant." Same for Brazil. The United Kingdom was only slightly better off. The mere continuation of current trends will ensure that "by the year 2000 the United Kingdom will simply be a small group of impoverished islands, inhabited by some 70 million hungry people, of little or no concern to the other 5–7 billion people of a sick world," he wrote in an earlier paper. Of course, it could be worse than that: Thermonuclear war or some variety of ecocatastrophe were distinct possibilities. "If I were a gambler, I would take even money that England will not exist in the year 2000, and give ten to one that the life of the average Briton would be of a distinctly lower quality than it is today." Not that Americans are in any position to gloat, Ehrlich cautioned. The United States is entering "the most difficult period ever faced by industrialized society." This dark new age may well see the end of civilization. Ehrlich noted that those in the burgeoning "survivalist" movement were stockpiling supplies in wilderness cabins—"a very intelligent choice for some people"—but he and his wife had decided to stay put. "We enjoy our friends and our work too much to move to a remote spot and start farming and hoarding," Ehrlich wrote. "If society goes, we will go with it."

The sulphurous smell of doom even wafted from the pages of mainstream newspapers. "Civilization as we know it in modern America may be in for a drastic change," concluded a four-part series of articles that ran in the Knight-Ridder chain of newspapers in December 1974. "The crisis burst into public consciousness with a dramatic rise in oil prices a year ago, threatening world depression. But as time has passed, it has become clear to both statesmen and scholars that far more than energy is involved. Suddenly, not one but a host of powerful forces has come together—intricately interrelated—to shake the very foundations of life in the modern industrialized world." A former secretary of the interior is quoted saying that in the near future, the interstate highway system "may very well be used primarily as a right-of-way for trains and for bicycling." Chicago's proud new Sears Tower may have an even more ignoble fate, the reporter noted. "Before this century is out, it may become a towering museum, as useless as the pyramids along the Nile, and just as symbolic of a bygone age."

Unless revolutionary changes were made at every level, argued Richard Falk, a legal scholar at Princeton University, in *This Endangered Planet,* "people will increasingly doubt whether life is worth living." And it would only get worse. After "the Politics of Despair" in the 1970s, Falk wrote, the 1980s would witness "the Politics of Desperation," the

1990s would see "the Politics of Catastrophe," and the twenty-first century would be "the Era of Annihilation." Other observers agreed. "The logical answer to the question 'has man a future?' is 'probably not.' Or, to be more accurate, man has many possible futures but the most likely ones are disastrous," wrote the British scientist Desmond King-Hele in *The End of the Twentieth Century?* "The 1980s could witness even greater catastrophes than the 1930s," warned a panel of international statesmen chaired by former West German chancellor Willy Brandt. French president Valéry Giscard d'Estaing was gloomier. He called the crises in energy, food, population, and economics the "four horsemen" of the modern Apocalypse.

"Look for the present sociological problems such as crime, riots, lack of employment, poverty, illiteracy, mental illness, illegitimacy, etc., to increase as the population explosion begins to multiply geometrically in the late '70s," wrote evangelist Hal Lindsey in *The Late Great Planet Earth.* "Look for the beginning of the widest spread famines in the history of the world. Look for drug addiction to further permeate the U.S. and other free-world countries." There would be "limited use" of nuclear weapons, Lindsey predicted, and American economic and military power would fade. The "United States of Europe" would form under a charismatic dictator and take control over the West. The Soviet Union would invade Israel, but the Red Army would be crushed by Europe. China would then march on the Middle East with a stupendous two-hundred-million-man force, only to be annihilated in the battle known as Armageddon. Finally, Jesus Christ would descend from heaven to smite Satan and establish God's kingdom on earth. With its strange mixture of biblical prophecy and hip lingo—the Rapture will be "the ultimate trip," Lindsey enthused—*The Late Great Plant Earth* became the top-selling book of the 1970s.

In 1970, futurist Alvin Toffler had argued in *Future Shock* that the human brain couldn't cope with the accelerating pace of change. We may all go mad, Toffler warned. By 1979—with rioters shouting "Disco sucks!"; millions of people scanning the clouds for heavily armed angels; and the president on TV talking about a collective nervous breakdown—that was one prediction that seemed exactly right.

THE AGONY OF NOT KNOWING

We want control. We *need* control. And bad things happen when we don't have it.

In an unsettling study, elderly residents of a nursing home were placed in rooms where everything was handled by others, right down to the arrangement of the furniture and the selection and care of a houseplant. With no decisions to make, their environment was pleasant but completely out of their control. Other residents of the home were given the same room and treatment, but they were asked to decide how the furniture would be arranged and they were asked to select and care for a plant. A year and a half later, 30 percent of the residents without control had died, compared to 15 percent of those with control. Plenty of other research points to the same conclusion: If we do not perceive ourselves to have at least a little control of our surroundings, we suffer stress, disease, and early death.

Control is such a fundamental psychological need that doing without it can even be torture. I mean that quite literally. I spent the better part of 2003 investigating torture in Egypt, Turkey, Uzbekistan, and elsewhere, and the essential point to emerge was that torture is not about physical pain. That is merely one of the torturer's tools. At its core, torture is a process of psychological destruction. And that process almost always begins with the torturer explicitly telling the victim he is powerless. "I decide when you eat and sleep. I decide when you suffer, how you suffer, if it will end. I decide if you live or die." That is the torturer's mantra.

Knowing what will happen in the future is a form of control, even if we cannot change what will happen. Torturers know this. It's why they avoid routines by constantly varying the time of interrogation sessions, what is done to prisoners, and how long it lasts. Often they will do things that make no sense—shout nonsense, make impossible demands—to further bewilder the prisoner. When all is uncertain, nothing is predictable, and that is terrifying. In an experiment disturbingly similar to torture, researchers in the Netherlands asked volunteers to experience a series of twenty electrical shocks while their bodies were monitored for sweating, rapid breathing, and elevated heart rates—physiological evidence of fear. Some of the participants were given twenty strong shocks. Others were given seventeen mild shocks interspersed randomly with three strong shocks. All participants were told in advance what sort of shocks they would get, which meant that what would happen was predictable for those receiving the twenty strong shocks but unpredictable for those receiving mostly mild shocks. The result: People who experienced the mild-but-unpredictable shocks experienced much more fear than those who got the strong-but-predictable shocks. Uncertainty is potent. And experienced interrogators know it. "The threat of coercion usually weakens or destroys resistance more effectively than coercion itself," noted a CIA manual on interrogation obtained in 1997 by reporters at *The Baltimore Sun*. "The threat to inflict pain, for example, can trigger fears more damaging than the immediate sensation of pain. . . . Sustained long enough, a strong feeling of anything vague or unknown induces regression, whereas the materialization of the fear, the infliction of some sort of punishment, is likely to come as a relief."

Given how devastating uncertainty and lack of control can be, it's not a surprise that we have some powerful psychological defenses against both. The "illusion of control" discussed earlier is a big one. Another is superstition.

When the anthropologist Bronislaw Malinowski studied the daily lives of native people living on the Trobriand Islands of the South Pacific, he noticed that while the islanders used magic rituals abundantly, they reserved them only for some activities. When they went after the plentiful fish in a sheltered lagoon, for example, they didn't use magic, but when they fished in the open sea, they did. That might have suggested it was the presence of danger that settled whether they used magic or not, but that explanation didn't fit other observations. The islanders used magic to keep insects from devouring their crops, for example, but they didn't in gardening generally. Malinowski realized that what made the difference was control. When the islanders felt their own work and skill would determine success or failure, they did not resort to magic; when the outcome involved chance or other factors outside their control, they did.

Expanding on Malinowski's insight, psychologists have demonstrated that resort to superstition rises and falls in tandem with stress and uncertainty. In a study conducted during the Gulf War, when Iraq was firing missiles at Israel, psychologist Giora Keinan found Israelis living in areas at risk were more likely to indulge in "magical thinking" than those who did not. In a later study, Keinan asked students to answer questions like "How is your health?" and "Has anyone in your immediate family suffered from lung cancer?" Students who were experiencing the stress of an impending examination were more likely to "knock on wood" after mentioning their good fortune than were students who were not under the gun. Researchers have even demonstrated that people who feel they lack control are more likely to see patterns that don't exist.

These are natural impulses, and they are automatic. Even someone who is fully aware of them, and knows how irrational they are, will feel the itch. "While I appreciate that carrying the same amount of tees in my pocket will not help me play a round [of golf] any better, or the action of always marking my ball on the green with a coin placed 'heads up' will not influence the outcome," noted British psychologist David Lavallee, who specializes in sports psychology, "I will probably continue to resort to such behaviors." Of course, the little superstitions of weekend golfers are trivial compared to the elaborate rituals professional athletes follow, which is precisely what we would expect to see: As the uncertainty and stress rise, so will the superstitious behavior. Researchers have even found that among elite professional athletes, superstition rises more prior to matches with higher stakes and more uncertain outcomes.

If this is a universal human tendency, there should be evidence at the level of societies and nations that when uncertainty increases—when economies turn sour, governments fail, wars loom—so does superstition. And there is. In a 1973 paper, Stephen Sales of Carnegie Mellon University examined data comparing the 1920s and the 1930s in the United States. Those decades were chosen because they were polar opposites: The first was a "low-threat environment" in which the economy experienced an unprecedented boom and the political scene was relatively calm; following that, however, was a "high-threat" decade featuring the Great Depression, frightening political turmoil, and a looming world war. As psychologists would expect, Sales found that interest in astrology was substantially higher in the 1930s. Sales then looked at the periods 1959 to 1964 and 1967 to 1970. The contrast between these two eras wasn't as sharp as that between the Roaring Twenties and the Depression-era thirties, Sales admitted—the earlier period had some frightening events and the latter wasn't so bad in many ways. But economic figures, opinion polls, and other data supported the conclusion that the earlier period was relatively low-threat compared to the turmoil at the end of the 1960s. And here again Sales found interest in astrology went up as times got scarier. Researchers who examined data from German archives covering 1918 to 1940—from the end of the First World War to the beginning of the Second—got the same results.

More controversially, Sales also looked at how uncertain times affect church memberships. Some churches strictly enforce a clearly defined moral and spiritual dogma, he noted: They insist there is only one truth and they know what it is. But others are more liberal: They tolerate a wide range of beliefs and behaviors. If people seek out sources of certainty in uncertain times, does membership in the more dogmatic churches go up at the expense of the more liberal churches? Comparing the 1920s and 1930s, Sales found they did. Later research covering more time periods got the same result.

It's too bad Sales did his research in 1973, and not a decade later, because his own time provided plenty of evidence on the subject.

"Astrology is having the greatest boom in its history," wrote Hal Lindsey in *The Late Great Planet Earth*. That's a touch hyperbolic, but Lindsey had a point. Throughout the 1970s, interest in mysticism and spiritualism mushroomed. "Although it possessed earlier antecedents," wrote historian Bruce Schulman, "the New Age emerged circa 1971." Along with gurus like Baba Ram Dass, psychics like Jeane Dixon enjoyed rapidly growing audiences—including, in Jeane Dixon's case, President Richard Nixon. The prophecies of Edgar Cayce—dead since 1945—found millions of readers, and Nostradamus returned to fashion yet again. Hal Lindsey was sure he knew why. "In talking with thousands of persons, particularly college students, from every background and religious or irreligious upbringing, this writer found that most people want reassurance about the future. For many of them, their hopes, ambitions, and plans are permeated with the subconscious fear that perhaps there will be no future at all for mankind."

Of course, for Lindsey, searching for answers in astrology and New Age mumbo jumbo was terribly misguided, as the only reliable prophecies came from the Bible. A huge and growing number of Americans agreed. After many years of decline, religion surged in the 1970s, although the aggregate numbers obscured dramatic disparities in the pews: Membership in Evangelical Christian churches exploded; Roman Catholic numbers held steady; but the liberal Protestant churches—Presbyterian, Episcopalian, Methodist—lost as much as 15 percent of their members in ten years. These trends are an exact fit with Sales's research.

Along with superstition and dogmatic religion, a third source of certainty, the conspiracy theory, flourished in the 1970s. "To the orderly mind of the conspiracy theorist, there is no such thing as randomness," wrote George Johnson, science writer and author of *Architects of Fear: Conspiracy Theories and Paranoia in American Politics*. In the 1970s, bug-eyed fantasists like Lyndon LaRouche developed substantial followings by assuring the dazed and confused that it all made sense. "Every coincidence, every accident, is meaningful. History is a war between good and evil in which everything unfolds according to plan."

Expert predictions were a fourth source of certainty, and they did as well, and for the same reasons, as horoscopes, line-by-line analysis of the Book of Revelation, and urgent revelations about who *really* killed the Kennedys. Predictions did away with complexity, incomprehension, and uncertainty. In their place was the gentle buzz of knowing. All one needed to do was to pick an expert and listen carefully. Maybe it was Howard Ruff, Paul Ehrlich, or any one of the others who were sure they knew what was coming. They all had compelling stories to tell and they told them well. And they had credentials—Ph.D.'s, posts in universities, or praise from important people. Anyone with a trace of rational skepticism wouldn't trust astrology or other flaky superstitions. For many, the same is true of religion, or at least the sort of dogmatic, literalist religion that claims to see tomorrow's headlines in the Bible. But expert predictions are different. Experts are smart, informed people. Treating their predictions as gospel seems perfectly rational, at least in a superficial sense, and when there is a psychological craving to be satisfied, a superficial appearance of rationality will do. The alternative, after all, is to reject expert prediction as a source of certainty. And if you do that—and you can't accept superstition, religion, or conspiracy theories—what are you left with? Nothing. And that's frightening.

"An uncertain future leaves us stranded in an unhappy present with nothing to do but wait," wrote psychologist Daniel Gilbert. The "unhappy present" Gilbert was referring to was the depths of the recession following the crash of 2008, but it could well have been the 1970s or any other particularly unsettled and uncertain time. In that environment, we want to know what will happen, even if what will happen is awful. Researchers found that people who received colostomies they knew would be permanent were actually happier six months after surgery than those whose colostomies might or might not be permanent, Gilbert noted. "People feel worse when something bad *might* occur than when something bad *will* occur." Anyone who has waited to hear if they have cancer or not, and experienced a strange sort of relief when their worst fear was confirmed, knows exactly what he means.

Our profound aversion to uncertainty helps explain what would otherwise be a riddle: Why do people pay so much attention to dark and scary predictions? Why do gloomy forecasts so often outnumber optimistic predictions, take up more media space, and sell more books?

Part of this predilection for gloom is simply an outgrowth of what is sometimes called "negativity bias": Our attention is drawn more swiftly by bad news or images, and we are more likely to remember them than cheery information. "The greater impact of bad than good is extremely pervasive," concluded a review of the extensive research. And for good reason. If your ancestor was picking berries on the African savannah a hundred thousand years ago and someone shouted, "Lion!"—bad news, indeed—he had to drop the berries and run, but if someone mentioned that lions hadn't been seen for days, he could shrug and keep working. "Survival requires urgent attention to possible bad outcomes," the review noted, "but it is less urgent with regard to good ones." People whose brains gave priority to bad news were much less likely to be eaten by lions or die some other unpleasant and untimely death than those whose brains did not, and so "negativity bias" became a universal human trait.

But uncertainty is the bigger force at work for the simple reason that it is usually when things are going wrong that we are most likely to worry, peer into the future, and be spooked by all that swirling uncertainty. In such times, optimistic forecasts are likely to feel wrong. Remember the availability heuristic and the human tendency to project today into tomorrow: When the economy tanks, or stocks crash, or terrorists attack, we intuitively conclude that the economy will slump further, stocks will slide deeper, or terrorists will strike again. At that time, the expert who predicts a sunny future is battling against people's intuitive judgments. And when those judgments are strengthened by confirmation bias, and the intuitive judgments of friends and neighbors, and the opinions of experts who see nothing but gloom ahead, that's not a fight the optimist will win. In contrast, the gloom-mongers have it easy. Their predictions are supported by our intuitive pessimism, so they *feel* right to us. And that conclusion is bolstered by our attraction to certainty. As strange as it sounds, we want to believe the expert predicting a dark future is exactly right, because knowing that the future will be dark is less tormenting than suspecting it. Certainty is always preferable to uncertainty, even when what's certain is disaster.

Of course, this suggests that all experts offer certainty. But many do not. Some experts routinely talk of possibilities and probabilities. They say things like "It may happen," "It's more likely than not," "There are several possible outcomes," and "Large uncertainties remain." These tend to be the foxes. Hedgehogs find such talk distasteful. To them, it sounds like hedging, maybe even cowardice. Hedgehogs value decisiveness. They are far more likely than foxes to flatly say, "It will happen," or "It won't." The words *inevitable* and *impossible* seldom pass the lips of foxes, but hedgehogs spray them like bullets from a machine gun.

It's not hard to guess which type of expert is more likely to draw an audience. People want certainty. It's the psychological payoff of expert predictions. But foxes seldom deliver it. They may narrow the number of possible futures and—cautiously—attach probabilities to each outcome, but that only *reduces* uncertainty. It doesn't dispel it. Hedgehogs, however, can be counted on to give people what they crave. They all but *ooze* certainty. And so, as we will see in the next chapter, hedgehogs dominate airwaves, best-seller lists, and public discussion.

Unfortunately, as Philip Tetlock proved and long experience shows, confidence doesn't make hedgehogs better able to predict the future. It makes them worse.

Whether it's Paul and William Paddock declaring mass starvation "foredoomed," Paul Ehrlich pronouncing the inevitable collapse of India and the American way of life, or Howard Ruff forecasting "an international monetary holocaust which will sweep all paper currencies down the drain and turn the world upside down"—and countless others in between—the 1970s were one long parade of pessimistic predictions. Most came from hedgehogs. And most were very, very wrong. Inflation didn't soar out of control, the economy didn't spiral downward, an age of scarcity did not begin, billions of people did not starve, the United States did not fade, civilization did not end, and Jesus Christ did not found God's kingdom on earth. And all those survivalists sitting in wilderness cabins watched their stockpiled food rot as the world went on without them.

It's easy to make fun of those whose prophecies came to naught. But to be fair, it's important to remember that many of the awful things predicted in the 1970s could have happened. They did not because, as always, history is contingent: The particular choices that were made, and the accidents that happened, took us in different directions. But they were real possibilities. What they were *not* was inevitable. It's also reasonable to conclude they were not nearly as probable as they seemed. Had the hedgehogs who predicted them thought more like foxes—beginning with the fact that the only certainty is uncertainty—their forecasts might have been at least a little more accurate. Of course, toning down the confidence of their predictions likely would have meant foregoing the pleasure of being treated like gurus and prophets with best-selling books. But at least their work wouldn't be embarrassing in hindsight.

"For the better part of the past two years nobody has been safe from the divinations of the new decade," wrote the essayist Lewis Lapham in 1979. "Almost without exception, the seers who look into the abyss of the 1980s predict catastrophes appropriate to the fears of the audience they have been paid to inform and alarm." And almost without exception, the seers were wrong. Still, it made no difference to the business of prediction. Even as the forecasts of the 1970s were going down in flames, experts declared it absurd to think the Soviet Union was on the verge of internal crisis (Arthur Schlesinger Jr., 1982), inevitable that the United States would plunge into another Great Depression (Ravi Batra, 1987), certain that Japan would be the next world-dominating superpower (Jacques Attali, 1991), and many more sure bets.

As always, people listened and put their money down.

6

Everyone Loves a Hedgehog

He is *"often wrong but he's never in doubt."*

— BRITISH POLITICIAN NORMAN LAMONT
EXPLAINS WHY A PUNDIT IS A FAVORITE
OF HIS

A recession is coming and it will be bad. The man on television is dead sure of that. "The basic problem of the American economy is that we have too much consumption and borrowing and not enough production and savings," he says. "And what's going to happen is the American consumer is basically going to stop consuming and start rebuilding his savings, especially when he sees his home equity evaporate." And since consumption makes up 70 percent of the economy, that means hard times are coming fast.

The man is Peter Schiff, an investment adviser and frequent commenter in the business media. The date is August 28, 2006. After years of dramatic increases, housing prices have flattened out. Four months later, they will start to nosedive. At the end of 2007, the American economy will slip into recession and home values will plunge. The American consumer will stop consuming and start rebuilding his savings. The economy will crumple.

Peter Schiff was right. He called it.

Schiff's famous prediction is immortalized on YouTube, along with similar calls he made prior to the disaster of 2008, in a tightly edited sequence of video clips. Released as the economy was crashing, the video spread like a California wildfire in an abandoned housing development. Some who watched were Schiff's fans. But for most people, what made the video so delicious was the humiliation it inflicted on a parade of arrogant pundits.

"I don't believe any of it, whatsoever," Arthur Laffer says in response to Schiff's 2006 prediction. In the clip, Laffer, an economist and investment adviser, has the bemused look of a scientist responding to a kook who thinks the earth is flat. "Savings are way down but wealth has risen dramatically. The United States economy has never been in better shape. There is no tax increase coming in the next couple of years. Monetary policy is spectacular. We have freer trade than ever before," Laffer says. "I think Peter is just totally off base. I don't know where he's getting his stuff."

"It's not wealth that's increased in the last few years," Schiff fires back. "We haven't increased our productive capacity. All that's increased are the paper values of our stocks and real estate. But that's not real wealth. When you see the stock market come down and the real estate bubble burst, all that phony wealth is going to evaporate and all that's going to be left is all the debt that we accumulated to foreigners."

"You're just way off base," Laffer scoffs. "There is nothing out there. We're going to have a nice slowdown but it's not going to be a crash." Ouch. The poor, pompous fool.

The clip that follows aired December 31, 2006, on Fox News. "Will homes be worth more or less in 2007?" the host asks.

"Prices will go up about ten percent," says a real estate agent named Tom Adions, a beefy man with long hair and a striking resemblance to the model Fabio. "And here's why. You're coming into a regular, normal market and in a regular, normal market that's about what you get."

Peter Schiff, what do you say? "Today's home prices are completely unsustainable. . . . [In 2007], you're going to start to see both the government and the lenders reimposing lending standards and tightening up on credit and you're going to see a lot of the speculative buyers turn into sellers and these sky-high real estate prices are going to come crashing back down to earth."

Over to Mike Norman, a Biz Radio host. "I agree with Tom," Norman says. "They're probably going to be up about ten percent." With slicked-back hair, dark suit, and gold tie, Norman is the panel's Gordon Gekko. He turns on Schiff with a cutting smirk. "I have no idea what Peter Schiff is talking about."

"Most of the profits that people have in real estate are going to vanish just like the profit in the dot-coms in 1999–2000," Schiff responds. The other pundits can be heard giggling. In split screen, Norman appears alongside Schiff, eyes rolling.

Next up is a clip from August 18, 2007. Like the tremors before a volcano explodes, the first rumblings of the subprime mortgage crisis were being felt. The stock markets were suffering, financial stocks in particular. So Fox News host Neil Cavuto asks Ben Stein, actor and business commentator, if people should be worried about those subterranean vibrations.

"The credit crunch is way overblown," Stein says. "The subprime problem is a problem but it's a tiny problem in the context of this economy. The storm is a problem but it's a tiny problem. Meanwhile, it's as if nuclear war had struck the financials and really struck the whole market. It's a buying opportunity, especially for the financials, maybe like I've never seen before in my entire life."

Peter Schiff appears. "This is just getting started. It's not just subprime. This is a problem for the entire mortgage industry. It's not just people with bad credit that committed to mortgages they can't afford.

It's not just people with bad credit who are going to see their home equity vanish. And it's not limited to mortgage credit. Americans are going to have a difficult time borrowing money to buy cars, to buy furniture, to buy appliances. Foreigners around the world have been lending money to us for years. They're now finding out that we can't afford to repay. This is going to be an enormous credit crunch. The party is over for the United States. We cannot continue to borrow beyond our means and consume foreign products."

Stein and Schiff lock horns. "Subprime is tiny. Subprime is a tiny, tiny blip," Stein insists.

"It's not tiny and it's not just subprime. It's the entire mortgage market."

"Well, you're simply wrong about that."

"No, I'm not."

Cavuto moves the panel along. Has the trouble peaked?

First up is Charles Payne, the author of *Be Smart, Act Fast, Get Rich*. "I think the worst is over," Payne says casually. Ben Stein agrees. "I think stocks will be a heck of a lot higher a year from now than they are now." Two other panelists say the same.

But then Cavuto returns to the skunk at the garden party. "The worst is yet to come," Schiff declares. "The fundamentals are not sound. They're awful. If the fundamentals were sound we wouldn't be having these problems." A panelist gasps in amazement.

On to stock picks, Cavuto says, "Ben, what do you like?"

"The financials, as I keep saying, are just super bargains," says Ben Stein. "I particularly like Merrill Lynch, which is an astonishingly well-run company."

"I like the financials too," says Payne. "Merrill isn't my top pick in the group. I think Bear is probably the cheapest, although the riskiest, and some of the others are better. But the financials are a great place, absolutely." The other panelists chime in with the same advice: People should load up on financials.

Again, Schiff appears on-screen to ruin the consensus. "Stay away from the financials. They're toxic. They're not cheap. They're expensive." Another incredulous gasp is heard. "There's a lot of losses coming up in the future. These financials are going to get hit and they're going to get hit hard. Don't believe what these forecasts are for future earnings."

Stein and Schiff bark at each other until Cavuto interrupts to say the show is over. "All right, Peter, I wish we had more time with you. I know you want to continue that exposé on Santa Claus."

In the final clip, it's late December 2007. The American economy is clearly hurting. Schiff warns that things will get much, much worse. But an expensively suited analyst disagrees. The first six months of the year will be a little ugly but then things will bounce back nicely, he says calmly. The Dow will break through 16,000.

Needless to say, the Dow did not break through 16,000 in 2008. In March of that year, the investment bank Bear Stearns collapsed. In September, the rest of the financial system melted down. More firms went under. Merrill Lynch—the "astonishingly well-run company" that Ben Stein recommended—was sold at a bargain price, like used furniture. The global credit system froze, stocks collapsed, and economies tumbled.

Peter Schiff was right. He called it.

But leave aside who called what for a moment and focus on what is true of every person in these clips, Schiff included. Without exception, they are confident. The message they give to audiences is that they *know* what will happen; they are *sure* of it. Not one of them offers a probabilistic forecast like "It's more likely than not" or "It's very probable but not certain." Not one of them acknowledges that these sorts of forecasts have a terrible track record. Not one of them mentions that if they were as accurate as they are confident, they would be billionaires—and billionaires don't do talk shows.

This is all too typical. The media superstars who tell us what will and won't happen are an overwhelmingly *confident* bunch. Talking heads on business shows are particularly cocksure but the other pundits who engage in prognostication—whether futurists, newspaper columnists, or the sages on television who tell us the fate of politicians and nations—share the same fundamental characteristics. They are articulate, enthusiastic, and authoritative. Often, they are charming and funny. Their appearance commonly matches the role they play, whether it's a Wall Street sharpie or a foreign affairs maven. They commonly see things through a single analytical lens, which helps them come up with simple, clear, conclusive, and compelling explanations for what is happening and what will happen.

They do not suffer doubts. They do not acknowledge mistakes. And they never say, "I don't know."

They are, in this book's terms, hedgehogs. Their kind dominates the op-ed pages of newspapers, pundit panels, lecture circuits, and bestseller lists.

Now, if this is true, and if it's also true that the predictions of hedgehogs are even less accurate than those of the average expert—who does as well as a flipped coin, remember—then a disturbing conclusion should follow. The experts who dominate the media won't be the *most* accurate. In fact, they will be the *least* accurate. And that is precisely what Philip Tetlock discovered. Using Google hits as a simple way to measure the fame of each of his 284 experts, Tetlock found that the more famous the expert, the worse he did.

That result may seem more than a little bizarre. Predictions are a big part of what media experts do, after all. Surely experts who consistently deliver lousy results will be weeded out, while the expert who does better than average will be rewarded with a spot on the talking-head shows and all that goes with it. The cream should rise, and yet, it doesn't. In the world of expert predictions, the cream sinks. What rises is the stuff that should be, but isn't, skimmed off and thrown away.

How is this possible? Very simply, it's what people want. Or to put it in economic terms, it's supply and demand: We demand it; they supply.

INTRODUCING THE RENOWNED PROFESSOR
DR. MYRON L. FOX

For as long as students have evaluated professors, professors have complained about student evaluations. They aren't based on substance, professors say. A charming, funny, and confident teacher will be rated highly whether the students actually learn or not, while a serious and challenging professor who isn't so charming, funny, and confident will suffer. This complaint isn't unique to professors, of course. It can be heard anywhere people are rated by others, but professors have a unique way of fighting back.

In the early 1970s, three psychologists from the University of Southern California devised a simple but brilliant experiment. At the center of it would be a distinguished professor named Dr. Myron L. Fox.

Dr. Fox didn't exist. The psychologists invented him, complete with a suitably impressive résumé. To play the role of Dr. Fox, they hired an actor who fit the popular image of a distinguished professor. The researchers then crafted an hour-long lecture on "mathematical game theory as applied to physician education" that was nonsense, and they coached the actor "to present his topic and conduct his question-and-answer period with an excessive use of double talk, neologisms, non sequiturs, and contradictory statements. All this was to be interspersed with parenthetical humor and meaningless references to unrelated topics." If substance were the basis of how people judge experts, Dr. Fox would be humiliated.

But Dr. Fox didn't just look the part of a distinguished professor. He talked it. He spoke with clarity, confidence, and authority. That was all that mattered. When Dr. Fox delivered his lecture at a teacher-training conference—before an audience consisting of psychiatrists, psychologists, and social-worker educators—the evaluations were positive across the board. Dr. Fox even got a perfect 100 percent "yes" on the question "Did he stimulate your thinking?" The researchers then showed a videotape of the lecture to a similar group and got more enthusiastic responses. A third showing of the videotape—this time to a group of educators and administrators enrolled in a graduate-level university class—garnered still more praise. "Considering the educational sophistication of the subjects," the psychologists concluded, "it is striking that none of them detected the lecture for what it was."

Clearly, people were impressed by Dr. Fox. Just as clearly, it wasn't his substance that impressed them. So what was it exactly? Was it the aura of "expertness" emanating from his title and his authoritative speaking style? Or was it simply the enthusiasm and confidence he projected? It's impossible to tell from the experiment itself, but the answer is likely both.

As social animals, we are exquisitely sensitive to status. An expert, in the appropriate circumstances, has considerable status. We respect that, even defer to it, whether consciously or not, sometimes with bizarre results. In a Texas study, researchers had a man at a street corner cross against a traffic light and watched to see how many other people waiting at the corner would follow the man's lead and cross the street. The critical variable? Sometimes the man wore ordinary street clothes. Other times, he wore a sharp business suit and tie. As the saying goes, the clothes make the man: Three and a half times more people followed the man across the street when he wore the business suit. An Australian experiment produced even odder results, thanks to the well-documented connection between status and perceived size. In a series of university classrooms, a man was introduced to the students as a visitor from Cambridge University. In some classes, the man was said to be a student at Cambridge. In others, he was a lecturer, or a senior lecturer, or a professor. Afterward, students were asked to estimate the visitor's height: With each step up the ladder of status, the man grew by half an inch.

The power of authority was most famously demonstrated in Stanley Milgram's classic experiment involving electric shocks administered to a supposed test subject by a volunteer. The shocks weren't real; the "test subject" was actually an actor. The real subject was the volunteer who flipped switches under the supervision of a white-coated scientist. As the shocks got to supposedly dangerous and even deadly levels, volunteers got anxious and upset. They sweated and moaned. They begged the scientist to stop. But very few refused to do as directed when the scientist told them to throw the switch. A less famous experiment that is perhaps even more disturbing started with a phone call to twenty-two nurses' stations in various hospitals and wards. The man on the phone identified himself as a physician and told the nurses to administer a large dose of a certain drug to a patient. The nurses had plenty of reason to refuse. They didn't know this supposed doctor; it was against hospital policy for doctors to direct treatments over the phone; the drug prescribed by the "doctor" hadn't been cleared for use; and the label of the drug clearly stated that the maximum daily dose was half what the "doctor" had ordered them to inject in the patient. Despite all this, 95 percent of the nurses got the drug and were on their way to the patient's room when the researchers put a stop to the experiment. In effect, the nurses stopped thinking independently the moment they heard the title "Dr."

"Con artists," notes psychologist Robert Cialdini, "drape themselves with the titles, clothes, and trappings of authority. They love nothing more than to emerge elegantly dressed from a fine automobile and to introduce themselves to their prospective 'mark' as Doctor or Judge or Professor or Commissioner Someone. They understand that when they are so equipped, their chances for compliance are greatly increased." Experts, TV producers, newspaper editors, and book publishers act in better faith than con men, one hopes. But they, too, intuitively understand that the trappings of authority make people much more likely to find the expert persuasive. It's why pundits on business shows wear expensive business suits. It's why "Ph.D." so often appears alongside the author's name on the covers of books, and why an economist from Harvard or Oxford or some other prestigious university is far more likely to have her university affiliation mentioned in an introduction than an economist from a lesser institution. It's why the CNBC host in the video clip I described at the start of this chapter introduced Arthur Laffer as "chief investment officer of Laffer Investments and former economic adviser to President Reagan." There may be no rational reason to introduce Laffer by citing a job he held decades earlier, but that's not the point. Much like the phrase *Harvard economist* and a con man's gold watch, it establishes authority at a level deeper than rationality. The audience may not consciously think, "He was an adviser to the president of the United States! He *must* be right!" But nudging us toward that conclusion is certainly the effect.

THE CONFIDENCE GAME

In much the same way, a strong, enthusiastic, confident speaking style has a power that transcends mere rationality—a power the psychologist Stephen Ceci demonstrated in an ingenious little experiment. For more than twenty years, Ceci had taught the same class in developmental psychology at Cornell University. Sometimes he taught it twice in one year, once in the fall semester and again in the spring semester. Using the same course structure, the same lecture outlines, the same material, it was all perfectly routine. But one year, in the break between fall and spring semesters, Ceci and some other professors attended a workshop taught by a professional media consultant. Each professor was videotaped giving a lecture. The consultant critiqued the performance and suggested changes that would make the delivery more expressive and enthusiastic. "Underscore points with hand gestures," the consultant might say, or "Vary the pitch of your voice." The substance of the lectures wasn't discussed. This was strictly about style.

Ceci sensed an opportunity. He would follow the media consultant's advice about speaking and gesturing in the next semester but otherwise teach his class exactly as he always had. Then he would compare the student evaluations from the fall and spring semesters. If his ratings were higher in the spring, he would know if the stylistic changes alone had made a difference. And they did. Ceci's ratings improved across the board. Students judged him to be more organized, more accessible, and more tolerant. They even considered him to be more knowledgeable, with his average score on a five-point scale rising from 3.5 to 4.

Ceci's experiment clarified things by taking expert status out of the equation, but it still leaves some ambiguity. What exactly was it in his new speaking style that people responded to? Was he more likable? Or was it simply the greater enthusiasm and confidence he projected? That's not clear. But other research suggests confidence is a critical factor. In one study that examined how one person persuaded another when they disagreed, researchers concluded that "persuasion is a function not of intelligence, prediscussion conviction, position with respect to the issue, manifest ability, or volubility, but of the expression of confidence during the discussion itself." Very simply: Confidence convinces.

Another group of researchers asked people to tackle various problems—math questions, analogy puzzles, forecasts—and state how confident they were that the answer they came up with was correct. Then they were put in groups and asked to decide collectively what the answer was and how confident they were that their answer was correct. The researchers found the group responses tended to match those of the most confident person in the group, whether that person was actually right or not. In a third study, people were asked to watch the videotaped evidence of an eyewitness to a crime. The researchers varied ten different variables, including the circumstances of the crime, how a police lineup was conducted, and the witness's confidence in her own judgment—in one version, the witness says she is 80 percent sure she correctly identified the suspect; in another, she says she is 100 percent sure. The only factor that made a big difference to every measured outcome was confidence. Researchers have also shown that financial advisers who express considerable confidence in their stock forecasts are more trusted than those who are less confident, even when their objective records are the same.

This research, and much more like it, suggests there is a "confidence heuristic": If someone's confidence is high, we believe they are probably right; if they are less certain, we feel they are less reliable. Obviously, this means we deem those who are dead certain the best forecasters, while those who make "probabilistic" calls—"It is probable this will happen but not certain"—must be less accurate, and anyone who dares to say the odds of something are fifty-fifty will be met with scorn. People "took such judgments as indications that the forecasters were either generally incompetent, ignorant of the facts in a given case, or lazy, unwilling to expend the effort required to gather information that would justify greater confidence," one researcher found.

This "confidence heuristic," like the "availability" and other heuristics, isn't necessarily a conscious decision path. We may not actually say to ourselves, "She's so sure of herself she must be right!" It's something that happens at the edge of consciousness, or even without any awareness at all. It is automatic and instantaneous. We simply hear the person speak and suddenly we have the sense that, yes, she is probably right. If someone suggested her confidence played a key role in our conclusion, we may deny it. After all, we didn't *think* about her confidence; we may not have even *noticed* her confidence. At least not consciously.

Using confidence as a proxy for accuracy isn't all that unreasonable. In general, people's accuracy really does rise as their confidence increases. The person who mutters, "Gee whiz, I think so, but I'm not sure," probably *is* less likely to be right than the one who shouts, "I'm right! I'm right! I'd stake my life on it!" Which is why a "confidence heuristic" would work. But as is true with all heuristics, the confidence heuristic is far from perfect.

One problem is overconfidence. As we saw, most people are far too sure of themselves, and this gives us trouble if we use confidence to gauge accuracy. Robert Shiller is an interesting illustration. Aside from his very impressive title—Yale economist—Shiller is the very antithesis of the loud, quick-talking, dead-sure-of-himself pundit. He speaks quietly and is often hesitant, even a little inarticulate. He qualifies his statements and mentions reasons why he might be wrong. He is seldom simple, clear, and certain. But he has a track record that includes correctly calling both the high-tech bubble of the late 1990s and the real estate bubble that followed, and that record got him airtime on business shows normally dominated by cocksure pundits. A July 2009 interview on CNBC was typical. The American real estate market was "still in an abysmal situation," Shiller said, but there was a great deal of diversity within the national market and "people have gotten very speculative in their attitudes toward housing." This made it possible that in certain regional markets "there could be another bubble." But "this is not my more probable scenario," he added. It was more likely that prices "will languish for many years." By the standards of TV punditry, it was a nuanced and thoughtful overview of a complex situation plagued with uncertainties. And people hated it. Posted on a Web site, the interview drew 170 comments. Most ignored Shiller altogether and instead offered dead certain predictions of the sort that are usually heard on TV. Some were contemptuous. "This guy is really hedging his bet. He doesn't want to be underexposed or overexposed. I sure wouldn't take advice from him." Bring on the blowhards. As British politician Norman Lamont once said, admiringly, of one of his favorite newspaper columnists, "He is often wrong but he's never in doubt."

Another problem with the confidence heuristic is that people may look and sound more confident than they really are. Con men do this deliberately. We all do, to some degree. Of course most of us don't do it as brazenly as con men—one hopes—but we all sense intuitively that confidence is convincing. And so, when we are face-to-face with people we want to convince, we downplay our doubts, or bury them entirely, and put on a brave face. And that's before competition enters the equation. A financial adviser doesn't just want to convince clients that he can forecast the stock market. He wants to convince clients that he can do it better than other financial advisers. So he beats his chest a little louder than the other guys. But the other financial advisers want to land the same clients, so they answer this chest-beating with even more vigorous displays of bravado. Psychologists Joseph R. Radzevick and Don A. Moore tested this dynamic with an experiment in which people were assigned the role of either "guesser" or "adviser." The job of guessers was to estimate the weight of people in photos. The more accurate they were, the more money they made. The advisers were to provide estimates, including indications of confidence in their accuracy. Guessers were free to choose any adviser's estimate, so advisers made money based on the number of guessers who took their advice. Not surprisingly, advisers were overconfident in the first rounds of the experiment. But they weren't punished for being inaccurate. In fact, guessers preferred the more confident advisers, and advisers responded by getting steadily more confident as the experiment progressed—even though their accuracy never improved. Competition "magnifies" overconfidence, the researchers concluded.

Most people are overconfident to begin with. When they try to convince others, they become even more sure of themselves. Reward them for convincing others, and have them compete for those rewards, and it's just a matter of time before they are insisting they are 100 percent certain what the future holds.

TELL ME A STORY

People love stories, both the listening and the telling. It's a central part of human existence, found in every culture, in every place, in every time. That universality suggests its origins are biological, and therefore evolutionary.

There are many potential advantages storytelling gave our ancestors. It allowed experience to be distilled into knowledge and knowledge to be transmitted. It strengthened social bonds. It provided an opportunity to rehearse possible outcomes. But at an even more fundamental level, storytelling is a work-sharing agreement: If I use my brain's "Interpreter" neural network to produce an explanation for one set of facts and you use yours to explain another, we can share our explanations by swapping stories. If all fifty members of the tribe do the same, we'll all get fifty explanations in exchange for doing the heavy lifting on one. That's an efficient way to make sense of the world.

For explanation-sharing to work, however, a story cannot conclude with "I don't know" or "The answer isn't clear." The Interpreter insists on knowing. An explanatory story must deliver. When the movie *No Country for Old Men* ends as the killer walks off with nothing resolved, it disturbs us because the narrative isn't complete. What happens next? How does it end? This nonending worked for a movie (and novel) that was intended to be unsettling, but a story normally has to wrap everything up and come to a clear conclusion. Only that will satisfy the Interpreter's hunger for order and reason.

Other elements of a good story are as universal as storytelling itself. It has to be about people, not statistics or other abstractions. It should elicit emotion. Surprise is valuable, thanks to our evolved tendency to zero in on novelty. It also helps if the story involves a threat of some kind, thanks to the "negativity bias" mentioned in the last chapter.

"Confirmation bias" also plays a critical role for the very simple reason that none of us is a blank slate. Every human brain is a vast warehouse of beliefs and assumptions about the world and how it works. Psychologists call these "schemas." We love stories that fit our schemas; they're the cognitive equivalent of beautiful music. But a story that doesn't fit—a story that contradicts basic beliefs—is dissonant. (And nobody but a few oddballs enjoys dissonant music.) This is why there is no such creature as a universally acclaimed pundit. The expert who makes a prediction based on an explanatory story that fits neatly with the basic beliefs of an American free-market enthusiast, for example, is likely to get the attention and applause of American free-market enthusiasts. But that expert is just as likely to get a cold shoulder from European social democrats. Same story, same evidence, same logic, but completely different reactions. This sort of disparity appears routinely. Will man-made climate change savage civilization if we don't act now? Many scientists, activists, and politicians make that case. Some people find their evidence and arguments very compelling. Others snort. Whether a person falls in one camp or the other isn't up to a coin toss. Their prior beliefs—their schemas—make all the difference. If I were to describe an American who thinks gun control doesn't work, Ronald Reagan was a great leader, and international terrorism is a major threat, which side of the climate change debate is he likely to come down on? What about an American who supports strict gun control, thinks Reagan was dishonest and dangerous, and the threat of terrorism is overblown? We all know the answer—the first person is much more likely to snort—even though with regard to evidence and logic, gun control, Ronald Reagan, and terrorism have absolutely nothing to do with climate change. But they do reveal a person's schemas.

The importance of explanatory stories in convincing others cannot be exaggerated. "Imagine that you are the vice-president of a fairly large corporation," researchers asked a group of forty-four advanced university students with some training in basic decision making. As vice-president, you have been given the job of selecting a law firm to put on retainer. Among other things, the firm must be good at predicting the outcome of litigation. So you ask them to review a hundred pending cases in detail, predict whether the plaintiff or the defendant will win, and say how confident they are on a scale from 50 percent to 100 percent. Now, the researchers directed, "outline the strategy you would use in evaluating the accuracy of each firm that took part in the exercise." The big winner? One might think it would be a statistical analysis of the firm's accuracy, but people weren't so interested in that. What they wanted to hear was a good explanation: *How* did firms make predictions? If the method sounds good, the predictions must be as well.

Statistics be damned. Tell me a story.

As it happens, I've been told that many times, almost word for word, by people who should know. As a money manager based in Houston, Texas, Mike Robertson is one. Handling two billion dollars of other people's cash, Robertson is the fifth-largest independent wealth adviser in the United States. His clients are all multimillionaires; two are billionaires. He knows what it takes to convince very rich people to take his advice. And what it takes is *not* statistical evidence of sound judgment.

"Do I trust you? Do I think you care about me? Do I think you know what the hell you're doing?" That's what matters, Robertson told me. Getting people to say yes requires the ability to connect on a personal level, to make the potential client feel you're caring and trustworthy. Robertson is a big, friendly, likable guy. He's got the human stuff covered. As for competence, he establishes that with a good story—a confident, clear, concise explanation of how he makes decisions that leaves the potential client nodding his head and saying, "Yes, that makes sense." Robertson's story is drawn from the demographic analysis of business guru Harry Dent and it's not complicated: "Instead of coming in with reams of research papers and all this kind of stuff, you sit down and talk about potato chips and motorcycles." Who eats potato chips like crazy? Fourteen-year-olds. "I've had two fourteen-year-olds. I can attest to that." So if demographic projections show growing numbers of fourteen-year-olds in the coming years, you buy potato chip stocks. Same with motorcycles. They may be a young man's dream but Harley-Davidsons are expensive, so Harleys are mainly bought by people in their late forties. "Everybody says, 'Yeah, absolutely. The last guy I saw riding that thing had gray hair.'" So the future number of people in their late forties tells you whether you should get into Harley-Davidson.

Robertson doesn't deny that his story is very simplistic, or that there's far more to his thinking. But he doesn't go further because this story is what people want. Anything more is needless complication. "You don't have to sit there and bring in all these charts and stuff," he says. "If you don't trust me, it won't make a difference."

Fundamentally, says Robertson, convincing others that he has a handle on the future is *not* a rational process. "Statistics are rational. People are not."

NOW PUT IT ALL TOGETHER AND
GO ON *THE TONIGHT SHOW*

"This is a little different for us," says Johnny Carson, the legendary host of *The Tonight Show*. After an hour kibitzing with the comedian Buddy Hackett about such weighty matters as Hackett's hair—"You can comb it till your nose drops off and it stays like that," Hackett observes— Carson will now moderate a debate about the fate of humanity. On one side is the journalist Ben Wattenberg. On the other is a familiar face. "Dr. Paul Ehrlich has been with us a few times before," Carson says. "He's a population biologist at Stanford University and his book *The Population Bomb* has sold nearly a million copies."

As one might guess from the brown suits, sideburns, and ads for cigarettes—"New Kent Menthol has got it all together!"—this unusual moment in television history took place in August 1970. As always, Carson sat at his desk. Ehrlich took the chair normally occupied by grinning movie stars, while Wattenberg sat on the couch reserved for sidekicks and second-tier guests.

Carson asked Ehrlich to get things started by summarizing the basic argument of his book. "The main premise is there are 3.6 billion people in the world today. We're adding about seventy million a year and that's too many," Ehrlich said. "It's too many because we are getting desperately short of food. Matter of fact, recent indications are that the so-called Green Revolution is going to be less of a success than we thought it was going to be." Ehrlich's deep voice is calm and steady and his words flow smoothly. His left elbow is propped casually on the edge of the chair. He's young, but with his suit and tie, his relaxed confidence, and "DR. PAUL EHRLICH" flashed on-screen, he is every inch an authority. He knows what he's talking about. And he knows what's coming. "The very delicate life-support systems of the planet, the things that supply us with all our food, ultimately with all our oxygen, with all our waste disposal, are now severely threatened. I would say that trained ecologists are divided into two schools. There's the optimistic school, of which

I'm a member, that thinks that if we should stop what we're doing now very rapidly, that there's some chance that we'll prevent a breakdown of these systems. There are others who feel that the changes in the weather, that the permanent poisons that we've already added to the planet, have already set in train the sequence of events that will lead to disaster. They feel it's already too late. I think the only practical thing to do is pretend that it's not too late. So we're in deep trouble and I'm worried about it."

Wattenberg gives a decent reply, but it's obvious from the beginning he's no match. His delivery is hesitant, and his message is diffuse, unfocused. He accepts some of what Ehrlich is saying but suggests it's "overstated" and should be more balanced, but his alternative vision is as fuzzy as Ehrlich's is sharp and vivid.

Wattenberg tries gamely to parry Ehrlich's attacks but Ehrlich is far too quick-witted. When Wattenberg claims, "The new cars have sixty percent less pollution," Ehrlich shoots back, "That's nonsense."

Wattenberg looks a little stunned. "Well, that's my data," he says.

"That's not your data. That's the automobile manufacturers' data for cars that have never run anywhere," Ehrlich responds.

Wattenberg leans back in his chair. "I can't debate the scientific data with you."

Ehrlich smiles gently. "True," he says. The audience laughs. It's like watching Muhammad Ali float like a butterfly and sting like a bee. You can't help but feel sorry for the poor chump in the ring.

Ehrlich delivers all the elements that make a powerful presentation— evident expertise, confidence, clarity, enthusiasm, and charm. He tells a story that is simple and clear and fits the audience's beliefs and current concerns. ("I consider the Vietnam War and racism to be part of the same mess," Ehrlich says. "So it's really one big crisis.") And Ehrlich is able to move from one element to the other as smoothly as Johnny Carson working his way through the opening monologue.

He is also unflappable. When Wattenberg delivers his best line—"I didn't believe it when Chicken Little said the sky was falling and I don't believe it when Dr. Ehrlich says it"—Ehrlich merely smiles. "I *am* a doomsayer because I do believe doom is coming," he responds. "And I would say Mr. Wattenberg is essentially in the position of the person saying, 'Well, you're trying to sell me life insurance but I've never needed any before.'" The audience roars. Johnny Carson laughs harder than he did at anything Buddy Hackett said. Even Wattenberg chuckles wryly.

Before the laughter fades, Ehrlich grins and says to the audience, "Can I turn professorial for a moment?" He holds up a blank notepad. "I want to produce a very simple equation." With a marker, he writes "$D = N \times I$." The D stands for damage to the earth's life-support systems, he says. The N is the number of people. The I is the negative impact of each person on the environment. "In other words, you've got two factors: How many people you've got and what the people do. Now, it's quite true that if we stop population growth now and leave our environmental impact high, you go down the tubes. If you cut down the environmental impact of each person, do things differently, and let the population continue to grow, the product remains the same and you go down the tubes. What you've got to do is operate on both of these things at the same time. You've got to both reduce the size of the population *and* you've got to reduce the impact of the individual."

It's a tour de force. Ehrlich has swatted away his opponent's best line, cracked up the audience, and then, after pivoting smoothly to the role of esteemed academic expert, delivered a lecture that is simple, clear, and compelling. Wattenberg lights a cigar and smokes in silence. He knows it's over. Ehrlich won.

When Buddy Hackett surprises everyone by wandering onto the set as the debate is wrapping up, Ehrlich finishes with an encore: Jumping up, he asks, "Can I have a kiss, Buddy? My mother wouldn't believe it." Buddy obliges. The audience applauds madly.

As much as the events and culture of the era, Paul Ehrlich's *style* explains the enormous audience he attracted. Today, *The Population Bomb* is thought of as a pioneering work that ushered in fears of overpopulation and famine. It was not. As a young undergraduate, Ehrlich was himself inspired by two books—*Our Plundered Planet* and *Road to Survival*—both published in 1948. By the time Ehrlich wrote his blockbuster in 1968, the "population explosion" had long been a routine topic of discussion in governments, think tanks, and the mass media— it made the cover of *Time* on January 11, 1960—and Ehrlich's basic arguments had been made in a very long list of books. What was different about *The Population Bomb* was its author.

Paul Ehrlich is a gregarious and delightful man, a natural performer. "Ask me questions and I'll try to give you honest answers or clever lies," he kids when I call for an interview. He may be seventy-seven years old, but he's as sharp as ever. "I was teaching a course in evolution at Stanford," he recalls when I ask how he became one of the most famous public intellectuals of his time. "I spent the first nine weeks of the ten-week course on where we came from and the last week on where we were going. The last week got to be popular on campus and people told their parents and I started to be asked to speak to alumni groups and I was finally asked to speak to the Commonwealth Club." That lecture was broadcast on radio, and the executive director of the Sierra Club heard it. He contacted a publisher he knew, and Ehrlich agreed to write a popular book. Ehrlich wanted to call it *Population, Resources, and Environment*— a rare case in which his sense of how to appeal to a mass audience failed him. But the publisher caught the mistake. Let's call it *The Population Bomb*, he said.

At the same time, Ehrlich recalls, "I got involved with some colleagues at Yale and started Zero Population Growth [ZPG] as an NGO. It didn't go anywhere until Arthur Godfrey sent a copy of *The Population Bomb* to Johnny Carson." A coveted invitation to *The Tonight Show* arrived and under the bright studio lights Ehrlich and Carson hit it off. "We had a wonderful time. We went for a long time." Carson let Ehrlich plug ZPG, to great effect. "When I went on *The Tonight Show,* ZPG had six chapters and six hundred members. Johnny had me back about three times in a few months and let me give the address each time. And it went to six hundred chapters and something like sixty thousand members."

Ehrlich was suddenly a rock star. "Articulate, witty, and with a flair for the dramatic, Ehrlich has scored well with personal appearances," noted a reporter in 1970. "Campus appearances invariably draw mobs. Recently, more than 2,000 were turned away from a lecture at Berkeley after the university administration had first assigned him to a seminar room for 30, then moved his talk to an auditorium that seated 500." In total, the confident, chatty, charming professor with the dire predictions was invited to talk with Johnny Carson and his millions of viewers more than twenty times.

For experts who want the public's attention, Paul Ehrlich is the gold standard. Be articulate, enthusiastic, and authoritative. Be likable. See things through a single analytical lens and craft an explanatory story that is simple, clear, conclusive, and compelling. Do not doubt yourself. Do not acknowledge mistakes. And never, ever say, "I don't know."

People unsure of the future want to hear from confident experts who tell a good story, and Paul Ehrlich was among the very best. The fact that his predictions were mostly wrong didn't change that in the slightest.

THE EHRLICH LESSON

Whether they know about Paul Ehrlich or not, every successful communicator knows the lesson of his example.

Politicians know the Ehrlich lesson: "Confident, clear, and simple" is standard operating procedure in political communications. When the Obama administration wanted a stimulus package approved, it issued a chart with two lines—the first was the American unemployment rate over the coming months and years with the stimulus package, while the second line, much higher than the first, showed unemployment without the stimulus package. There was no ambiguity, no uncertainty. Just two lines stretching into the future. Which line would you like? Time passed. And reality scoffed: The unemployment rate shot past both lines. But politicians know predictions are about convincing people *today*, not being right *tomorrow*. When Danish prime minister Anders Fogh Rasmussen addressed scientists in the lead-up to the Copenhagen climate conference of 2009, he implored them to give politicians the sort of conclusions they could use to sell the public on a course of action. "I need fixed targets and certain figures," he said, "and not too many considerations on uncertainty and risk and things like that." Accuracy isn't imperative in politics, certainty is.

Other policy makers know this lesson too. That's why they engage in "overarguing," as Greg Treverton, a former vice chair of the U.S. National Intelligence Council, calls it. "Senior decision makers communicate with one another, their organization, and the public by using narratives—stories that combine statements of goals, assumptions about the world, and plans of action. When they craft these narratives, policymakers strive to appear more certain than they actually are, knowing full well that a storyline acknowledging their underlying uncertainty would undermine their authority in policy debates."

Many scientists have also realized that speaking as science itself speaks—complex, ambiguous, uncertain—is a sure way to be ignored. If they want funding and public support, they have to follow the lead of their colleague Dr. Ehrlich and deliver bold, confident predictions. The same is true of activists and nongovernmental organizations. And "futurists," forecasters, and other gurus who work the corporate lecture circuit. It's especially true among those who put together business forecasts; managers and executives know that someone who wishes to keep her job will not announce to a roomful of superiors that the future is complex, unpredictable, and out of her control—no matter how true that may be.

But more than all the rest, the news media know the lesson of Paul Ehrlich.

The worst offenders are the opinion columnists, talk-show hosts, and bloggers who issue predictions about as often as most people breathe. "It's the least intellectually taxing question that somebody can ask or the least intellectually taxing answer somebody can give, and one of the least challenging discussions for an audience," noted veteran journalist

Jeff Greenfield. "You're not actually talking about history, culture, facts. You're talking about what one of my law school professors used to call breezy speculation, or the initials thereof. And in an era when there's more and more talk on cable, the cheapest thing you can do on television is to bring people into the studio and have them talk, and the easiest kind of talk is to say what's going to happen." Imagine something that would be interesting if it happened; let your Interpreter cobble together an explanation for why it could happen; spin it into an entertaining story. In far too many cases, that's all there is to pundits' predictions. "We are very good at making up these grand theories about what's about to happen," writes Paul Wells, a Canadian political journalist. "After they don't happen, we are at least as good at forgetting our earlier mistaken certitude."

Pundits aside, the news is filled with simple, clear, and confident predictions. It's the entrenched way of doing things—so entrenched, in fact, that even a disastrous failure of forecasting like the crash of 2008 cannot convince the media to do things differently. The cover of the July 2009 edition of *Money* magazine—to take one of literally hundreds of examples—promised to reveal "How to Profit in the New Economy: The Five Big Changes Ahead, and What They Mean for Your Investing, Spending, and Career." Alongside it on the newsstand, *BusinessWeek* offered a look at "Housing Market 2012." Neither article mentioned the catastrophic failure of articles like these to see 2008 coming. Instead, they tell readers that the American economy will grow almost 6 percent in 2012 and median home values will rise 7 percent. There will be strong job growth in Colorado. Housing supply will be tight in Oregon. And in 2019 the percentage of the American workforce that is freelance, temporary, or self-employed will be precisely 40 percent.

This sort of certainty is so routine we seldom stop to marvel at how ridiculous it is. And it's not just the business press—it's even found in *science* news. The May 2, 2009, cover of the popular British science magazine *New Scientist* blared, "Swine Flu: Where It Came from, Where It Will End, How to Protect Yourself." At the time, the first wave of the flu had just started spreading outward from Mexico, and no scientist would have dared suggest the future course of the virus was so neatly predictable that they could say "where it would end." This critical fact can be found deep in the text of the article—"All this means the virus could go pandemic. Or it might not"—but the cover is not marred by a trace of uncertainty. Neither is the headline: "The Predictable Pandemic."

"Journalists, whose base currency is 'fact,' have little patience with contingent possibilities. Most are disposed to seeing their job as turning the unknown into the known," observed John Huxford, director of journalism studies at Villanova University. In 2008, when the National Academy of Sciences (NAS) brought together scientists in Washington, DC, to discuss the risks posed by an electromagnetic "solar storm," the group agreed the threat was real. A particularly severe storm could damage electrical grids, the report noted. However, "it is difficult to understand, much less predict, the consequences." But when the *New Scientist* reported on the group's conclusions, that uncertainty was swept aside. Instead, an extreme scenario prepared by private consultants for the NAS committee became the dramatic foundation of the entire article. "It is midnight on 22 September 2012 and the skies above Manhattan are filled with a flickering curtain of colorful light," it begins. "All the lights in the state go out. Within 90 seconds, the entire eastern half of the U.S. is without power. A year later and millions of Americans are dead and the nation's infrastructure lies in tatters. The World Bank declares America a developing nation. . . . It sounds ridiculous. Surely the sun couldn't create so profound a disaster on Earth. Yet an extraordinary report funded by NASA and issued by the U.S. National Academy of Sciences in January this year claims it could do just that." Well, it *could*.

Far too often, the track record of the experts offering predictions simply isn't a concern for the producers and editors who shape the news. In the dismal winter of 2009, like a ghost from the past, Howard Ruff appeared on CNBC and other business shows. The author of the 1978 best seller *How to Prosper During the Coming Bad Years* had a huge following during the inflation-racked years of the late 1970s and early 1980s, but when inflation collapsed, the economy turned around, stock markets got bullish, and Ruff looked out of touch. When he kept calling for inflation, recession, and misery all through the 1980s and 1990s, he faded from public view. But in 2009, after more than three decades sounding the alarm about hard times ahead, Ruff was back on TV at the age of seventy-eight. In an interview later that year, he told me it wasn't because TV producers were taking his ideas seriously again now that hard times had actually come. "I spent some money on a PR firm," he said. Ruff had a good story to tell, and he was available. That was enough.

Experts who have neither a thrilling story nor money for a PR firm find the media simply isn't interested in hearing from them. In 1999, Ross Anderson, a professor of computer science at Cambridge University, was that sort of expert. His not-so-thrilling story involved Y2K, the programming glitch—years had been recorded with two digits, not four—which could cause computers to mistake the year 2000 for 1900 and do all sorts of odd things as a result. Systems would fail and the failures would cascade, putting corporations and governments in danger, according to a large and growing number of consultants who offered to fix the problem for a fee as big as the threat. Many insisted it was even worse than that. The economy would suffer, vital services would break down, and there could be social unrest. It could even cause the end of the world as we know it—or "TEOTWAWKI," as believers liked to call it. Political leaders didn't go that far, but most Western governments took the threat very seriously. "I do not want to seem irrational or a prophet of doom, but there is a possibility of riots," the head of the UK's task force on Y2K said in 1997. No one really knows how much was spent on the problem, but most estimates put it in the hundreds of billions of dollars.

All big British institutions were concerned about Y2K, but Cambridge had more reason to be worried than most. With seven thousand employees and a vast array of computer systems—operating in everything from state-of-the-art scientific labs to advanced medical treatments to an aerial photography unit—the opportunities for failure were legion. A readiness committee was struck, with Ross Anderson as the technical adviser, and Anderson got an idea. Given the vast diversity of Cambridge's computer systems, a thorough analysis of each system's vulnerability to the Millennium Bug, and the cost to fix them, would provide a reasonably good sense of the level of vulnerability in a great many other settings. That may seem elementary, but in fact, little of this sort of hard analysis had been done. Almost all the noise around Y2K was based on little more than speculation, some of it informed, much of it not. So Anderson got to work, and he soon had good news. The threat wasn't nearly as bad as it was portrayed in the media and fixing it had cost Cambridge less than a hundred thousand pounds.

This was important information, Anderson thought. He brought it to the attention of the British civil service, but no one wanted to touch it. "Officials seemed worried in case the precautions they'd taken were criticized as unnecessary," Anderson later wrote. So he contacted "a number of prominent journalists." Still, no one was interested. Why would they be? Anderson wasn't saying Y2K was a hurricane about to make landfall, or that the whole thing was a fraud. He was saying there was a real problem but it probably wasn't severe and could be fixed at reasonable cost. That's a *lousy* story. It's a bit complicated, and it's boring. But Anderson didn't give up. Two weeks before the moment of truth, the university's press office sent a media release to hundreds of news organizations. "I can't predict the future but now we've gone out and looked at a lot of systems, I'm much less worried than I used to be," Anderson said in the release. "Lots of things may break, but few of them will actually matter." That release generated a grand total of four radio interviews, three of them brief—no more than a few raindrops in the raging monsoon of Y2K coverage.

Ross Anderson was too modest. He *did* predict the future: His study was a remarkably accurate forecast of what actually happened when 1999 became 2000. But that didn't matter, any more than it mattered that Paul Ehrlich's predictions failed. It's the Paul Ehrlichs the media and the public want to hear from, not the Ross Andersons.

The incentives are as obvious as they are huge—TV spots, newspaper interviews, best-selling books, lucrative lectures, corporate consulting contracts, the attention of the public and people who matter. Anyone who wants these things, whether for selfish or selfless reasons, must follow the lead of Paul Ehrlich. "Breathless hype," observed journalist Michael Lind, is what "wins readers for journals and newspapers and makes the careers of pundits who aspire to bloviate at Davos before an audience of the trendy rich."

Be simple, clear, and confident. Be extreme. Be a good storyteller.

Think and talk like a hedgehog.

A SWING AND A MISS! AND NOBODY CARES. . . .

Still, there's a problem. People may want to hear from absurdly confident experts, and the media may make such experts stars. But stardom means lots of people are listening. If the expert is lousy at forecasting the future, lots of people will see his predictions crash and burn. He will be humiliated and they will stop listening. So for all the incentives pushing experts to pump up their predictions, there must be a countervailing incentive to tone it down. Or so we might think. In reality, there is little accountability for predictions, and while big calls that go bad *should* damage the reputations of those who make them, they seldom do.

One of the most extreme voices in the Y2K fiasco belonged to social critic James Howard Kunstler. "If nothing else, I expect Y2K to destabilize world petroleum markets," Kunstler wrote, and the effects of that will be as bad as, or worse than, those of the 1973 oil embargo. Industrial agriculture will collapse. "Spectacular dysfunction" will plague car-dependent cities. Supply chains will crumble. "I doubt that the Wal-Marts and Kmarts of the land will survive Y2K." That was the minimum-damage outcome. He actually expected things to get much worse. "The aggregate economic effect of these [computer system] failures will be a worldwide deflationary depression. I will not be surprised if it is as bad in terms of unemployment and hardship as the 1930s." Expect "international political and military mischief." And look out for the United States to seek salvation in some "charismatic political maniac."

In the long and rich history of failed predictions, few forecasts have been more wrong. But Kunstler shrugged it off. So what if Y2K didn't destroy civilization? *Something* would. And soon. In 2005, Kunstler published *The Long Emergency,* a frantic, sweaty tour of all the things that could go horribly awry, and surely will, plunging us all into "an abyss of economic and political disorder on a scale that no one has ever seen before." One might think that after Kunstler's Y2K pratfall, people wouldn't pay for him to be their tour guide to the future, but *The Long Emergency* was a best seller and Kunstler—a wildly entertaining speaker—became a fixture on the lecture circuit, where he is paid significant amounts of money to tell audiences they are doomed.

The 2003 invasion of Iraq left failed predictions lying about the landscape like burnt-out tanks. The first army of pundits defeated by reality were the pessimists who thought the invasion itself would turn into a long, massive battle between two huge armies, or that the battle for Baghdad would become "another Stalingrad." Then it was the optimists who predicted that Saddam Hussein's vast arsenal of weapons of mass destruction would be unearthed, that the American soldiers would be embraced as liberators, that a flourishing democracy would get up and running quickly, that a reborn Iraq would cause the spirit of reform to sweep across the Middle East, that the terrorist "swamp" would be drained. And a square in Baghdad would be named after George W. Bush by the grateful Iraqi people. They were all wrong, but the careers of the pundits who made these predictions were not among the war's casualties. Consider David Brooks and William Kristol. Writing in *The Weekly Standard* prior to the invasion, Brooks and Kristol relentlessly urged the United States to war. A failure of nerve would lead to disaster, they insisted, while an invasion would work wonders in the Middle East and at home. "If the effort to oust Saddam fails, we will be back in the 1970s," wrote Brooks. "We will live in a nation crippled by self-doubt. If we succeed, we will be a nation infused with confidence. We will have

done a great thing for the world, and other great things will await."
In March 2003, on the eve of the invasion, both men put it all on the
line. "Events will soon reveal who was right, Bush or Chirac," Brooks
wrote. "History and reality are about to weigh in," Kristol added, "and
we are inclined to simply let them render their verdicts."

History and reality did weigh in: Far from the quick and glorious
adventure Brooks and Kristol expected, the invasion of Iraq became a
nightmarish occupation that drained American blood, treasure, and
confidence. And yet, this had no apparent effect on the career of either
man. In September 2003, David Brooks was hired to write a column in
The New York Times, the world's leading newspaper, instantly becoming
one of the most influential voices in journalism. In December 2007,
Kristol received the same punishment.

The case of Brooks and Kristol is extreme but far from unique. Dick
Morris, the former Bill Clinton pollster who is now a conservative commentator, routinely makes predictions that are as confidently expressed
as they are wrong—a classic being his 2006 book *Condi vs. Hillary,* which
foresaw a 2008 presidential election contest between Democratic nomi-
nee Hillary Clinton and Republican candidate Condoleezza Rice. Morris's mistakes apparently make no difference to his demand as a televised
talking head. The same is true of the Anglo-Canadian-American pundit
Mark Steyn. As the British writer Geoffrey Wheatcroft helpfully summarized in 2006: "Apart from predicting that George Bush would win
the 2000 presidential election in a landslide, Steyn said at regular intervals that Osama bin Laden 'will remain dead.' Weeks after the invasion
of Iraq, he assured his readers that there would be 'no widespread resentment or resistance of the Western military presence'; in December 2003,
he wrote that 'another six weeks of insurgency sounds about right, after
which it will peter out'; and the following March he insisted that 'I don't
think it's possible for anyone who looks at Iraq honestly to see it as anything other than a success story.'" Steyn's most endearing quality, Wheatcroft noted with dry British wit, is his "enviable self-confidence." And
apparently, that is enough. In 2006, Steyn published *America Alone: The*

End of the World as We Know It, which predicted that Europe would soon be swamped by fecund Muslims, leaving the United States alone in the struggle to save Western civilization from the Islamic hordes. Despite its author's demonstrated inability to predict matters somewhat less complicated than the fate of continents and civilizations, *America Alone* became a *New York Times* best seller and a hugely influential tract among American conservatives.

And finally, there's Paul Ehrlich himself. It was clear by the 1990s that the dire forecasts Ehrlich had made in the 1970s had come to nothing, but that didn't slow the shower of awards Ehrlich enjoyed that decade. There was the Gold Medal Award of the World Wildlife Fund International; the John Muir Award of the Sierra Club; the Volvo Environmental Prize; the Blue Planet Prize of the Asahi Glass Foundation; the Tyler Prize from the University of Southern California; the Heinz Award, created by Teresa Heinz, billionaire wife of U.S. senator John Kerry; the Sasakawa Prize from the United Nations; and the MacArthur Fellowship, nicknamed the "Genius Award." Ehrlich also won the Crafoord Prize of the Royal Swedish Academy of Sciences, which is widely considered the Nobel of environmentalism. Many of these honors stemmed, at least in part, from Ehrlich's research as a biologist, which is respected in his field, but they often were given for popular work like *The Population Bomb* and *The End of Affluence.* The Crafoord Prize citation specifically noted Ehrlich's "numerous books on global environmental problems, such as overpopulation, resource depletion, nuclear winter, and greenhouse effects. It has been said that with Rachel Carson he is the one person with the greatest importance for present-day awareness of the imminent global catastrophe." The citation does not say precisely what that imminent global catastrophe may be; two decades later it's still not clear. No matter. In 2009, the Programme for Sustainability Leadership at the University of Cambridge surveyed its "alumni network of over 2,000 senior leaders from around the world" and asked them to choose the best books ever written about sustainability. The result was a list of fifty books the university billed as "the wisdom of our age." *The Population Bomb* was number four.

Ehrlich's colleague John Holdren—who cowrote many pessimistic and prediction-filled articles with Ehrlich in the 1970s and 1980s—got a slightly tougher time of it when he faced a Senate confirmation hearing in 2009. In a 1971 article cowritten with Paul Ehrlich, Holdren had declared that "some form of ecocatastrophe, if not thermonuclear war, seems almost certain to overtake us before the end of the century." Senator David Vitter asked Holdren if he thought that "was a responsible" thing to write. "First of all, I guess I would say that one of the things I've learned in the intervening nearly four decades is that predictions about the future are difficult," Holdren joked. "That was a statement which, at least, at the age of twenty-six, I had the good sense to hedge by saying 'almost certain.'" And that was that. The Senate approved Holdren's appointment, making him science adviser to the president of the United States.

It seems we take predictions very seriously, until they don't pan out. Then they're trivia.

IT'S A HIT! AND THE CROWD GOES WILD!

People may ignore misses, but a prediction that *succeeds* is another matter entirely. We not only pay attention to hits when they happen in front of our eyes, we go looking for them. We even fabricate them.

Whenever a major event happens, a hunt begins. Who called it? Someone must have—because a major event that was not predicted would lead to the psychologically disturbing conclusion that the world is in some degree unpredictable, unknowable, and uncontrollable. After the terrorist attacks of September 11, 2001, the need to know someone had predicted the awful event was palpable, and within days, an e-mail flashed from person to person, around the world, with an answer: Nostradamus had called it. As usual with chain e-mails, it mutated as it was passed along, but the core of the e-mail was this statement, in typically cryptic language: "In the City of God, there will be great thunder. Two Brothers torn apart by Chaos. While the fortress endures, the great leader will succumb." People were stunned. "Two brothers torn apart by Chaos"? That has to be the Twin Towers! The news spread almost as fast as news of the event itself. But if people had been even slightly skeptical and made a quick Google search, they would have discovered that Nostradamus didn't write those words. A high school student in Canada did. His name is Neil Marshall. In 1997, as an assignment for a co-op work placement, he created a Web site. At the time, he was annoyed that so many people believe that the notoriously vague pronouncements of Nostradamus predict anything, so he wrote "a little piece on why I think Nostradamus is a crock," including some ominous pronouncements he concocted in the style of the sixteenth-century Frenchman. Almost immediately after the 9/11 attack, someone either deliberately misrepresented Marshall's mockery, or they misunderstood what he had written. Either way, people got what they wanted—an accurate prediction of the disaster—and they passed it along to millions of others hungry to believe, thus making Marshall's point in spectacular fashion.

The hunt for the successful prediction seldom comes up with such a patently absurd result, but it always comes up with something. After the crash of 2008, the lucky Nostradamus was Peter Schiff, who went from being just another talking head on business shows to a guru with a best-selling book and the sort of fame that makes it impossible to take a stroll in Manhattan without someone wanting to shake your hand. What's intriguing about these successes is that they are universal. No matter what happens, someone turns up to claim the prize. What this phenomenon demonstrates is not that the universe is predictable but that vast numbers of people are making predictions and, like lotteries, when such large numbers are involved, the chances of someone winning the grand prize are high even though the chances of any particular person winning are tiny. Imagine, for example, a parallel universe in which 2008 was essentially the opposite of the year we experienced. Economies roared, real estates values took off, and stock markets went through the roof. In that universe Peter Schiff would have continued to enjoy undisturbed strolls in Manhattan. But there would still be a man anointed as the guru who called it: His name is Robert Zuccaro, who had taken the daring gamble some years before of publishing a book called *Dow 30,000 by 2008*. Of course, it's always possible that someone hailed for predicting a major change really did call the change in a meaningful sense, but the more likely explanation is that he, like a lottery winner, got lucky. And he's likely to get lucky a second time because, thanks to the "illusion of prediction" and our poor intuitive sense of randomness, people seldom attribute a predictive hit to anything but skill.

What makes this mass delusion possible is the different emphasis we put on predictions that hit and those that miss. We ignore misses, even when they lie scattered by the dozen at our feet; we celebrate hits, even when we have to hunt for them and pretend there was more to them than luck. This discrepancy is so extreme and pervasive, it even has a name. It's the "Jeane Dixon Effect," coined by the mathematician John Allen Paulos in honor of the American psychic. Dixon was renowned for having made several accurate predictions, including the assassination of President John F. Kennedy, or so the media often said. Close examination of these alleged hits suggests there is much less to them than meets the eye. But more importantly, the very long list of Dixon's misses—the USSR would put the first man on the moon, China would start a world war in 1958, Richard Nixon would win the election of 1960, et cetera—was simply ignored.

This is a little odd, when you think about it. We don't just want predictions, after all. We want *accurate* predictions. But it's impossible to judge the accuracy of predictions if we zero in on the hits and ignore the misses. So why is so much attention given to hits while misses usually are treated as trivia or ignored altogether?

CUI BONO?

The most obvious factor is self-interest. When there's a hit, there is also a guy who wants you to know he nailed it; when there's a miss, the responsible party would very much like the prediction to be quietly forgotten. You can be sure Robert Zuccaro would prefer that his name not appear in this book.

The selective editing of predictions is particularly easy for newspaper columnists, who need only to stay on a topic when events confirm their predictions and switch when they don't—as veteran *New York Times* columnist Anthony Lewis did to great effect. Lewis started writing about population growth, food shortages, and the coming age of scarcity in the late 1960s. In 1969, he described Paul Ehrlich's predictions as "frighteningly convincing," and his praise for *The Limits to Growth* report—"One of the most important documents of our age!"—was emblazoned prominently on the cover of the paperback. When the oil embargo of 1973 caused gas stations to run dry, store shelves to empty, and prices to soar, Lewis declared it to be proof the Cassandras were right. "The authors [of *The Limits to Growth*] understandably find some grim vindication in events," he noted, before going on to quote Dennis Meadows saying things would only get worse. And again, in 1981, as the American economy sank into the most severe recession since the Great Depression and oil prices soared to previously unimaginable highs, Lewis gave his readers a stern I-told-you-so. "When the question of resources was introduced to public consciousness in the book *The Limits to Growth*, critics mocked its warning. They said economic mechanisms and human effort could always overcome scarcity. But all around us now, less than a decade later, we see the effects of resource limits. Oil is the obvious example. The pressure of demand, to which the producers reacted as the textbooks said they should, has made oil an expensive commodity. We know it is going to become more expensive." But it didn't become more expensive. In fact, four years later, the price of oil collapsed, and it stayed in the basement for two decades. But as far as I can tell, Lewis didn't write about that. Some of his other omissions are even more startling. In 1974, with the food crisis mounting, Lewis wrote repeatedly about the dire situation in South Asia. In November 1974, for

example, he wrote that "to avoid starvation deaths in the tens of millions, South Asia will depend increasingly on outside food aid. By early
in the next century, on the population projections, the aid needed would
equal total United States agricultural production." In 1975—*the very
next year*—India did well enough to decline all international food aid.
In the years that followed, India's food production grew rapidly, and
fears of a nation-destroying famine were forgotten. But Lewis had other
things to write about, and he never gave his readers the good news.

When protests rocked Iran in the spring of 2009, experts rushed to
the ramparts and fired volleys of predictions. There were so many predictions, pointing to so many outcomes, that almost any conclusion to
the turmoil would produce an expert who had "predicted" it, noted
sociologist Charles Kurzman. "In a year's time, some of these experts
will crow that events have confirmed their analyses. Others will quietly
remove this week's remarks from their Web sites." No prediction is too
big to be quickly and efficiently forgotten. Even when a prediction is
tied to a very precise date—as few are—it can still disappear down the
Orwellian memory hole. "The sun rose on 1 January 2000 like the lights
coming on at an orgy," British journalist Nick Davies wrote about the
Y2K scare. "Everybody who had been so busy—the journalists, the governments, the bug-related businesses and the computer experts—all
picked themselves up, hoped nobody was looking, and quietly tiptoed
away."

The self-interest of the person doing the predicting is not the only
one that favors hits over misses, however. The media, too, has much at
stake. Almost every news story involves comments from experts, often
including predictions. Whether readers and audiences value these stories depends on how credible they seem to be, and one of the best ways
to boost the apparent credibility of the story is to boost that of the expert. Mentioning hits but not misses does just that. In 2009 and 2010,
the Canadian economist Jeff Rubin was quoted in countless stories
about oil prices, which are Rubin's specialty, and the stories routinely
noted Rubin's "oracular reputation," as *Newsweek* put it. Rubin "accu-

rately predicted oil's surge during the last decade," reported *Business-Week*. He has been "deadly accurate," wrote the *National Post*. "In 2006, he predicted oil would hit $150 a barrel in 2008." All these statements are true but what none of these stories mentions is that in the first half of 2008, Rubin saw oil prices going nowhere but up. "Don't think of today's prices as a spike," he told *The Toronto Star*. "Don't think of them as a temporary aberration. Think of them as the beginning of a new era." Nine months later the price of oil crashed, and a chart of that year's oil prices looks remarkably like a spike. That's not to say Rubin won't be right in the long term, but he definitely missed the spectacular drop in oil prices that year—and news stories definitely don't mention it.

Of course, experts *are* occasionally hauled into the public square and pilloried for making a failed prediction. Sometimes it happens because a journalist does her job better than most. Or particularly after there's been a dramatic turn of events, it's a sort of scapegoating, in which one prognosticator is made to suffer for the sins of many. In the years leading up to the bursting of the tech bubble at the end of the 1990s, for example, countless pundits insisted that the old rules of valuation had been thrown out in the new economy and stocks would keep right on soaring. When stocks crashed, millions of people suffered. Someone had to be blamed, and so James Glassman and Kevin Hassett, the authors of *Dow 36,000*, were singled out and vilified. It wasn't that their prediction was especially bad. Indeed, many pundits had been far more bullish. But Glassman and Hassett were unlucky enough to publish their book shortly before the bubble burst, and its immediate success gave them a high profile. The title of their book also vividly summarized the hype that fueled that giddy, delusional era. They were ideal scapegoats.

More often, however, it's self-interest that holds experts responsible for their words. For decades, antienvironmentalist commentators have mocked Paul Ehrlich, not out of some high-minded concern for accountability but because discrediting Paul Ehrlich is a handy way of discrediting anyone who warns against environmental threats. It's not accuracy

they want to advance, it's their agenda. But these sorts of attacks sel-
dom do much damage because the self-interest that motivates them is
too obvious. In fact, among environmentalists, the insults flung at
Ehrlich by right-wing critics are only perceived to polish his armor;
Ehrlich himself actually boasts about being attacked by the likes of Rush
Limbaugh.

Self-interest also explains why Arthur Laffer, Ben Stein, and the other
pundits who squared off against Peter Schiff were humiliated by that
YouTube video. Holding them to account wasn't the reason the video
was produced and released. As the title makes clear—"Peter Schiff was
right"—the purpose was to tout Schiff's hit. Laffer, Stein, and the rest
were merely collateral damage. It's also worth noting that, however
embarrassing the video may be, the pundits in it are still working the
media circuit—including Ben Stein, who writes a column on economics
in *The New York Times*.

That said, financial commentary is one field where predictive failures
are noticed—and mocked. But so often it's competitors who gleefully
play up the pratfalls of others, limiting the impact of the criticism. And
sharp words about failed predictions are essentially forbidden where
they are most needed: The media do not want talking heads highlight-
ing the failed predictions of other talking heads on air. After all, if a
guest destroys the credibility of the pundits who appear on a show, he
also destroys the credibility of the show.

Arianna Huffington, founder of the liberal Web site The Huffington
Post, demonstrated the existence of this unspoken rule in a December
31, 2009, appearance on CNBC. "I'm sorry, Larry," Huffington said to
Larry Kudlow, the show's voluble and opinionated cohost. "You and I
have known each other for a long time. I have no idea why anybody's
still listening to you." In 1999, Huffington said, Kudlow had written in
The Wall Street Journal that the Dow would top 50,000 by 2020.

Kudlow was not pleased. He categorically denied having made any
such prediction, he denounced Huffington's "ad hominem" attack, and
he quickly and firmly directed the conversation elsewhere.

But Huffington wouldn't let go that easily. After a commercial break, she held up a copy of Kudlow's prediction and read it. Kudlow sat frozen. His cohost intervened—"Let's just move on for the sake of conversation"—and steered the discussion to politics and predictions about the elections of 2010.

Finally, at the end of the segment, Kudlow let loose. "Just let me say, Arianna, insofar as your personal attack on me, I am a great believer in American free-market capitalism for the long run. Unlike you, I have never changed my stripes. You were a conservative Newt Gingrich supporter, then you flip-flopped to a liberal. I stay the course. We may get to Dow fifty thousand or not. I don't recall ever making that forecast. But in the long run, in the long run, economic freedom and free-market capitalism will keep this country great. I say that on New Year's Eve. I will keep that point of view. And I have not changed my point of view for my entire adult life."

Huffington tried to respond but Kudlow cut her off. "We're going to move on," he said. "I just want to make a response. We gave you time, Arianna. I don't like ad hominem stuff. It's a cheap shot. You're trying to promote your Web site. That's your right as an American."

"It's not a cheap shot," Huffington squeezed in. "I'm just telling you what you said. You're denying what you said."

Kudlow waved her off. "Don't drag us through the mud."

Kudlow's cohost wrapped things up. "Happy New Year!" he gushed. And that was that.

YESTERDAY'S NEWS

In 1993, *New York Times* book critic Christopher Lehmann-Haupt was glum. He'd just read Paul Kennedy's new book *Preparing for the Twenty-first Century,* which warned that soaring populations would combine with diminishing resources and worsening environmental problems to produce disaster. "When you come to the end, you are so depressed you barely have strength to close the book," he wrote. His only criticism of the author was that Kennedy had suggested there were still uncertainties in play so the grim future he foresaw would not necessarily come to pass. "Kennedy whistles past the graveyard," Lehmann-Haupt wrote.

What makes this review revealing is that in the early 1970s Christopher Lehmann-Haupt reviewed—and praised—several books whose themes were identical to Kennedy's. The only difference was that the earlier books said the decade that would decide everything would be the 1970s: Either there would be major change then or we were all doomed. One of the books Lehmann-Haupt reviewed was Paul Ehrlich's *The End of Affluence,* which predicted, as we have seen, that American prosperity was finished no matter what. It also made a long string of precise predictions about the end of oil, food shortages, mass famines, and the collapse of India. By 1993, it was clear that most of the forecasts in Ehrlich's book and the others reviewed by Lehmann-Haupt had completely failed. And yet in his review of Paul Kennedy's book, Lehmann-Haupt didn't mention that Kennedy's claims had been routinely made in the 1970s, or that those earlier predictions had fallen flat. Instead, Lehmann-Haupt faulted Kennedy for refusing to declare our doom inevitable.

So why didn't Lehmann-Haupt mention the many failed predictions of the 1970s? A cynic would say it was deliberate. He's pushing an agenda and he doesn't care if his readers are properly informed. I don't think that's right. I think he simply forgot. Why would he remember books he had read more than two decades earlier? It was 1993, after all. Oil was cheap, people were getting fat, and the economy had done reasonably well for most of the previous decade. Food shortages? Overpopulation? The "energy crisis"? That was so 1970s. People hadn't talked about any of it for years. You can't blame Lehmann-Haupt if *The End of Affluence* had vanished from his memory.

This is another huge reason we notice hits but ignore misses: If a prediction about a subject hits, that subject will probably be in the news and people will be talking about it, but if the prediction misses, the subject is likely yesterday's news and nobody will be talking about it. If Paul

Ehrlich's predictions in *The End of Affluence* had been right, you can be sure that overpopulation and food shortages would have been very hot topics in 1993—and Christopher Lehmann-Haupt would remember Ehrlich's book. But they weren't right. By 1993, overpopulation and food shortages were as dated as bell bottoms and disco, and Lehmann-Haupt had forgotten the predictions he had once found so compelling.

"Three-quarters of *news* is 'new,'" an editor once told me. News happens *today*. If a famine happens now and an expert predicted it a decade ago, that old prediction is news. But if the famine *doesn't* happen, that old prediction is not news. It is merely old. In 2006, political scientist John Mueller contacted a *Wall Street Journal* reporter about a cover story on terrorism she had written for *National Journal* magazine two years earlier, shortly after the presidential election of 2004. In the story, the reporter quoted experts who predicted that the threat would rise in the months following the election. "Bin Laden, having uttered his warning, will be marshaling his resources to make good on his promise that Americans will not be able to avoid a new 9/11. It'll be a race against time," an expert said at the end of the article. Nothing remotely like that happened, so Mueller asked the reporter if she would write a follow-up piece noting that the prediction had failed. Probably not, she suggested politely. "It's hard to do stories that do not have a hard news component." Of course, if there *had* been terrorist attacks, you can be sure there would have been stories about the expert who predicted them. But with no terrorist attacks, there was no "new" news, and thus no reason to write a story about the expert who blew smoke.

Heads: I win. Tails: You forget we had a bet.

There's not much risk for experts who make predictions.

CAPRICORNS ARE HONEST, INTELLIGENT, HARDWORKING, GULLIBLE. . . .

Self-interest and media amnesia aside, the more profound reason we notice hits and ignore misses lies in human psychology.

In 1949, psychologist Bertram Forer asked his students to complete a personality test. Later, he gave them a personality profile based on the test's results and asked them to judge the test's accuracy. Everyone was impressed. They were sure the test had really nailed who they were, which was odd because everyone had been given the same profile. Forer had assembled it out of vague statements—"You have a tendency to be critical of yourself"—culled from a book on astrology.

"The root of all superstition is that men observe when a thing hits, but not when it misses," wrote Sir Francis Bacon. The "Forer Effect" is one demonstration of this universal tendency. It's what makes horoscopes so appealing. When we read a string of statements—"A business opportunity is promising," "New love beckons," "A figure from the past makes contact"—the hits and misses are not equally weighted. Those that seem to fit our circumstances grab our attention and are remembered, while those that don't are scarcely noticed and quickly forgotten.

That much is obvious. But bear in mind that hits and misses don't come with labels. It's a matter of perception whether something is a hit or a miss, which makes language important. The more ambiguous the wording is, the more a statement can be stretched, and since we want hits, that's the direction in which things will tend to stretch—a tendency astrologers, psychics, soothsayers, and prophets have understood since the dawn of time. When the notoriously vague Oracle of Delphi was asked by King Croesus of Lydia whether he should attack the Persian Empire, the oracle is said to have responded that if he did he would destroy a great empire. Encouraged, the king attacked and lost. Croesus hadn't considered that whether he won or lost, a great empire would be destroyed. Nostradamus also knew better than to be precise. All the sixteenth-century sage's predictions were written in such fuzzy, poetic images—"Serpents introduced into the iron cage where the seven children of the king are taken"—they could be taken to mean almost anything. And they have been. For centuries, people have insisted that a careful reading of the master's work reveals that Nostradamus predicted the present—even though it is only by constantly reinterpreting the same writing that his admirers keep Nostradamus on top of the day's events.

Mysticism invites this sort of gullibility but incense and spooky stories aren't necessary for the human mind to go to absurd lengths to discover hits, or even turn misses into hits. This truth is neatly illustrated in a book simply called *Predictions*. Published in 1956, it's a compilation of old cartoons and illustrations that made predictions about the future. One cartoon shows a map of Russia as a ravenous bear that has swallowed almost all of Europe and Asia and has its jaws open for its next meal: Japan. In a caption, the author describes the cartoon as "too accurate for comfort." He thought this because, in 1956, Soviet Russia was a superpower threatening to dominate all of Europe and Asia—and since the cartoon had been drawn in 1904, more than fifty years earlier, it seemed astonishingly prescient. To come to that conclusion, however, the author had to overlook a lot of history. In fact, the cartoon was a commentary on rising tensions between Japan and Russia that exploded into war in 1905. Russia was crushed. Russia then suffered a civil insurrection. Less than a decade later came the First World War, another defeat, the loss of vast territories, revolution, and civil war. A decade after *that* came mass starvation. Then Russia was nearly annihilated by Nazi Germany. Only *forty years after the cartoon was published* did Russia achieve the superpower status that made an observer in 1956 think this cartoon was an amazing hit instead of the spectacular miss it really was.

Simply reading a list of old predictions reveals our unfortunate bias. The misses may produce a chuckle or two, but they are soon forgotten. A hit, on the other hand, leaps off the page and is remembered. I often experienced this phenomenon in doing the research for this book. One day, for example, I was thunderstruck to read the following in a newspaper column Anthony Lewis wrote in 1969: "The increasing carbon dioxide in the air gradually warms the oceans and could, it is feared, eventually melt the polar ice caps at a rate fast enough to flood the coasts of our continents. Daniel Patrick Moynihan, counselor to President

Nixon, warned here this week that the atmosphere's carbon dioxide content would grow 25 percent by the year 2000." That's more or less the current theory of man-made climate change, which didn't become scientific orthodoxy until the 1990s. Talk about a hit! But then I reminded myself that in the late 1960s and early 1970s, there were several hypotheses about climate change floating about. Some called for warming. Some for cooling. Some of those raising alarms of the day said either was possible. If someone in 1969 had made a short list of those theories, including a "no change" option, and then chosen one outcome entirely at random, she would have had a good chance of successfully "predicting" the future. But more to the point, I was so focused on this supposedly successful prediction that I paid little attention to others that appeared in the same column. They included "Competition for food and raw materials is going to become savage as populations grow." And "People and engines are using up oxygen at an alarming rate: one transAtlantic jet burns 35 tons. . . . One day, suddenly, the world's billions of creatures may literally be struggling for a last breath." The hit may have been more apparent than real but it still had the power to overwhelm some spectacular misses.

PETER SCHIFF WAS RIGHT!

Which brings us back to the amazing Peter Schiff. As the title of that famous video says, he was right. When so many pundits were saying everything was fine with the American economy, he said it would crash. And it did. Peter Schiff was right.

That time. In a sense. Sort of.

"The dollar is going to start to fall. And as the dollar falls, you're going to have significant flows out of U.S. financial assets from all around the world. And that is going to send interest rates through the roof. And when that happens, this whole consumer-led, borrow-and-spend economy is going to come tumbling down. Then we're going to have a real recession." That was Peter Schiff in a television interview that was not included in the famous "Peter Schiff Was Right" video. The year was 2002. "The bear market began in 2000," Schiff said. "It's probably going to last another five or ten years. I think the bulk of the downside is going to happen in the next couple of years." And how much "downside" would there be? "My prediction for the NASDAQ is that it's going to fall to around five hundred. Right now, it's about seventeen hundred. It's got a long way to go down. Dow Jones is still above ten thousand. Probably going to fall to between two thousand and four thousand. But it might go below two thousand."

Even if we are so generous as to stretch the time frame of Schiff's prediction to 2009—and it's clear he was actually talking about the first half of the decade—this looks bad. The dollar did decline from 2002 to 2008, but it didn't send interest rates through the roof and it didn't cause a recession. In fact, when the crisis of 2008 hit, investors ran to the American dollar, pushing it up significantly. There also was no rampant inflation, another of Schiff's predictions. The stock markets did decline for about a year following his forecast, but they then rose steadily for four years, with the Dow hitting a peak of 14,000 in late 2007. And even in the darkest days of the 2008 crash, the markets never sank to anywhere near the depths Schiff forecast—the Dow hit bottom at 6,500 but surprised most observers, including Schiff, by bouncing back above 10,000 months later.

But Schiff didn't let any of this dent his confidence. "While the housing bubble was inflating, I was telling people to rent. I was telling people to get out of tech stocks in 1998 and 1999. They kept rising, but then they collapsed, and I turned out to be right," Schiff said in May 2008, when the American economy was sinking and his star was on the rise. "The reality is I don't think I've been wrong on anything," Schiff said in a May 2008 interview. If Schiff were right about his dazzling predictive powers, investors who took his advice must have really cleaned up in the year of Schiff's alleged vindication. But they didn't. "The year that Schiff became a star prognosticator on TV was also one of the worst periods ever for his clients," *Fortune* magazine reported. "In most cases the foreign markets he likes got hit even harder than the U.S. in 2008 and even more surprising to Schiff, the U.S. dollar rallied strongly as investors rushed to the perceived safety of Treasuries." Schiff provided some other reasons to question his claims of perfection in May 2008. "I think the stock market is heading lower," he predicted. He was right about that. "Gold is going to be twelve hundred to fifteen hundred dollars by the end of the year." Off by several hundred dollars on that one. "Oil prices had a pretty big run and might not make more headway by the end of the year. But we could see a hundred fifty to two hundred dollars next year." Oil crashed; it was less than forty dollars at the end of the year and it spent most of 2009 around seventy dollars. "At a minimum, the dollar will lose another forty to fifty percent of its value. I'm confident that by next year we'll see more aggressive movements to abandon the dollar by the [Persian] Gulf region and by the Asian bloc. That's when the stuff really hits the fan." Stuff hit the fan in 2009, but not that stuff.

But it's not the misses that dazzle. In December 2008, *New York Times* business columnist Joe Nocera gushed about the "Peter Schiff Was Right" YouTube video. "One thing that makes it amazing is how unflinching Mr. Schiff is, how unyielding, how matter-of-fact, no matter how scornful and sneering the response from the other talking heads. Even when they laugh at him, he keeps coming back," Nocera wrote. "The other thing that makes it amazing, of course, is that Mr. Schiff absolutely nailed the current crisis—and did so many, many months before the rest of us could feel the first tremor." True enough. But it's somewhat less amazing if you bear in mind that Schiff has been making essentially the same prediction for the same reason for many years. And the amazement fades entirely when you learn that the man Schiff credits for his understanding of economics—his father, Irwin—has been doing the same at least since 1976. Now, even if we generously give Schiff unqualified credit for calling 2008, that means the combined record of Peter and Irwin Schiff is something on the order of one in thirty-two. As the old saying goes, even a stopped clock is right twice a day—which produces a record of one in twelve. It seems only reasonable that prognosticators should be required to do better than stopped clocks before we declare them gurus.

Nocera's judgment of Schiff's accuracy may be doubtful but he's absolutely right about Schiff's style. He is articulate, passionate, and authoritative. And he is absolutely, unswervingly, unconquerably sure of himself. Just like the other hedgehogs who dominate the talk shows, best-seller charts, and lecture halls.

They may be wrong far more often than they are right. They may do worse than flipped coins and stopped clocks. But they never fail to deliver the certainty that we crave.

And we never fail to ask for more.

POSTSCRIPT: HANG THE INNOCENT

On the very short list of pundits who suffered for making bad predictions, one name must take top spot.

Norman Angell was British but he spent part of his youth knocking about the American West, working as a journalist, a cowboy, a laborer, and a homesteader. In the years prior to the First World War, he wrote an internationally renowned essay and turned it into a hugely influential best-selling book. He became a member of Parliament, a lecturer, and a statesman. In 1933, he won the Nobel Peace Prize.

But all that is forgotten. The sole reason that Norman Angell's name continues to appear in print today, the only thing for which this remarkable man is remembered, is a prediction he made in 1909.

The economies and financial systems of the major powers were now intertwined, Angell noted in a pamphlet entitled *Europe's Optical Illusion*. It followed that in a war between the major powers, "the victor would suffer equally with the vanquished," wrote historian Barbara Tuchman, summarizing Angell's views, "therefore war had become unprofitable, therefore no nation would be so foolish as to start one." And so the major powers would never again go to war with each other, Angell concluded with impeccable logic and terrible timing: Five years later, Europe exploded in war and the great powers spent much of the next half century doing what Angell said they would never do again.

Norman Angell has been mocked ever since. Even now, almost a century after Angell's prediction failed so spectacularly, his name routinely appears in print as a warning against foolish optimism or economic determinism or the perils of making predictions. No one has ever suffered more for a prediction that failed.

And that is deeply unfair, for the simple reason that Norman Angell never predicted there would be no war.

What Angell actually argued in *Europe's Optical Illusion* and in the many best-selling editions of the book that followed—under the title *The Great Illusion*—was that the interconnections of the economic and financial systems meant that a victorious nation would suffer more than it gained if it attempted to profit from war by looting national banks or otherwise plundering the defeated. This was a limited thesis. It left open the possibility that nations could reap political or strategic gains in war. It also did not deny the possibility that nations would go to war despite their self-interest, since Angell never thought that individuals and groups are always guided by strict rationality. So war was not impossible, in Angell's view; it was merely unprofitable, in a precise and limited sense.

Tuchman's summary of Angell's views, quoted above, is simply wrong. And Tuchman was far from the first to misrepresent what Angell wrote.

Almost from the moment Angell's book was published, his argument was simplified and sexed up: Victors *always* lose more than they gain; war is *always* contrary to self-interest; therefore no one would be so stupid as to launch a war in the modern world; therefore no one ever will. It wasn't only critics who made this mistake. So did many of Angell's ardent admirers. "What shall we say of the Great War of Europe, ever threatening, ever impending, and which never comes?" wrote David Starr Jordan, president of Stanford University, in 1913. "We shall say that it will never come." Even though Angell's work was discussed at the highest levels in London and other capitals, even though dozens of study groups were created to pore over *The Great Illusion,* the misunderstanding persisted. Angell later pinned some of the blame on his writing. There was a "fundamental defect of presentation in a book that was highly, at times extravagantly, praised for its clarity and lucidity," he wrote. Angell's biographer, Martin Ceadel, thinks the titles—both *Europe's Optical Illusion* and *The Great Illusion*—added to the confusion because they didn't make clear that the "illusion" in question wasn't the *threat* of war but the *profitability* of war. "Angell would have been spared much heartache had he called his book *The Economic Contradictions of Aggression* or some similarly substantive formulation that would have clarified that he was disputing neither the possibility of war nor the utility of defense," Ceadell wrote.

Angell struggled mightily to set the record straight. "War is, unhappily, quite possible, and, in the prevailing condition of ignorance of certain politico-economic facts, even likely," Angell wrote to the *Daily Mail* in 1911 after the newspaper claimed Angell had argued "war is impossible." Angell wrote many such letters. "You are good enough to say that I am 'one of the very few advocates of peace at any price who is not altogether an ass.' And yet you state that I have been on a mission 'to persuade the German people that war in the twentieth century is impossible.' If I had ever tried to teach anybody such sorry rubbish I should be altogether an unmitigated ass," Angell wrote in 1913. "Personally, not only do I regard war as possible, but extremely likely. What I have been preaching in Germany is that it is impossible for Germany to benefit by war, especially a war against us; and that, of course, is quite a different matter."

It did no good. In 1914, the First World War exploded. As the most famous of the many experts who had said—or were believed to have said—that there would be no war, Norman Angell was singled out. He was the scapegoat.

Angell fought back in letters and lectures and interviews, but it was no use. In 1933, when Angell was awarded the Nobel Peace Prize for his tireless antiwar activism, the citation prominently denounced the claim that he had said war was impossible. Not even that helped. Among those less informed than the Nobel committee, Angell's reputation was permanently stained. Angell even complained that he had to avoid getting involved with causes he supported lest he "might taint others with the derision which has grown from this falsehood or confusion."

In 1952, when Angell published his autobiography, a sympathetic reviewer in *The New York Times* noted how absurd it was that Angell had suffered so much for so little reason. Even the critics' description of Angell was cockeyed, the reviewer noted. They called him "starry-eyed," an ivory-tower academic, a theorist out of touch with reality, but he was, in fact, a much-traveled and experienced journalist. And, no, the reviewer stated emphatically, he had *not* claimed war was impossible. Still, five decades later, in the very same newspaper, a writer mocked "the starry-eyed British economist Norman Angell" who had claimed war was impossible.

One might think Angell would have been left in peace after he died in 1967, at the age of ninety-five, but the torment continued posthumously, thanks largely to Barbara Tuchman. Tuchman didn't merely repeat the myth of Angell's prediction. She repeated it in *The Guns of August,* a 1962 examination of the causes of the First World War that won the Pulitzer Prize, deeply impressed President John F. Kennedy, and became a massive best seller that shaped the popular understanding of the war that launched the twentieth century. Tuchman chiseled the myth into marble.

And so, decades after he died, Norman Angell continues to be mocked as the fool who said war was impossible, while the many fools who actually said war was impossible lie undisturbed in their graves. There really is no justice in the matter of predictions.

7

When Prophets Fail

When the facts change, I change my mind. What do you do, sir?

—JOHN MAYNARD KEYNES

The cataclysm would be swift, terrible, and awesome. At sunrise on the morning of December 21, tectonic plates would lurch and buckle. The entire west coast of the Americas, from Seattle to Chile, would crumble into the Pacific Ocean. Floodwaters would surge across the heart of the continent, creating a vast inland sea stretching from the Arctic Circle to the Gulf of Mexico. Tens of millions would die and the United States would all but vanish.

Marian Keech, the American psychic who experienced this terrible premonition of the future, planned on being far away that fateful morning in 1955. Hours earlier, at the stroke of midnight, she and her small band of believers would be met by the aliens who had warned Keech of the coming doom. Together, they would board a flying saucer and zoom off into outer space.

History records that on December 21, 1955, the United States was not destroyed and Marian Keech did not leave the planet. Given these facts, it follows that Keech's prediction was wrong. How could it be anything else? The prediction was clear and the timing was precise. The predicted events did not happen, ergo, the prediction was wrong. No person of sound mind would dispute it. Or so one might think. But as psychologist Leon Festinger demonstrated in a legendary study, a mind deeply committed to the truth of a prediction will do almost anything to avoid seeing evidence of the prediction's failure for what it is.

In 1955, Festinger and his colleagues were working on a new psychological theory when they heard about Keech's prophecy and saw a chance to put their thinking to a real-world test. Posing as laypeople, the psychologists joined Keech's group, which they dubbed the "Seekers." (All the names used by Festinger were pseudonyms, as they didn't wish to subject Keech and her followers to more ridicule.) What they found were ordinary midwestern Americans. Marian Keech was a middle-aged housewife remarkable only for the strange beliefs she concocted from a variety of popular sources. "Almost all her conceptions of the universe, the spiritual world, interplanetary communication and travel, and the dread possibilities of atomic warfare can be found, in analogue or identity, in popular magazines, sensational books, and even columns of daily [news]papers," wrote Festinger and his colleagues. The Seekers may have let their imaginations run loose but they weren't in any sense mentally ill.

Among Keech's most ardent supporters were Thomas and Daisy Armstrong, a couple who had worked as Christian missionaries before a shared interest in the occult led them to UFOs and prophecies. When Keech had her vision of the disaster to come—she believed she could psychically "channel" the aliens, which allowed them to take control of her hand and write messages with a pen and paper—it was Daisy who claimed to find "corroborating evidence" in the literature on UFOs. And it was Thomas who brought others to Keech. As a physician, Thomas was a respected authority figure. "A tall man in his early forties, Dr. Armstrong had an air of ease and self-assurance that seemed to inspire confidence in his listeners."

Keech had little interest in spreading the word. The Seekers contacted the media, but only briefly. Mostly, they refused interviews. Even in the days leading up to December 21, when reporters from the major national newspapers and wire services were knocking on Keech's door, they were shunned. Not surprisingly, Keech's following grew slowly, to a total of thirty-three people who were affiliated to some degree. Of these, eight had committed to the prophecy by quitting a job or doing something else that showed they strongly believed the cataclysm would occur. These true believers were well aware of how much they had on the line. "I have to believe the flood is coming on the twenty-first," one said to a researcher on December 4, "because I've spent nearly all my money. I quit my job, I quit comptometer school, and my apartment costs me a hundred dollars a month. I have to believe."

The days and hours counted down. On what the Seekers believed would be the last night of the world as they knew it, they gathered in Keech's house. Midnight approached. "The last ten minutes were tense ones for the group in the living room. They had nothing to do but sit and wait, their coats in their laps," Festinger wrote. Midnight struck. Nothing happened. Keech's followers sat in silence. At five minutes past midnight, someone noticed that the time on a different clock was four minutes to midnight. Clearly, the first clock was running fast. All attention shifted to the second clock.

Three more minutes passed. "And not a plan has gone astray!" Keech squeaked nervously. A fourth minute slipped by and midnight struck again. Still, nothing happened. Where was the flying saucer? Channeling the aliens, Keech announced there had been a short delay. Again they sat in silence. "Occasionally someone shifted in his chair or coughed but no one made a comment or asked a question." The phone rang. A reporter wanted to know what was happening. No comment.

In the hours that followed, the tension dissolved into confusion. Maybe "time didn't mean anything," one man suggested. Maybe the event happened a thousand years ago. Maybe it will happen a thousand years from now. Others didn't accept that. Something had gone wrong. "Well, all right," Keech said finally. "Suppose they gave us a wrong date. Well, this only got into the newspapers on Thursday and people only had seventy-two hours to get ready to meet their maker. Now suppose it doesn't happen tonight. Let's suppose it happens next year or two years or three or four years from now. I'm not going to change one bit. I'm going to sit here and write and maybe people will say it was this little group spreading light here that prevented the flood. Or maybe if it's delayed for a couple of years there'll be time to get people together. I don't know. All I know is that the plan has never gone astray. We have never had a plan changed. And you'll see tomorrow the house will be full of them and we'll have an open house and I'll need every one of you to answer the phone and maybe they'll ask us to go on television. I'm not sorry a bit. I won't be sorry no matter what happens."

It was three A.M. The group looked back at the original prophecy. They had misread it, some decided. It was a mistake, for example, to read a reference to "parked cars" that would take them somewhere literally. Parked cars don't move. They're parked. So clearly that was *symbolic* language. Happily, at that very moment, the aliens sent a message via another channeler in the group. The message confirmed that "parked cars" was symbolic of the believers' physical bodies, and their physical bodies had indeed been present at midnight. The flying saucer in the prophecy was also symbolic. It stood for spiritual knowledge. Thus, the prophecy hadn't failed at all. It had been fulfilled.

Some eagerly agreed with the new interpretation, but Keech balked. The woman who channeled the new interpretation was offended. Do you have a better explanation? she huffed. No, Keech conceded. But "I don't think we have to interpret it, we don't have to understand everything. The plan has never gone astray. We don't know what the plan is but it has never gone astray." The group wasn't satisfied but Dr. Armstrong urged others to keep the faith. "I've given up just about everything. I've cut every tie. I've burned every bridge. I've turned my back on the world. I can't afford to doubt. I have to believe."

Keech started to cry. "They were all now visibly shaken," Festinger wrote, "and many were close to tears."

The Seekers milled about, bewildered and hurt. But at 4:45 A.M.,

Marian Keech excitedly asked everyone to gather in the living room. She had received a message from the aliens, she said. Or rather, she had a message from God—for He was the ultimate source of the words from above. "For this day it is established that there is but one God of Earth, and He is in thy midst, and from His hand thou has written these words," the message read. "And mighty is the word of God—and by His word have ye been saved—for from the mouth of death have ye been delivered and at no time has there been such a force loosed upon the Earth. Not since the beginning of time has there been such a force of Good and light as now floods this room and that which has been loosed in this room now floods the earth." The group had shown such faith that God had chosen to avert the catastrophe, Keech explained. So the prediction hadn't been wrong. In fact, it had been proved right! "This message was received with enthusiasm by the group," Festinger noted.

Keech channeled another message, which essentially repeated the first and directed the group to go out into the world and spread the word. At this, one man got up and left, but "the rest of the believers were jubilant." Of course, this explanation flatly contradicted the earlier message about the prophecy being "symbolic," but the group didn't see a contradiction because the earlier message was never mentioned again.

In the hours and days that followed, Keech and her slightly diminished band of followers were transformed. They issued press releases, published flyers, called reporters, and described in great detail to anyone who would listen how they had saved the world. In a channeled message, the aliens further directed Keech to lift the long-standing ban on photographs. In fact, they directed, the group should "make special efforts to please photographers."

The Seekers also became keenly interested in the news itself. Keech excitedly noted a story in the newspaper about an earthquake that had happened five days earlier in Nevada. More evidence the prediction was right! And when they learned that earthquakes had struck Italy and California on December 21 itself, the Seekers were delighted. "It all ties in with what I believe," Keech proudly declared.

To an external observer, the prediction had clearly and conclusively failed. But to Marian Keech and the others committed to its truth, this simply could not be. The prediction was true. And nothing could prove otherwise.

MAKING EVERYTHING FIT

The theory Leon Festinger was developing in 1955 is now a foundational concept of modern psychology. It is cognitive dissonance.

The human mind wants the world to make sense, Festinger noted. For that to happen, our cognitions—our thoughts, perceptions, and memories—must fit together. They must be consonant. If they aren't, if they clash, and we are aware of the contradiction, they are dissonant. And we can't be comfortable in the presence of cognitive dissonance. It has to be resolved. Distraction—"Think about something else!"—is the simplest solution. But sometimes it's impossible to ignore the thoughts crashing into each other and we have to deal with it. That may take the creation of new cognitions or the alteration of existing ones, or they may have to be forgotten altogether. However it's done, it *must* be done, because dissonance is a highly aversive emotional state. Like a bad headache, we *must* make it go away.

Say you're a cop walking the beat. You see a man park a car and get out. He seems a little unsteady on his feet. Is he drunk? You walk over. He makes a flippant comment and you shove him backward. He stumbles and hits his head. He's bleeding. Now what? You're a decent person and a trained professional—and you hurt a man for no good reason. Those cognitions do not fit together. Worse, they go right to the heart of your self-definition. The cognitive dissonance is throbbing. How do you resolve it? You can't take the shove back, and you can't forget it, at least not instantly. But what you can do is change your perception of the man and the incident. Maybe the way he spoke to you was really offensive, aggressive, almost threatening. Maybe *he deserved it*. Like morphine easing a headache, the new cognition—*he deserved it*—dissolves the dissonance, and you feel better.

We engage in this sort of rationalization all the time, though it's seldom as explicit and conscious as I've made it out to be. It happens, for example, anytime we make a difficult decision. By definition, difficult decisions involve factors pointing in opposite directions. Should I buy this stock? Should I quit my job? Should I get married? In every case, there are reasons for and against, and so, no matter what choice we finally make, we will have done it despite reasons that suggest we should not. That creates dissonance and is the reason we rationalize these tough calls by playing up the factors that supported our decision while belittling those that didn't. This transforms the decision. Before, it was hard, but afterward we are sure that the decision was the right one. In the classic demonstration of this tendency, psychologists interviewed people lined up to place a bet at a racetrack. "How likely is it you will win?" they asked. On average, people gave themselves a "fair" shot. They also interviewed people *after* they placed their bets; they said they had a "good" chance of winning. The researchers were particularly amused when a man who had been interviewed on his way to placing a bet sought them out immediately after putting his money down. He wanted to let them know he'd changed his mind. He had rated his chance to be fair, he said, but now he was sure it was "good. No, by God, make that an excellent chance."

But things get really interesting after the race is run. At that point, there's hard evidence about the decision. What happens if the evidence says, "You were wrong"? Sometimes people don't fool themselves. They see the evidence for what it is and they say, "I was wrong." But that reaction is much less likely than one would expect, because people tend to be "cognitive conservatives"—meaning they stick with existing beliefs far more than is reasonable.

In one experiment, researchers showed people a pair of notes. One of these is a genuine suicide note, they said, but the other is a fake. See if you can tell which is which. After guessing, they were told if they were right or wrong. This process was repeated twenty-five times. Or at least this is how it seemed to the test subjects. In reality, the results weren't real. They were randomly assigned: Some people were told they were excellent at the task, having correctly spotted twenty-four out of twenty-five of the genuine suicide notes; others were told they were average, getting seventeen right; and the rest were told they had done a lousy job, getting only ten right. But after giving people this bogus evidence, and letting them form a belief about how good they were at spotting genuine suicide notes, the researchers let them in on the secret. These results are meaningless, they said. They tell you nothing about how good you would be at this task. Then the researchers asked three questions: How many correct guesses do you think you actually made? How many correct guesses do you think the average person would make? If you did a similar test a second time, how many correct guesses would you make? The researchers found that people who had been told falsely that they were excellent at the task tended to rate their ability above average while those who had been told they were lousy at it rated themselves to be below average—which clearly demonstrated that the initial results swayed perceptions even though everyone knew the initial results were meaningless. "It is clear that beliefs can survive potent logical or empirical challenges," wrote psychologists Lee Ross and Craig Anderson in a summary of the many studies on the subject. "They can survive and even be bolstered by evidence that most uncommitted observers would agree logically demands some weakening of such beliefs. They can even survive the total destruction of their original evidential bases."

The people in the suicide-note experiment obviously did not have a strong commitment to what they believed about their suicide-note identification skills. That makes the persistence of their beliefs all the more remarkable because, thanks to cognitive dissonance, how *committed* we are to a belief makes a big difference when we are faced with proof that the belief is wrong. A casual bettor at the racetrack who puts five dollars on a horse he thinks will win doesn't have a lot on the line. He never claimed to be an expert, and it's only five bucks. But someone who bets a thousand dollars, who lives for the racetrack, who prides himself on knowing horses, who brags to anyone who will listen that his pick is a sure thing—he's going to have a much harder time saying, "I was wrong." In psychological terms, the cognitive dissonance experienced by the first bettor will be mild. Confront him with the evidence—"You were wrong! Admit it!"—and he may just shrug and nod. Yes, he made a bad call. So what? But the second bettor will suffer the cognitive equivalent of a migraine. Instead of admitting he was wrong, he is far more likely to rifle the medicine cabinet of his mind for a soothing rationalization. Maybe the track was muddier than he'd thought, or the jockey made a stupid mistake. Whatever. There *has* to be an explanation. Anything to make the cognitive pain go away.

An excellent place to see how strong commitments can skew our thoughts and perceptions is in the political arena. To many people, politics is something they think about only during election campaigns or not at all. But for party stalwarts or ideological warriors, politics is a constant passion that matters deeply. It is a big part of their personal identity, and these committed citizens who follow politics closely tend to be very knowledgeable. So who's more susceptible to mistaken or distorted thinking about politics? I suspect most people would assume that the less interested, less informed, and less involved citizens are, but cognitive dissonance theory suggests the opposite: It's the more interested, more informed, and more involved citizens who are more committed to their beliefs. Greater commitment produces more cognitive dissonance when facts don't fit beliefs, and this prompts more effort to rationalize the problem away— to *make* the facts fit the beliefs. And this is just what researchers have found, many times. The deficit of the U.S. federal government decreased 90 percent between 1993 and 1996, so there was no question what the right answer was when Americans were asked in 1996 if the deficit had decreased, increased, or stayed the same. And yet only one-third of respondents said the deficit had declined. Forty percent said it had increased. Now, some of that result comes from simple ignorance. Polls consistently find large chunks of the public get basic factual questions wrong. More revealing was the partisan split: Slightly more than half of Republicans said the deficit had increased a lot or a little, compared to 37 percent of independents and 31 percent of Democrats. Why the difference? The president was a Democrat, and the thought of a Democrat successfully defeating the deficit did not sit easily in Republican minds. And, no, this isn't just a Republican thing. Surveys in the late 1980s, years after the decade-long plague of inflation had finally been stamped out, revealed a similar partisan split—except this time the president was a Republican and it was Democrats whose perceptions were unreasonably negative. In the face of such bias, mere facts don't stand a chance. "Political knowledge does not correct for partisan bias in perception of 'objective' conditions, nor does it mitigate the bias. Instead, and unfortunately, it enhances the bias; party identification colors the perceptions of the most politically informed citizens far more than the relatively less-informed citizens." And bear in mind that this research didn't separate less committed Democrats and Republicans from their fiercer comrades. It's a safe bet that if it had, it would show bias growing in lockstep with commitment: In the mind of the True Believer, belief determines reality, not the other way around.

After Japan attacked the United States at Pearl Harbor, General John DeWitt was sure American citizens of Japanese origin would unleash a wave of sabotage. They must be rounded up and imprisoned, he insisted. When time passed and there was no sabotage, DeWitt didn't reconsider. "The very fact that no sabotage has taken place is a disturbing and confirming indication that such action *will* be taken," he declared. As the reader may realize, DeWitt's reasoning is an extreme example of the "confirmation bias" discussed earlier. Confirmation bias is cognitive dissonance at work: Having settled on a belief, we naturally subject evidence that contradicts the belief to harsh critical scrutiny or ignore such evidence altogether. At the same time, we lower our standards when we examine supportive evidence so that even weak evidence is accepted as powerful proof. And if, like DeWitt, we're desperate to shore up a crumbling belief we are deeply committed to, we are likely to drop our standards altogether—and say something as silly as "the absence of evidence that I am right proves I am right."

When the clock struck midnight on December 21, 1955, Marian Keech was even more compelled to defend her belief than DeWitt had been in 1942. Her commitment to the prediction was massive. It was the centerpiece of her understanding of how the universe worked; her name and prophecy were in newspapers across the country; people had abandoned jobs and families to join her. When the flying saucer didn't appear and the sun rose on an ordinary day, the cognitive dissonance she experienced must have been knee-buckling. Keech's more ardent followers suffered similarly, because they, too, had completely committed themselves. Only the peripheral members of the group, whose belief and commitment were modest, escaped severe mental turmoil.

For Leon Festinger, that was the moment of truth. The reaction of Keech and her followers to that moment would put cognitive dissonance theory to the test. In the months leading up to December 21, 1955, Festinger made three of his own predictions: First, those Seekers who were only modestly committed would accept that the prediction had been proved wrong and would drift away; second, those who were heavily committed would find rationalizations that would allow them to maintain their belief in the prediction, even if they had to twist themselves into mental knots to do it; third, the remaining faithful would greatly boost their efforts to spread the word in order to have their beliefs affirmed by the interest and support of others.

That is precisely what happened. Leon Festinger was a better prophet than Marian Keech.

EXPERTS ON THE DEFENSIVE

One might think the experts who took part in Philip Tetlock's landmark study suffered little cognitive dissonance when they were told just how bad their predictions had turned out to be. After all, Tetlock had carefully drafted his questions so there would be no doubt about whether a prediction was right or wrong after the fact, and the experts in his study had been guaranteed anonymity, so they wouldn't be publicly humiliated. And Tetlock is a quiet and gentle man who tried, as he says, "to put it as nonjudgmentally as I could." Surely, under these encouraging circumstances, the experts would look at the evidence, shrug, and say, "I guess I was wrong."

Some did. But Tetlock noticed that those who were frank about their failure tended to be those who didn't think prediction was even possible. "They would say, 'I didn't think I could do predictions but I was humoring you and I wanted to be helpful,'" Tetlock recalls with a laugh. These experts tended to be foxes, not surprisingly. Much less forthcoming were experts who thought prediction *is* possible, especially hedgehogs. When Tetlock reviewed their failed predictions with them, they dug in and fought back with an impressive arsenal of mental defenses. They weren't really wrong, they insisted. Things *almost* turned out as they had predicted. Or they still might. And anyway, the prediction got thrown off by an "exogenous shock" that no one could possibly have foreseen and that shouldn't be held against them. Reviewing the excuses made by Tetlock's experts, psychologists Carol Tavris and Elliot Aronson offered this succinct and withering summary: "Blah blah blah."

This defensiveness doesn't surprise psychologists because, while the experts in Tetlock's experiment may have had nothing on the line in public, they still had a significant commitment at stake. "Our convictions about who we are carry us through the day and we are constantly interpreting the things that happen to us through the filter of our core beliefs," Tavris and Aaronson wrote. "When experts are wrong, the centerpiece of their professional identity is threatened," and that generates cognitive dissonance. It may not have been as severe as that suffered by General DeWitt or Marian Keech, but it was enough to inspire some vigorous rationalizing. All humans are talented rationalizers—as Michael Gazzaniga demonstrated with his research on the "Interpreter"— but experts are particularly good at it. Not only are their brains stuffed with information about the subject at hand, giving them more raw material to work with, but experts are experienced at generating a hypothesis, assembling arguments, and making a case. If they do not restrain their thoughts with self-scrutiny and reason, they can easily spin failure until it seems meaningless, or very close to a success, or even a triumphant vindication.

The forms rationalization can take are limited only by human creativity, and we are a very creative species. But two varieties of rationalizing deserve special mention because they are heard so often when predictions fail.

The first line of defense of the failed prophet—whether preacher or Ph.D.—is to insist that while it may appear that the time frame of the prediction has passed, a closer examination reveals the clock is still ticking. Marian Keech and the Seekers did this quite literally when they stopped watching the clock that showed midnight had come and gone and turned to one that showed there was still time left. This sort of evasion often happens in apocalyptic religious movements. In the early nineteenth century, for example, an American sect called "Millerites" identified 1843 as the year in which biblical prophecies of the end of the world would be fulfilled. When the sun rose on January 1, 1843, William Miller, the movement's founder, refined his forecast by declaring that the end would come sometime between March 21, 1843, and March 21, 1844, "according to the Jewish mode of computation." For various reasons, many believers became certain the big day was April 23, 1843. When that came and went, they chastised themselves for having made an obvious error. They then decided the real date was the last day of the year. When it, too, passed uneventfully they settled on March 21, 1844. Again, nothing happened. "There was strong and severe disappointment among the believers," Leon Festinger wrote in *When Prophecy Fails*, "but this was of brief duration and soon the energy and enthusiasm were back to where they had been before and even greater." Another date was determined—October 22, 1844—and belief was so strong that some farmers didn't bother to plant their fields that summer, knowing they would be in heaven before winter came. When the world still didn't go down in flames, the Millerites finally conceded that perhaps their core belief was not entirely correct. Amid acrimony and accusations, the sect finally dissolved.

A second major line of defense lies in memory, a fact that is not often recognized because far too many people misunderstand what memory is and how it works. We think memory is a collection of permanent records, like a shoe box full of photographs. A photo may be lost now and then. And some are a little fuzzy and hard to make out. But generally, we assume, memory is an accurate and unchanging reflection of past experiences and feelings. For better or worse, the reality is very different. Memory is an organic process, not a recording. While memories can remain sharp and fixed for decades, they can also evolve, sometimes subtly, sometimes dramatically. These changes aren't random. Memories serve the present: We misremember in ways that suit the needs of the moment. Have a falling-out with an adult sibling and you can be sure your childhood memories of that sibling will grow darker, with good memories fading and bad memories growing more vivid; repair the relationship and the memories will get sunnier too. Change your mind about an issue and your memories are likely to change as well, leading you to erroneously believe that your current opinion is the opinion you have always held—which is why people very commonly deny having changed their minds when they clearly have. As the years pass and we learn and grow and change, our old selves can even become strangers to our present selves. In 1962, researchers asked seventy-three fourteen-year-old boys questions about such emotional subjects as their families, sexuality, politics, and religion. More than three decades later, the same boys, now forty-eight years old, were asked to search their memories and recall how they'd felt when they were fourteen. "The men's ability to guess what they had said about themselves in adolescence was no better than chance." Memories can even be cobbled together out of nothing more than desire and scraps of real memories. Psychologist Carol Tavris describes a vivid memory she has of her father reading her a children's storybook called *The Wonderful O*. It is a cherished image, as Tavris's father died when she was very young and this was a direct link to him. It was also false. Tavris was stunned to discover that *The Wonderful O* was published *after* her father had died.

The obvious sincerity of these distorted memories underscores an absolutely essential point that is too often missed: There is nothing dishonest about any of this. We can't consciously change our memories. Nor can we distinguish between a changed memory and the original. When we make a statement based on what we recall, we assume that our memories are accurate. If that assumption is incorrect, the statement will be false, but it will not be a lie. This distinction was lost in 2008 when Hillary Clinton—who was campaigning for the Democratic presidential nomination—told audiences about the time her plane landed at a Bosnian airport in the 1990s and she had to run from sniper fire. It was a thrilling story. But when reporters looked up video of the event, they found nothing more exciting happened that day than a little girl giving flowers to a smiling Hillary Clinton. Clearly, the story was false, so Clinton was hammered for lying. But did that make sense? Clinton had visited Bosnia as first lady of the United States. Her every footstep had been recorded by TV cameras and stored in archives. She knew that. She also knew that her every word on the campaign trail was being scrutinized by the media and the opposition. Why would she tell an easily exposed lie for so little gain? A much more plausible explanation is that her memories evolved to serve the needs of the present—a present in which Clinton was constantly making speeches and giving interviews in which she described herself as an experienced, tough, "battle-tested" leader. She didn't lie. She really believed what she said. And no one, I suspect, was more shocked by that video than Clinton herself.

The ease with which memories change to suit the needs of the present makes them an ideal tool for resolving cognitive dissonance. If, for example, an esteemed expert thinks the sudden collapse of the Soviet Union is close to impossible, and then the Soviet Union collapses, that expert may pay a cognitive price—unless his memory of what he believed before the collapse undergoes a suitable evolution. Maybe he hadn't thought it was close to impossible, maybe instead he had thought it was a significant possibility, or even more likely than not that the Soviet Union would fall. If the expert's memory recalls it that way, he could say that he had seen the whole thing coming—and there wouldn't be a trace of cognitive dissonance.

This may seem extreme, even absurd. It's hard to believe that people can delude themselves so badly. But it is precisely what Philip Tetlock discovered when he asked his experts in the 1980s about the likelihood of a Soviet collapse and then went back to them, after the collapse, and asked them to recall what they had predicted. In every case, the experts remembered their earlier predictions incorrectly. And always the mistake they made leaned in the same direction: They remembered themselves rating the likelihood of a Soviet collapse much higher than they actually did. "It was a big distortion," Tetlock says. On average, the shift was about 30 or 40 percentage points. So an expert who had actually thought there was only a 20 percent chance of a Soviet collapse would remember having thought the odds were 50/50 or even that it was more likely than not. There were more extreme cases in which experts who had said there was only a 10 or 20 percent chance of a collapse remembered themselves rating it a 60 or 70 percent chance. There was wide variation in the extent to which Tetlock's experts suffered hindsight bias, of course, but the variation wasn't random—hedgehogs tended to be more afflicted than foxes.

As startling as these results may be to laypeople, they replicate what psychologists have known for decades. "Hindsight bias" is a well-documented phenomenon: Once we know the outcome of anything, we will tend to think that outcome was more likely to happen than we would have if we had judged it without knowing the outcome. It's a potent force that can even alter our memories of how we thought and felt in the past. Psychologist Baruch Fischhoff demonstrated the bias by giving students information about the early-nineteenth-century war between Britain and the Gurkhas of Nepal. Based on this information, Fischhoff asked the students, estimate the likelihood of the war ending in a British victory, a Gurkha victory, a stalemate with no peace settlement, or a stalemate with a peace settlement. The information given to one group included only the military forces available to the two sides and other factors that may have had an effect on the result. A second group was given this information along with the actual outcome—a British victory—and asked to estimate the chances of each outcome without regard to what actually happened. Knowing how history played out made all the difference: Those who knew the British won rated that outcome to be much more likely than those who did not. Fischhoff confirmed his findings by telling other groups that the actual outcome was a Gurkha victory or one of the two stalemate results. In each case, knowing the supposed outcome drove up the estimated likelihood of that outcome. In another version of the experiment, the researchers asked people not to let their awareness of the outcome influence their judgment. It still did. In a final experiment, Fischhoff had students estimate the likelihood that certain events in the news would take place; months later, well after it was clear that the events had or had not taken place, Fischhoff went back to the students and asked them to recall how likely they had judged the events to be. The hindsight bias was obvious: If the event actually occurred, they recalled themselves thinking it was more likely than they actually had; if it didn't occur, they underestimated how strongly they had felt it would.

Hindsight bias is universal, but the degree to which we suffer it varies. After a football team wins a game, for example, all fans are likely to remember themselves giving the team better odds to win than they actually did. But researchers found they could amplify this bias simply by asking fans to construct explanations for *why* the team won. So merely knowing an outcome gets hindsight bias started, but having a satisfactory explanation for it really cranks the bias up. "Of course the team won. The defense is third in the league and the other team's star was injured a week ago. It was obvious they'd win. I knew it all along." This fact means experts are particularly susceptible, because by definition, they know lots about their subject, and for most, identifying causal connections is almost habitual. So it is only to be expected that they are better than laypeople at constructing after-the-fact explanations for why some event happened.

Tetlock also conducted hindsight studies using less spectacular events than the collapse of the Soviet Union—whether Quebec would separate from Canada, what would happen to apartheid South Africa, whether the European monetary union would come together, and so on—and he found that the hindsight bias wasn't as extreme as it had been in the case of the Soviet collapse. So it seemed cognitive dissonance was also in play. An expert who spends his life studying international politics and who believes his expertise gives him insight into the future won't be pleased when he fails to foresee an important event, but being surprised by one of the biggest events of the century is a huge challenge to his very identity, which sets off a five-alarm blaze of cognitive dissonance and a proportionate mental response. Memories aren't just tweaked, they are airbrushed top to bottom. Just as the Soviets themselves did, the expert's mind drastically changes the recorded past to suit the needs of the present, and he is left with the comforting belief that he knew it all along.

Unlike Philip Tetlock's experts, the experts on talk shows, best-seller lists, and the op-ed pages of major newspapers are far from anonymous. When they make predictions, their public reputations are at stake. Their connections, their meetings with movers and shakers, their invitations to Davos, are all on the line. So is cash. An expert who is perceived to provide genuine insight into the future owns a golden goose, but if that perception is lost, so is the goose. Everything that Tetlock's experts had on the line in his experiment, these experts also have, plus so much more.

"Suppose an individual believes something with his whole heart," wrote Leon Festinger. "Suppose further that he has a commitment to this belief, that he has taken irrevocable actions because of it; finally, suppose that he is presented with evidence, unequivocal and undeniable evidence, that his belief is wrong; what will happen? The individual will frequently emerge, not only unshaken, but even more convinced of the truth of his beliefs than ever before." In 1955, Marian Keech and her followers illustrated this profound insight. Today, plenty of experts and their followers keep proving Leon Festinger right.

JAMES HOWARD KUNSTLER

James Howard Kunstler is an American but he doesn't like much about the United States. A journalist, social critic, and novelist, Kunstler is famous for his firecracker writing style and his bleak views on suburbia, consumerism, and popular culture. "Our practices and habits in place-making the past half-century have resulted in human habitat that is ecologically catastrophic, economically insane, socially toxic, spiritually degrading, and fundamentally unsustainable," he wrote in a typically frenzied burst. "We have built a land of scary places and become a nation of scary people."

Kunstler first heard about the Y2K computer glitch in 1998. It was a revelation. "For five years, I have been flying around the country telling college lecture audiences and conference-goers that our fucked-up everyday environment of strip malls, tract houses, outlet malls, parking lots, and other accessories of the national automobile slum was liable to put us out of business as a civilization," he wrote in an April 1999 essay. "I asserted that the culture growing in this foul medium had gotten so bloated and diseased that it would succumb sooner rather than later to its own idiot inertia. I still believe that today. It is both a conviction and a wish, because to go on in our current mode would be culturally suicidal." Kunstler had no doubt that the slouching beast that is American society would stumble and collapse into the dirt. He likened it to "evolutionary biology, where organisms achieve their largest scale and greatest complexity at the cost of their ability to adapt to changes in their surroundings. They flourish during periods of extraordinary stability and die off when conditions destabilize. The United Parking Lot of America seemed to me to be just this sort of overgrown, overly complex organism." But what exactly would kill the creature? When Kunstler heard about Y2K, he had his answer. "I now see Y2K as the mechanism that will force events to a tipping point much more quickly and surely."

As we saw earlier, Kunstler's Y2K predictions were very specific and very grim. At a minimum, Y2K would cause a crisis similar to the 1973 oil embargo. But that was just the beginning of the possibilities. There could also be "a worldwide deflationary depression," Kunstler wrote. "I will not be surprised if it is as bad in terms of unemployment and hardship as the 1930s." War and dictatorship were distinct possibilities. Kunstler was also clear about the timing. "Y2K will not 'strike' at the midnight hour on 1/1/00," he wrote. "It will unfold fractally as a series of events over the next several years, with accelerating disruptions across the remainder of 1999, a 'spike' of failures around New Year 2000, and a ripple of consequences accumulating, amplifying, and reverberating for months and even years afterward. I expect problems with business and government to be evident by the middle of 1999."

The problems were not evident by the middle of 1999, nor did they appear when 1999 rolled over into 2000. An elevator or two got stuck, but Y2K did not cause a war, a depression, or a recession. It didn't even crash a plane. Just as the failure of a giant sea to cover most of North America demonstrated that Marian Keech's prediction was wrong, the failure of Y2K to cause any notable disaster would seem to be clear disconfirmation of James Howard Kunstler's forecast. But does Kunstler see it that way? In response to an e-mail, Kunstler fired back an 850-word message that can be summarized in one short sentence: I was right.

"What we've been seeing during the past decade might be understood as a kind of 'meta' event, of which the Y2K episode was an early chapter," he began. "Overall, this meta-event has been about systemic socioeconomic collapse as a result of overinvestments in hypercomplexity.... We are seeing now, ten years later, a full playing out of these trends in the collapse of banking and capital finance, and consequently in the real economy of ordinary business activity and households." After some more in this vein, Kunstler connected it to the Millennium Bug. "Y2K was, in my opinion, an early apprehension of the dangers of growing hypercomplexity." In the late 1990s, computerization "came on very quickly and it began to dawn on people paying attention that there might be dangerous unintended consequences in turning over control of so many vital activities to complex machines and their algorithms."

But what exactly does this have to do with the rather straightforward fact that what he predicted would happen did not happen? After two paragraphs about Y2K "in the psycho-social realm," Kunstler acknowledged that "as the 'rollover' date approached, I took the position that we were in for a lot of trouble. The trouble, as it turned out, was averted. This is the part of the story usually overlooked by those who mock the Y2K episode. Billions of dollars were spent, and scores of thousands of man-hours were dedicated, to mitigating this problem. . . . There were no 'cascading' failures of the kind that were most feared. Lots of systems did fail, but not a critical mass of the largest and most critical ones. The Y2K incident passed into history as a joke. I don't think it was a joke. I regard it still as a legitimate potential catastrophe that was averted."

There are several striking elements in Kunstler's response. First, he understates his prediction—he called for considerably more than "a lot of trouble"—and overstates the actual damage done by Y2K. This closes some of the gap between the two, easing the cognitive dissonance.

More important is his claim that Y2K was a catastrophe averted by lots of money and hard work. A key fact Kunstler doesn't mention is that throughout 1998 and 1999, there was a steady stream of reports from corporations and governments saying that they were working hard, spending lots of money, and their systems would not fail in the rollover. In his April 1999 essay, Kunstler scoffed at these claims. "A lot of the information released to the public so far has been self-serving and of questionable value—for instance, reports of Y2K readiness released by government agencies whose chief interests might be 1) covering their own asses, and 2) trying to quell public concern that could escalate to panic," he wrote. So Kunstler was either wrong about Y2K or he was wrong about Y2K remediation efforts. In either event, he made a mistake. But looking back, he doesn't see any error.

Another omission in Kunstler's response is considerably more revealing. Anyone even slightly familiar with the Y2K issue knows there is a standard response to the claim that Y2K would have been a catastrophe if vast sums hadn't been spent to fix the problem. It is this: Some corporations and countries—notably Italy, Russia, and South Korea—did *not* spend vast amounts on Y2K remediation. Their efforts were haphazard at best, and all through 1999 these laggards were criticized for putting themselves and others in jeopardy. But on January 1, 2000, they suffered no worse than anyone else. Korea Telecom did "nothing" about Y2K, noted Cambridge University computer scientist Ross Anderson in a BBC interview. "It took the view that, hey, if it breaks we'll fix it. Then you have British Telecom, which was spending five hundred million pounds on bug-fixing. And they couldn't both be right. They were using the same sort of equipment on the same sort of scale. The fascinating thing that we observed in the end is that the Koreans called it right." Whether or not this is conclusive, it *is* important evidence and anyone who wants to honestly assess Y2K must deal with it. But Kunstler didn't even acknowledge it. That's willful blindness, which is precisely what a psychologist would expect to see in a highly committed individual suffering the pangs of cognitive dissonance.

Following the failure of his prediction, Kunstler, like Keech before him, became even more convinced of the beliefs that led him to make the prediction. In 2005, he published *The Long Emergency,* which reads like an expanded version of his Y2K essay, with the one important exception that Y2K itself has vanished. The sole reference comes when Kunstler mocks those who think fears of "peak oil" are "another fantasy brought to us by the same alarmists who said that the Y2K computer bug would bring on the end of the world as we know it." Readers are not told that Kunstler was one of those alarmists.

Whether *The Long Emergency* is prescient or silly is something that cannot be decided today because the forecasts Kunstler makes extend decades into the future. We can be reasonably sure, however, that no matter what happens, James Howard Kunstler will believe he was right.

ROBERT HEILBRONER

Anyone who has studied economics, even briefly, has probably come across Robert Heilbroner's *The Worldly Philosophers,* a study of the lives and ideas of the great economists that has been a staple of economics classes since it was first published in 1953. But Heilbroner, an American economist, was also a prolific social critic with a keen interest in figuring out how the future would unfold, and he laid out his predictions in a series of books and essays spanning decades. One is particularly famous—and particularly useful for present purposes.

Heilbroner wrote *An Inquiry into the Human Prospect* in 1972 and 1973. The mood was one of "puzzlement and despair," he noted. "There is a question in the air, more sensed than seen, like the invisible approach of a distant storm, a question I would hesitate to ask aloud did I not believe it existed unvoiced in the minds of many: 'Is there hope for man?'" Like a god standing at the crest of Olympus, Heilbroner gazed across history and the globe and rendered his verdict: Not really. "The outlook for man, I believe, is painful, difficult, perhaps desperate, and the hope that can be held out for his future prospects seems to be very slim indeed. Thus, to anticipate the conclusions of our inquiry, the answer as to whether we can conceive of the future other than as a continuation of the darkness, cruelty, and disorder of the past seems to me to be no; and to the question of whether worse impends, yes."

The first of the nightmares afflicting humanity is the population bomb. "The demographic situation of virtually all of Southeast Asia, large portions of Latin America, and parts of Africa portends a grim Malthusian outcome," Heilbroner wrote. And don't look to the Green Revolution for salvation. The technical obstacles to growing more food may be insurmountable, and if they were overcome, it would be a disaster—because it would "enable additional hundreds of millions to reach childbearing age," which would make everything worse. Thus, there are only two possible futures. "One is the descent of large portions of the underdeveloped world into steadily worsening social disorder." There would be starvation, stunted children, declining life expectancies. Nations would descend into near anarchy. The alternative, which Heilbroner thought more likely, is the rise of "iron" governments, "probably of a military-socialist cast," that would hold things together with brute force. These governments would not be so forgiving of the gap in wealth between the world's haves and have-nots, Heilbroner believed, making it likely there would be war between the poor world and the rich. And with nuclear weaponry becoming cheap and easy to develop—even terrorists would have nuclear arsenals—these wars could mean annihilation. But Heilbroner didn't think it would come to that. It was "more plausible" that the dictators of the poor world would engage in nuclear blackmail—threatening to incinerate the rich world if suitably large and regular cash payments were not made.

But that wasn't the worst of it, in Heilbroner's view. A more fundamental threat came from the environment and dwindling resources. Pollution would steadily worsen and demand for oil would soon outstrip supplies. Worse still, the climate would change. Industrial activity generates heat as a by-product, Heilbroner wrote, and so, if industry keeps growing, it will eventually generate so much heat the earth will cook. Industrial activity would have to stop or all human life—perhaps all life—would be consumed. In any event, "one irrefutable conclusion remains. The industrial growth process, so central to the economic and social life of capitalism and Western socialism alike, will be forced to slow down, in all likelihood within a generation or two, and will probably have to give way to decline thereafter."

So is humanity doomed? Not at all, Heilbroner assured his readers. "The human prospect is not a death sentence. It is not an inevitable doomsday to which we are headed, although the risk of enormous catastrophes exists." It's more like "a contingent life sentence—one that will permit the continuance of human society, but only on a basis very different from the present, and probably only after much suffering in the period of transition." Unfortunately, that new basis would be brutal authoritarianism in the United States and other developed countries because only such governments would have the strength to see us through the dark days ahead. These new regimes would feature a government that "blends a 'religious' orientation with a 'military' discipline," Heilbroner wrote. The closest thing to it was China under Mao Zedong. "Such a monastic organization of society may be repugnant to us," Heilbroner wrote with some understatement, "but I suspect it offers the greatest promise of making those enormous transformations needed to reach a new stable socio-economic basis."

So that was the human prospect: Maoist China or extinction.

Even by the standards of the early 1970s, this was grim stuff from a leading intellectual, and it got a lot of attention. But what makes *An Inquiry into the Human Prospect* stand out today is that the book was republished in 1980 and again in 1991, and both times Heilbroner added commentaries after each that looked at what he had written in light of what had happened as the years passed.

In his first retrospective, written in 1980, Heilbroner begins with what appears to be an admission that he was a little off base. "I am acutely aware that things do not look quite the same today as they did when I wrote this opening chapter," he began. The "atmosphere of siege" has lifted. "The rumblings of a civilizational malaise" are not heard so much. But this doesn't mean Heilbroner was wrong. It means that people are increasingly deluded about humanity's prospects—which are as awful as ever. True, Heilbroner acknowledges, the population problem has changed dramatically thanks to surprising downturns in fertility rates all over the world, but "if the cancer is now spreading less rapidly, it is still spreading." There have been "several serious famines since *The Human Prospect* first appeared," he notes, and more are sure to come. And while the poor nations have not yet produced authoritarian governments bent on war with the rich world, well, just wait. Nuclear weapons are even cheaper now. And poor nations with oil ("a fast-disappearing resource") could choke the life out of rich countries—although rich countries like the United States and Canada could retaliate with "food power" because "each year the Asian and African countries" import more food to keep their populations from starving.

As for the environmental predicament, Heilbroner felt in 1980 that he was just as right as he had been in 1973. "I see little need to alter the thrust of my original argument, even though, since the first edition appeared, the attention of scientists has been directed at the climate problem from a somewhat different perspective than its long-term heating-up from the release of combustion energy," he wrote. "The emphasis today is on a short-term effect that results from the release of carbon dioxide into the atmosphere as a by-product of combustion. There, the CO_2 forms an invisible 'pane' of gas that acts like the glass in a greenhouse, trapping the reflected rays of the sun, and warming the atmosphere just like the air in a greenhouse." Note what Heilbroner has done here: In 1973, he predicted that the heat produced as a by-product of industrial activity would warm the atmosphere, putting the very existence of life in jeopardy. That was one of many climate-change hypotheses making the rounds at the time, but by 1980, most scientists had decided it was wrong. And yet, Heilbroner didn't conclude that his prediction had been even a little wrong. Instead, he acknowledged "a somewhat different perspective"—as he describes the rise of a completely different theory that happens to lead to a similar conclusion. It's as if someone predicted Muslim insurrections would cause the collapse of the Soviet Union and then boasted when the Soviet Union collapsed for reasons that had absolutely nothing to do with Muslims.

Heilbroner's 1991 commentaries are even more interesting because, by then, major changes had happened. Resource prices had fallen and the world was awash in cheap oil. The Green Revolution had produced huge increases in food in the developing world. Equally significant was what had not happened in the almost two decades since *An Inquiry into the Human Prospect* was first published. There was no war between the poor world and the rich. Nuclear weapons had not proliferated. Authoritarianism had not flourished. In fact, it was clear that freedom, not authoritarianism, was on the rise. In 1973, 46 percent of countries in the world were rated "not free" by Freedom House, the internationally respected NGO; 25 percent were "partly free"; 29 percent were rated "free." By 1980, when Heilbroner wrote his first retrospective, 35 percent were not free, 33 percent were partly free, and 32 percent were free. By 1991, the Iron Curtain had been raised and the percentage of "not free" countries had fallen by half to 23 percent; 35 percent were partly free; free countries were now the largest category at 42 percent. History had delivered exactly the opposite of what Heilbroner had expected.

Still, Heilbroner saw nothing significantly wrong with his 1973 forecast. "Specific predictions, estimates, and measurements have all changed, but only marginally. The basic assessment remains. With them also remains the demanding, uncomfortable, despairing—but not defeatist—prospect for humanity." How could Heilbroner draw that conclusion in 1991? By writing nothing about oil and resources, food supply, the fate of freedom, or other subjects that were critical to the original forecast. Thus he was spared unpleasant encounters with facts that had changed in ways that contradicted his beliefs.

Heilbroner did note the fall of the Soviet bloc, however. He had to. It was 1991, the collapse of the East Bloc had already happened, and the final crumbling of the USSR was taking place as he wrote. This was a problem, because Heilbroner had argued that both capitalist and socialist systems would be strained by environmental pressures, and the latter had a better chance of coping. "That conclusion has been dramatically proved wrong," he wrote, at least "for the form of socialism known as communism." This was admirably forthright, but Heilbroner quickly added that it didn't really change anything. "The great challenge affecting all socioeconomic orders in the twenty-first century remains the approach of ecological danger," he wrote. "Twenty years have not affected that outlook one iota."

Of course, he may still be right about that last statement. But it's hard to escape the conclusion that for Robert Heilbroner the human prospect was grim, and it would remain so no matter what happened.

LORD WILLIAM REES-MOGG

"We got some things wrong but we got enough right to justify writing them," Lord William Rees-Mogg, the former editor of *The Times* of London, says about the three thick volumes of prognostication he and James Dale Davidson, an American investment adviser, published between 1987 and 1997. This is British understatement. Looking back in 2009, Rees-Mogg thinks he and Davidson nailed pretty much all the important trends and events of our time. "We got basically the decline and fall of the Soviet Union right. We saw, though we got the timing wrong, the weaknesses which led to the crisis of the economic system. We even got the attack on the Twin Towers right, in that we pointed to the vulnerability of the Twin Towers as symbolic of the vulnerability of modern society." When I ask what he got wrong, Rees-Mogg acknowledges being off on timing occasionally. "We were much too early" in calling the crash of 2008, he says. And the high-tech crash of 2000: "I became very bearish about the American economy, and nervous about it, as early as the mid-nineties."

Yes, the timing. That's always the tricky part. But Rees-Mogg's view of what can and cannot be predicted is modest, he says. "The point of this kind of forecasting is to explore trends that people need to look out for. You obviously can't both foresee the future and foresee the timing of the future. You sometimes get it right. You sometimes get it wrong. But you can help people to understand the process in which they're involved, in which the world is involved, at this time." And in that sense, Rees-Mogg and Davidson did a fine job. "I think that our general view of the world fits reasonably well with what happened."

I'm sure he does believe that, but I suspect few others would agree.

The basic vision of Rees-Mogg and Davidson's first book of predictions, written in 1986, is summed up nicely in the title: *Blood in the*

Streets: Investment Profits in a World Gone Mad. "The best time to buy is when blood is running in the streets," the authors quote Nathan M. Rothschild as saying. Rees-Mogg and Davidson saw lots of blood and buying ahead.

Fundamental trends, particularly technological trends, are driving events, they argue. The world is rapidly approaching "an electronic feudalism, an environment in which cheap and effective high-tech weapons will give increasing numbers of disgruntled groups a veto over almost any activity they do not like." When every thug and terrorist can buy cheap missiles, the power of national military forces will be dramatically weakened. The United States will suffer worst. "The sun is setting now on the American Empire, as it once set on the British Empire. As it does, shadows fall on formerly safe streets everywhere. The political equivalent of youth gangs, petty local leaders, are reaching for their guns. They will make the rules now. Rules that are enemies of progress. Rules that are a way of saying 'nothing may pass this way without my say-so.' Rules that tax or inhibit trade. Rules that usurp and confiscate investment—the way street bullies take whatever they can get away with."

International trade will give way to protectionism, real estate values will plunge, and stock markets will crash. Debt default will sweep the world. Nations will splinter and crumble. How bad will it get? There are obvious parallels with the Great Depression, the authors wrote, but it's much worse than that. "We suspect that the forms of the nation-state would remain, as in Lebanon, as indeed, the form of the old Roman Empire was preserved, like an unburied mummy, throughout the Middle Ages. We could be slowly entering a period as violent and murky as the feudalism of old." And the transformation of the world is already well under way. "Economies, even in Europe and the United States, have begun falling into their foundations, like old houses with rotten beams."

In 1991, Rees-Mogg and Davidson published *The Great Reckoning: How the World Will Change in the Depression of the 1990s.* Although their earlier predictions had been "considered improbable or even ridiculous," the authors wrote, subsequent events had proved them right.

Stock markets plunged in October 1987, mere months after the publication of *Blood in the Streets*. Communism collapsed in the Soviet Union and Eastern Europe and was on the verge of death in China, just as they had predicted. The "multi-ethnic empire" the Soviets had inherited from Czarist Russia was crumbling right on schedule. And so much else was bang on. "We predicted the increase in protectionism, intensified terrorism, and more." True, humanity hadn't plunged into a global depression, the authors acknowledged. But just wait. The signs were everywhere.

Having established their prophetic prowess, Rees-Mogg and Davidson repeated and expanded the gloomy prognosis of *Blood in the Streets*. "We expect the 1990s to be a decade of escalating economic and political disorder unparalleled since the 1930s." Economies around the world will experience a "deflationary collapse" and the United States will not be able to bail anyone out because the American economy will itself be crippled. "The simultaneous decline in the relative power of both the United States and the Soviet Union is bound to be fundamentally destabilizing, economically as well as politically." At a time when Third World dictators are getting nuclear weapons and using terrorists to "deliver them by overnight express," the world will be without a leader. "Smaller and smaller groups will gain military effectiveness. Violence will tend to reassert itself as the common condition of life." Disintegration will sweep the globe. "We will see the breakup not just of the Soviet Union . . . but Canada, China, Yugoslavia, Ethiopia, and other countries." East Germany will become democratic in the newly unified Germany but "much of Eastern Europe, like the Soviet Union itself, has a future much like the past of Latin America"—meaning rule by uniformed thugs. Eventually, in the twenty-first century, international order may be restored by the rise of a new global policeman. But it won't be the United States. "If there is to be a new hegemonic power in the world, it is likely to be Japan."

And the same forces of disintegration will be felt within the United States, Rees-Mogg and Davidson warn. Gangs and terrorists will become increasingly powerful as high-tech weapons proliferate. Suburbs will decay and grow dangerous while inner cities turn into war zones. Los

Angeles, Chicago, Houston: "Practically every city with a large under-
class is at risk." New York will suffer worst. "By the year 2000, New York
could be a Gotham City without Batman."

In 1997, Rees-Mogg and Davidson returned with *The Sovereign Individual: Mastering the Transition to the Information Age*. After the usual
list of predictions the earlier books got exactly right, Rees-Mogg and
Davidson repeat their familiar themes and forecasts, along with a few
new twists. Y2K will be huge. And cyberterrorism looms. But the biggest threat is the millennium itself, the authors say. They see cycles in
history, and the year 2000 marks the end of the biggest. "More than 85
years after the day in 1911 when Oswald Spengler was seized with an
intuition of a coming war and 'the decline of the West,' we, too, see 'a
historical change of phase occurring . . . at the point preordained for it
hundreds of years ago.' Like Spengler, we see the impending death of
Western civilization, and with it the collapse of the world order that had
predominated these past five centuries, ever since Columbus sailed west
to open contact with the New World. Yet unlike Spengler we see the
birth of a new stage in Western civilization in the coming millennium."

The year 2000 did see the death of many dot-com stocks. But Western civilization? That's a stretch, as is Rees-Mogg's positive assessment
of these forecasts.

In the twenty years that followed *Blood in the Streets*, protectionism
did not dominate. Globalization did. Trade barriers fell to historic lows
and the economies of many developing countries—notably China,
India, and Brazil—grew faster than ever. The Soviet Union and Yugoslavia did break up—Yugoslavia was already falling apart when Rees-Mogg
and Davidson put it on the endangered list—but disintegration did not
become a global trend. In fact, the European Union expanded rapidly
into Eastern Europe, bringing the continent a degree of unity and order
it had not enjoyed since the glory days of the Roman Empire.

As for the United States, the general trend was up. The latter half of
the 1990s, in particular, saw a roaring economy, soaring stocks, and
swelling federal government surpluses. With the greatest of ease, the

United States bailed out Mexico and other foreign nations that suffered economic crises. And far from turning into urban wastelands, American cities enjoyed a renaissance; New York, in particular, was transformed for the better. At the same time, American geopolitical power grew so dramatically that, by the mid-1990s, a French minister famously complained that the United States had moved beyond superpowerdom and become a globe-dominating "hyperpower." International security improved as well. Instead of the rising bloodshed Rees-Mogg and Davidson predicted, the long-term rise in democracy continued, interstate wars became increasingly rare, civil wars became less common, and all wars became less deadly. There was also a steep decline in the number of genocides and mass killings.

The United States and the world took a big hit in 2008, of course. But even in the worst days of that crisis, neither America nor the world looked like the dystopian horror forecast by Rees-Mogg and Davidson. More crucially, *Blood in the Streets* and the other books made it clear that the disaster they predicted was *imminent,* not decades off.

As for terrorism, it continued to plague humanity in the years after Rees-Mogg and Davidson published their books, as it always has. But it did not escalate in frequency: The annual number of international terrorist attacks, which had been rising since the 1960s, peaked in 1991 at 450 incidents; it then fell steadily and substantially until 2000, when there were 100 incidents. Nor did terrorism go nuclear or high tech, as Rees-Mogg and Davidson had predicted. The 9/11 attacks were carried out by nineteen men armed with nothing more sophisticated than box cutters and plane tickets.

Rees-Mogg's claim to have predicted the breakup of the Soviet Union is only slightly less tenuous. The pair's whole argument was that technological change was empowering small groups and individuals and that this would fracture nations everywhere, the Soviet Union being only one. As their larger point is clearly wrong, it's not unreasonable to think it was only luck that they called the fall of the Soviet Union correctly. After all, a few hits are to be expected when you publish three thick books stuffed with predictions—a simple truth demonstrated nicely by British astrologers whose collective forecast of what would happen in the 1980s was wrong about almost everything except the assassination of Egyptian president Anwar Sadat.

But even if Rees-Mogg and Davidson are credited with predicting the collapse of the USSR, would an impartial observer agree with Rees-Mogg that his books' "general view of the world fits reasonably well with what happened"? I doubt it. And yet I don't doubt that Rees-Mogg is sincere in his assessment because he very much wants it to be true, and a yearning mind is a creative mind. Unmistakable failures are forgotten. Other memories are altered subtly, so they appear less wrong or almost right. Rationalization and confirmation bias multiply the hits. And time frames are stretched and stretched until finally something that looks even slightly like the prediction appears and the desperate prophet is able to shrug and say, "I was only off on timing."

That's how cognitive dissonance works.

PAUL EHRLICH

The sentence by which *The Population Bomb* should be judged is not the famous introduction: "The battle to feed all of humanity is over." Nor is it the frightening elaboration in the second sentence: "In the 1970s the world will undergo famines—hundreds of millions of people are going to starve to death in spite of any crash programs embarked upon now." No, the sentence that makes all the difference is the third sentence of the book: "At this late date nothing can prevent a substantial increase in the world death rate, although many lives could be saved through dramatic programs to 'stretch' the carrying capacity of the earth by increasing food production."

Paul Ehrlich's analysis of the world situation in the late 1960s and early 1970s boiled down to something very simple: The birthrate is far higher than the death rate, and as a result the population is soaring. This often happens in nature. Rabbits, mice, deer, and lots of other species multiply rapidly when the environment allows them to. But it always ends badly. The population grows and grows until it exceeds the capacity of the environment to sustain it. Then it is cut down by starvation, disease, and predators. The swelling human population has reached that horrible moment, Ehrlich believed. People will starve. Disease will flourish. Instability and war will grow. Combined, this will produce "a substantial increase in the world death rate."

Of course, there is an alternative to these sorts of tragedy. A "birthrate solution," as Ehrlich called it, would see the birthrate lowered to equal the death rate and stop the population from growing. But by 1968, with more than three billion people on the planet, it was too late. The population is already so big, Ehrlich argued, and the margin between global food demand and global food production is so thin, that not even swift and determined action on the birthrate will stop the calamity from striking in the 1970s. It is, as Ehrlich wrote a year later, "the most dramatic crisis *Homo sapiens* has ever faced."

This means checking on the accuracy of Ehrlich's forecast is remarkably easy. What happened to the death rate? As for the time frame, that's clear too. Ehrlich mentioned "the 1970s" over and over. He also wrote that "the next nine years will probably tell the story." At one point in *The Population Bomb,* he did, however, allow that the catastrophe could be delayed a little, into the 1980s. And in later editions of *The Population Bomb,* he changed the second sentence of the book to say that there would be famines in "the 1970s and 1980s." A generous observer might say those two decades are the time frame of his prediction.

So what happened? According to the definitive source—the United Nations' world *Demographic Yearbook*—the world death rate in the period 1965 to 1974 was thirteen per thousand population. In the period 1980 to 1985, it was eleven. In 1985 to 1990, it was ten. So there was no "substantial increase in the world death rate," as Ehrlich predicted. There was instead a substantial *decrease.* That trend continued, incidentally. In the period 2005 to 2010, the world death rate was nine.

Paul Ehrlich made a precise, measurable prediction. And it failed. In fact, what happened was the *opposite* of what he said would happen. Does Ehrlich acknowledge this? Not in the least. In two lengthy interviews, Ehrlich admitted making not a single major error in the popular works he published in the late 1960s and early 1970s.

To do this, Ehrlich has to ignore death rates. Not once in our interviews did he mention them, nor do they appear in the many other published interviews I've found. There is, however, a brief reference to death rates in a retrospective he and his wife, Anne, published in 2009: "We are often asked what happened to the famines *The Bomb* predicted, as if the last four decades were a period of abundant food for all," the Ehrlichs wrote. "But, of course, there were famines, essentially continuously in parts of Africa. Perhaps 300 million people overall have died of hunger and hunger-related diseases since 1968. But the famines were smaller than our reading of the agricultural literature at the time led us to anticipate. What happened? The central factor, of course, was the medium-term success of the 'Green Revolution' in expanding food production at a rate beyond what many, if not most, agricultural experts believed likely. As a result, there wasn't a general rise in the death rate from hunger—although there have been periodic regional rises in South Asia and Africa, and the world may now be on the brink of another major crisis." Forced to confront the blatant gap between his prediction and what happened, Ehrlich downplays what he actually wrote, fudges the evidence, and erases the time frame—suggesting he is about to be proved right any day now.

I asked Ehrlich to summarize his predictive record for me. He responded: "The main things, of course, that I predicted was that there was going to be continued hunger, that we would not solve the hunger problem in the foreseeable future, and since there are more hungry people now than when I made the prediction, that seems like a valid one. I predicted that if we were to keep putting crap in the atmosphere, we were going to get climate change, although at that time we didn't know if there would be heating or cooling. . . . I was too pessimistic about the speed with which the Green Revolution would spread. It did reduce the large-scale famines and more or less transform the whole thing into hunger spread around the world rather than famines as concentrated as I would have expected. I shouldn't say 'as I would have expected' [but] 'as the agricultural scientists I talked to expected' because it's not my area of expertise. I totally missed the problems with the destruction of the tropical forests. I did predict that there were going to be novel diseases, and of course we've had AIDS since, so that was an accurate prediction." Notice that the only flat-out mistake Ehrlich acknowledges is missing the destruction of the rain forests, which happens to be a point that supports and strengthens his worldview—and is therefore, in cognitive dissonance terms, not a mistake at all. Beyond that, he was, by his account, off a little here and there, but only because the information he got from others was wrong. Basically, he was right across the board.

The specific claims Ehrlich makes in his summary are all dubious, as careful examination reveals. To take just one example, Ehrlich did *not* predict "that there was going to be continued hunger." He predicted there would be massive famines *over and above* existing levels of hunger, which is why the death rate would rise. So while it may be superficially impressive that *The Population Bomb* predicted "hundreds of millions" would starve to death and "300 million people" died of hunger since 1968, it's very misleading. For one thing, the book's time frame was ten or twenty years, not forty. For another, Ehrlich upped the predicted death toll to "a billion or more" in the 1974 book *The End of Affluence.* But most importantly, the "300 million" figure doesn't show an *increase* in hunger and starvation. It only shows that hunger and starvation weren't eliminated.

The more telling problem with Ehrlich's summary of his record is what's not there. There's the end of affluence, for one. It was a key theme in all his writing. He even published a book with that title. "In our opinion, the last decades of the twentieth century will initiate a worldwide age of scarcity," Ehrlich wrote in 1974. "There will be no more cheap, abundant energy, no more cheap, abundant food, and soon the flow of cheap consumer goods will suffer increasing disruption and rising prices." It would be the most difficult period ever faced by industrial society, Ehrlich predicted. Society might crash.

Another gap in his summary is the fate of foreign countries, including the supposedly inevitable collapse of India, the decline of the United Kingdom into poverty and hunger, and many other dire forecasts. "We are facing, within the next three decades, the disintegration of an unstable world of nation-states infected with growthmania," he wrote in *The End of Affluence*. Again, he made no mention of any of this. When I asked Ehrlich if he recalled any predictions he had made about particular foreign countries, he said he could not.

Like the experts in Tetlock's experiment who were sure they had forecast the fall of the Soviet Union, hindsight bias and cognitive dissonance—and the distortion, rationalization, and forgetting they produce—have led Paul Ehrlich to the happy conclusion that his predictions were essentially correct. And it is very unlikely anything could convince him otherwise. The famous Simon–Ehrlich bet is proof of that.

In the 1970s, Julian Simon, who died in 1998, was a business professor at the University of Maryland who became tired of the constant gloomy talk from the likes of the Club of Rome and Paul Ehrlich. People are endlessly inventive, Simon argued. If we start to run out of one thing, we'll find more efficient methods of using it or substitute something else. And since human ingenuity is the ultimate source of wealth, the more people there are, the better off we'll be. Ten billion? No problem. Twenty billion? All the better. Simon's beliefs may have been radically unlike Ehrlich's, but he shared with Ehrlich a fondness for sweeping, confident statements about the future. As Ehrlich's fame grew, Julian Simon became the Anti-Ehrlich.

In 1980, Simon attacked the doomsters in the august pages of *Science*. The journal was deluged with angry letters. Ehrlich was especially livid. He and Simon exchanged furious claims and counterclaims, with each man accusing the other of ignoring his arguments and distorting the evidence. On and on it went until, finally, there came the bet.

Simon believed that human ingenuity would steadily drive the price of resources downward, contrary to the growing scarcity and rising prices expected by Malthusians like Ehrlich. So he offered to bet anyone that the price of any resource over any time would fall. Ehrlich announced he would "accept Simon's astonishing offer before other greedy people jump in." Together with John Holdren and two other scientists, Ehrlich agreed that he and Simon would buy a thousand dollars' worth of five key metals—copper, tin, chrome, nickel, and tungsten—in 1980. They would be sold in 1990. If the sale price, in 1980 dollars, were higher, Ehrlich would win and reap the profit. If the proceeds were lower, Simon would win and Ehrlich would pay him the difference.

Ten years passed, and the metals were worth considerably less in 1990 than they had been in 1980. Simon won. Ehrlich sent a check to his rival.

Ehrlich insists to this day that the bet proved nothing. There was a recession "in the first half" of the 1980s that "slowed the growth of demand for industrial metals worldwide," he wrote. "Ironically, a prominent reason for the slower industrial growth was the doubling of world oil prices in 1979. Indeed, the price of oil probably was a factor in the prices of metals in both years, being unprecedentedly high in 1980 and unprecedentedly low in 1990." So Simon wasn't right. He was lucky. Whether there's something to this or not—I don't find it convincing—what's more interesting about this defense is that, in the 1970s, Ehrlich stated repeatedly that oil scarcity had arrived and the price of oil would only go up. So his rationale for dismissing the bet is based on something he predicted would not happen. It's also interesting that in the decade *after* the bet, oil stayed cheap, but the price of metals, and most other commodities, continued to fall. If Simon and Ehrlich had renewed their bet in 1990, Ehrlich would have lost again.

In 1995, Julian Simon issued another challenge, as he often did. "Any trend pertaining to material human welfare" will improve in future, Simon claimed, and he'd put money on it. Ehrlich and Stephen Schneider, a climatologist at Stanford University, said they'd take Simon's bet based on fifteen indicators, including emissions of sulfur dioxide in

Asia, the amount of fertile cropland per person in the world, carbon dioxide levels in the atmosphere, the harvest per person from oceanic fisheries, and so on. Simon refused. He said he'd accept a bet only on direct measures of human welfare, such as life expectancy and purchasing power. It was another demonstration that Simon, like Ehrlich, sometimes used extreme rhetoric that could be embarrassing if someone called him on it.

Another way the two men resembled each other is that they were both bad at predicting the future. In the two editions of Simon's book *The Ultimate Resource*, published in 1981 and 1996, he wrote the following: "This is a public offer to stake $10,000, in separate transactions of $1,000 or $100 each, on my belief that mineral resources (or food or other commodities) will not rise in price in future years, adjusted for inflation. You choose any mineral or other raw material (including grain and fossil fuels) that is not government controlled, and the date of settlement." This was extremely bold language. Simon wasn't merely saying that, in general, over long periods of time, resources would tend to get cheaper. He said *any* resource, over *any* time period. Still, it held up in the 1980s, and again in the 1990s. But in the first decade of the twenty-first century, the price of oil, food, most metals, and other commodities broke with the trend of the previous twenty years and soared upward. That couldn't happen, according to Simon. But it did.

THE FANS

A final way in which Paul Ehrlich and Julian Simon resemble each other is the devotion of their many admirers. Remember that the expert who makes a prediction isn't the only one committed to it. Particularly when predictions involve big issues, they can become a fundamental part of a person's understanding of reality. They can even inspire life-changing actions. In the 1970s, some Americans who believed Paul Ehrlich's predictions had only one child, or none, as he advised. That's a big commitment based on a strong belief, and one does not simply shrug and walk away from a conviction like that. "Suppose an individual believes some-thing with his whole heart," Leon Festinger wrote a decade before Paul Ehrlich published *The Population Bomb*. "Suppose further that he has a commitment to this belief, that he has taken irrevocable actions because of it; finally, suppose that he is presented with evidence, unequivocal and undeniable evidence, that his belief is wrong; what will happen? The individual will frequently emerge, not only unshaken, but even more convinced of the truth of his beliefs than ever before."

"Ehrlich has in fact been right about all of his predictions, except in terms of where and when they would occur," wrote one blogger in 2009. Comments like this litter the Internet. Like Ehrlich himself, his fans minimize, evade, and rationalize, avoiding the obvious evidence that Ehrlich's predictions failed. A common dodge is that the alarm raised by *The Population Bomb* spurred people into action and it was those actions that forestalled the predicted disasters. "If Mr. Ehrlich hadn't written *The Population Bomb* in 1968," a letter to a Las Vegas newspaper argued in 2010, "would the technology to increase crop yields ever have been developed? Would millions of people all over the world have made the decision to limit the size of their families?" A few minutes with Google would have revealed to Ehrlich's defender that the Green Revo-lution began with the work of Norman Borlaug and colleagues in 1944, that it was delivering huge increases in agricultural yields years before *The Population Bomb* was published, and that Ehrlich repeatedly scorned those who claimed the Green Revolution or any other techno-logical fix could forestall the coming famines. He would also have dis-covered that fertility rates in the developed world had, with the exception of the postwar baby boom, been on a downward trend since the late nineteenth century, while even more dramatic declines in fertility rates happened in a long list of developing countries that have never heard of Paul Ehrlich or his book. But he didn't spend those few minutes with Google because he already had what he wanted—a rationalization that soothes cognitive dissonance the way aspirin quiets a headache.

The determination of fans to deny their idols make mistakes can sometimes even exceed that of the idols themselves. After James Howard Kunstler sent me his assessment of his Y2K forecast, he posted it to his Web site and was praised by his admirers. "Bravo on your Y2K piece," wrote one. "If anything, you've understated your case," wrote another fan, in what must be the first recorded instance of someone accusing James Howard Kunstler of understatement.

Sometimes it seems absolutely nothing can dismay believers. It may have been more than ninety years since Oswald Spengler wrote *The Decline of the West,* and the last sixty of those years may bear no resemblance to the future forecast by the glum German, but still, on Wikipedia, one finds the earnest claim that "no significant prediction of Spengler's in *The Decline of the West* has yet been refuted by events." An assertion that cannot be falsified by any conceivable evidence is nothing more than dogma. It can't be debated. It can't be proven or disproven. It's just something people choose to believe or not for reasons that have nothing to do with fact and logic. And dogma is what predictions become when experts and their followers go to ridiculous lengths to dismiss clear evidence that they failed.

A few years ago, I was standing near Red Square, in Moscow, on the day that used to mark the October Revolution, and I watched as a group of sullen old Communists milled about, taking swigs from brown paper bags. Now and then, someone would shake a bony fist at bored police officers and shout a slogan of some sort. "What are they saying?" I asked my translator. "'The victory of socialism is assured,'" she said.

Right, I thought. Marx was only off on timing. Keep the faith, comrades.

8

The End Is Nigh

The Commanding General is well aware the forecasts are no good. However, he needs them for planning purposes.

—KENNETH ARROW, NOBEL LAUREATE
ECONOMIST, RECALLING THE RESPONSE
HE AND COLLEAGUES RECEIVED DURING
THE SECOND WORLD WAR WHEN THEY
DEMONSTRATED THAT THE MILITARY'S
LONG-TERM WEATHER FORECASTS WERE
USELESS

In 1906, when my grandfather was born in that English village, the people around him may have thought he was a lucky baby with a golden future ahead. But it's tempting to think we would have known better.

After all, by 1906, Britain did not dominate all competitors as it had thirty years before. Many nations were rapidly industrializing, including the United States, and Germany was not only challenging Britain for the economic and scientific lead, it threatened to dominate Europe politically and militarily. Even the German navy was growing rapidly,

forcing Britain to engage in an expensive shipbuilding race if it hoped
to maintain the supremacy of the Royal Navy on which Britain and its
far-flung empire depended. There may have been many experts who
said there would never be a war between the Great Powers, but there
were some who were sure war was coming. And others feared that if
there were a war, new technologies—explosives, machine guns, subma-
rines, airplanes—would make it more terrible than any in the past.

Couldn't an intelligent person have put the pieces together and seen
the disaster ahead? And if the scope and horror of the First World War
had been predicted, surely it would have been obvious that Europe would
wane and the two powers on the periphery of the Western world—the
United States and Russia—would come to dominate the twentieth century? Some think so. "If the forecasting on technology had been combined with the forecasting on geopolitics, the shattering of Europe might
well have been predicted," wrote the political scientist George Friedman
in his 2009 book *The Next 100 Years.* "So, standing at the beginning of
the twentieth century, it would have been possible to forecast its general
outlines, with discipline and some luck."

And if that was possible at the beginning of the twentieth century, is
it not possible to do the same at the beginning of the twenty-first? Friedman insists it is. His book is an attempt at just that.

But what Friedman doesn't tell his readers is that for every one correct prediction at the end of the nineteenth century and beginning of
the twentieth (explosives and machine guns will make war deadlier, for
example) there were countless others that were dead wrong (the machine
gun, the airplane, radio, and the submarine were all said to make war
impossible). Without benefit of hindsight, how does one separate the
few valuable nuggets from the mountain of fool's gold? Friedman does
not say. And assuming it could be done, by what craft are the nuggets
forged into a map of the coming century? Friedman is vague on that too.
And did anyone *actually do* what Friedman confidently asserts could
have been done? He mentions no one. That may be because, as far as I
can determine, no one did. Brilliant people like John Bates Clark tried.

But read today, their efforts are downright funny. The clock's still tick-ing on F. E. Smith's century-long look forward in *The World in 2030,* but I'm reasonably confident that in 2030, India will not be a loyal daughter of the British Empire, as forecast, and the only people citing Smith's book will be historians interested in the Britain of 1930 and critics of future babble like me. You may call that a prediction if you wish.

But no matter how many times the best and brightest fail, more try. And they never doubt they are right. In his best-selling 2009 book *Why Your World Is About to Get a Whole Lot Smaller,* economist Jeff Rubin expresses serene confidence that the price of oil is only going up and he tells us what this will mean for the world and how we live—all without the slightest concern for the fact that very smart people have tried and failed to predict the future of oil prices for more than a century. The French intellectual Jacques Attali is a more egregious case. In 2009, almost twenty years after Attali published *Millennium*—and long after it was clear that essentially nothing predicted in *Millennium* would come to pass—he published *A Brief History of the Future: A Brave and Contro-versial Look at the Twenty-first Century.* George Friedman, too, is undaunted by the failure of past forecasts. Among them is his 1992 book *The Coming War with Japan,* which concluded that Japan would "once more seek to become an empire of its own, dominating the western Pacif-ic and eastern Asia," and this would lead either to "a long, miserable cold war" with the United States or to a rematch of the Second World War.

Experts who cannot learn from their own stumbles are beyond help, but it is possible for the rest of us—experts and laypeople alike—to adopt a considered, reasonable skepticism about predictions. Pundits "fore-cast not because they know," wrote economist John Kenneth Galbraith, "but because they are asked." We could stop asking. But if we insist on asking—and we probably will, unfortunately—we must at least think carefully about what we are told. Typically, when an expert presents a prediction in the form of a confident, well-told story that resonates with our values and our sense of how the world works, we don't think to ask whether the expert's past predictions give us any reason to think he's right this time. His story resonates, and that's good enough. The prediction is praised as "plausible" and "compelling." It garners readers, audiences, and sales. The expert who made it is invited here and there to repeat it, and he or she is asked to provide other plausible and compelling insights. Time passes, and, eventually, the accuracy of the prediction is revealed. If it's a miss, it is quietly forgotten and never discussed again. If it's a hit, it is celebrated—even if a little thought would reveal the alleged hit is very likely nothing more than a coincidence. Take H. G. Wells's 1933 prediction of a Second World War, which I mentioned at the beginning of the book. It's often said Wells was startlingly accurate; he was even right when he foresaw the war starting in a dispute between Germany and Poland over the German city of Danzig (which had been cut off from the rest of Germany when Poland was created after the First World War). So here is the father of futurology nailing the biggest event of the twentieth century—and demonstrating that grand-scale prediction is possible. But I'm afraid this is credulity on stilts. For one thing, the Nazis and other German nationalists were fiercely militaristic and they routinely called for a violent revision of the international order created at the end of the First World War. They were particularly incensed that Danzig had been cut off from Germany. The danger was obvious to anyone who read a newspaper, and in Britain, as historian Richard Overy observed, "guessing when war would come became a morbid parlor-game of the 1930s." Wells was also far from alone in picking 1940 as the start date. So did John Maynard Keynes. So, too, did an English preacher who thought Adolf Hitler was the Antichrist and the war would mark the beginning of the events prophesied in the Book of Revelation. And remember that Wells's prediction is found in *The Shape of Things to Come*—a book whose depiction of the course and conclusion of the war does not resemble what happened and which goes on to describe *a whole century* of future history that looks nothing like what unfolded. Thus Wells's dazzling prediction was, in fact, a banal observation combined with a lucky call on timing.

And yet, I must admit, skepticism about prediction is not easy to accept. One big reason is that it *feels* wrong, thanks to hindsight bias. Remember: Once we know an outcome, we judge the likelihood of that outcome to be higher than we would if we did not know it. We even adjust our memories to suit this bias, and, as Philip Tetlock showed, hindsight bias can transform a judgment of "this is very unlikely to happen" into a memory of "I said it was very likely to happen." This distortion has an especially unfortunate consequence: By giving us the sense that we could have predicted what is now the present, or even that we actually *did* predict it when we did not, it strongly suggests that we can predict the future. This is an illusion, and yet it seems only logical— which makes it a particularly persuasive illusion.

Hindsight bias is also responsible for an unfortunate misperception that can be heard almost any time someone frets about the future. "Things are uncertain," someone says. "Not like it was in the past." The first part of that statement is accurate; the second is not. The future is *always* uncertain, whether it is the future we face right now or the future people faced a century ago. But when we look back, hindsight bias causes us to see much less uncertainty than we do today. We remember the 1990s, for example, as the decade of soaring stocks and not much else. It was, as it's often called, a "holiday from history." We don't think of the 1990s as the decade in which we worried that Japan would swallow the United States, that there would be massive casualties in the Gulf War of 1991, that nuclear weapons from the crumbling Soviet Union would fall into the hands of terrorists, that the American government would be bankrupted, that the Asian meltdown of 1997 would lead to a global depression, or that Y2K would cripple infrastructure and leave us eating baked beans from the can in a candlelit basement. None of those things happened and we don't remember ourselves worrying so much that they would. In fact, lots of us *did* worry—the record is clear. But because of hindsight bias, we don't remember the uncertainty to the extent that we felt it at the time, and so we think that the future we face now is much more uncertain than the future we faced in the past.

The profound perceptual distortion caused by hindsight bias can make almost anyone nostalgic for the good old days. At the end of his life, my grandfather looked ahead at the world I would live in and he saw nothing but uncertainty and darkness. So many things could go so wrong. He worried for me. But *his* life? It had been sweet. This man who had seen his family's prosperity swept away, who had lived through two world wars, who had raised a young family in the worst depression in history—he was convinced he had lived in the best of times. It was the *future* that frightened him. This illusion is pervasive and yet it is seldom recognized. In books, articles, blogs, and broadcasts, we call our time the "age of uncertainty," believing that there is something uniquely uncertain about this moment. But the phrase *age of uncertainty*, which has appeared in *The New York Times* 5,720 times, made its debut there in 1924, while *uncertain times* has appeared 2,810 times, starting in 1853. The same illusion inspires frantic hand-waving about the supposedly unprecedented "roaring current of change" we are experiencing. Ecologist William Vogt expressed that sentiment perfectly when he wrote, "We live in a world of such rapid and dynamic change as man, in his hundreds of thousands of years of existence, has never known." But Vogt wrote that in 1948, a year after W. H. Auden published his famous poem *The Age of Anxiety*. And the phrase *roaring current of change* comes from Alvin Toffler's massive best seller *Future Shock*, which was published in 1970. In that book, Toffler warned that the pace of change in modern life was so torrid it was causing a crippling mental condition he dubbed "future shock." To historians, *future shock* sounded an awful lot like *neurasthenia*—a diagnosis that was popular for several decades after the American physician George Beard invented it in 1869. *Plus ça change,* as the French say.

Granted, the level of uncertainty and the pace of change do vary from place to place and time to time, and there may well be good reasons to judge one moment more uncertain or unsettled than another. But our perception of *this* moment in *this* place seldom comes from a careful and rational assessment of the facts. It's a permanent condition: We *always* feel the uncertainty and change we are experiencing now is greater than ever. That feeling makes us hunger for predictions about the future. Particularly rapid social change like that experienced during the 1970s adds to the hunger; shocks like the oil embargo of 1973 or the crash of 2008 multiply it.

And then there's the experience of having a baby. There's nothing a new mother or father wants to know more urgently than what the world will be like for their child. In a 1975 episode of *All in the Family*—the television show that perfectly captured American life in a difficult decade—Mike and Gloria learn they will have their first child. At first, they're thrilled. But then Mike starts worrying about "world problems." The air and water are "poisoned," the planet is overcrowded, "and there's not enough food to go around." What would they be bringing a child into? He couldn't really answer that question but he wanted to, desperately. And so he did: The future would be awful. He was sure of it. And his moment of joy was lost.

Whether sunny or bleak, convictions about the future satisfy the hunger for certainty. We want to believe. And so we do.

I PREDICT YOU WILL OBJECT

But still, one may protest, prediction *is* possible. And indispensable. "When the United States invaded Iraq, it was based on a prediction of what would happen," George Friedman responded when he was asked about claims that prediction is impossible. "When investors placed their money with Bernie Madoff, they were predicting that it was a good investment. When we cross the street we predict that the car standing at the light won't suddenly press the accelerator. All of us, in our daily lives, must make the best prediction available on every level. Prediction is built into our existence."

He's right. Almost everything we do is influenced by an explicit or implicit judgment about the future, whether that future is five seconds or five decades from now. A plan to meet someone for dinner is always based on a long list of assumptions about what will happen, and what won't, between the moment the decision is made and dinnertime. Saving for retirement is based on a prediction that the institutions you entrust with your money will not collapse, that the investments will generate a satisfactory return, and that you will not die before you get your gold watch and clean out your desk. Our collective decisions, too, are based on predictions. For example, if we support raising gas taxes to encourage conservation, that support is based on a prediction: Do this thing and there will be a certain result in the future. So we really do predict all the time. It's an essential and unavoidable part of life, as the English soccer star Paul Gascoigne inadvertently demonstrated when he firmly declared, "I never make predictions and I never will."

It's also true that lots of our predictions are quite reliable. Essentially everyone who crosses the street on the assumption that the car stopped at the red light won't suddenly charge forward will be proved right. There may be rare exceptions, but millions of people make the same prediction every day and get the same result every time. We may not know the statistics, but we see this phenomenon play out on street corners daily. That's valuable input. It tells us that if we make the same call, it's likely to be right. Insurance companies do something similar. They know, for example, that millions of male, white, middle-aged, modestly overweight Americans have come and gone over the years and they know that by examining the vast quantity of data generated by those millions of lives, they can predict how long a male, white, middle-aged, modestly overweight American is likely to live. The predictions they make are quite reliable. Selling life insurance wouldn't be a profitable business if they weren't. Similarly, every year, there are millions of cars on the roads of Britain driving millions of passenger miles and generating heaps of data. Those numbers can give us an excellent sense of how many fatalities there will be next year—it's a safe bet that it will be close to this year's total—and the risk the average Briton will face when he gets behind the wheel.

Of course, things get harder when we ask a question like "During the next five years, will the government of Sweden be ousted in a military coup?" There aren't millions of Swedish governments whose experience can be compiled and analyzed. But there have been many decades of stable governance in Sweden, and there's no sign of Swedish colonels with delusions of grandeur. So it's safe to say the likelihood of a military coup in Sweden is very low. But it's not zero: No matter how unlikely it may be, it is still possible there could be a military coup in Sweden.

That's a critical caveat. It applies to all predictions, even the most reliable. It's always possible that a driver's mind will wander as he waits for the light to turn green, leading him to accelerate into pedestrians who predicted he would not. It's very unlikely. But it's possible—just as it's possible that a male, white, middle-aged, modestly overweight American could be struck and killed while crossing the street five minutes after signing a million-dollar life insurance policy. You never know. Even normally reliable big-scale forecasts can be thrown off by surprises. In 1973, war in the Middle East led to an oil embargo that caused soaring gas prices in the United States and a decision by the American government to conserve gasoline by lowering highway speed limits; some combination of the higher cost of gas and the lower speed limit caused the largest one-year drop in traffic fatalities ever—a reduction that could not possibly have been forecast at the beginning of this chain of events.

Uncertainty is omnipresent. Even the forecasts of eclipses and ocean tides—the pinnacle of predictability—are not and never will be absolutely certain because we live in a universe littered with comets and asteroids big enough to gouge a big chunk out of the planet or blow the moon to smithereens. Thus, the most that we can ever hope to do is distinguish between *degrees* of probability with reasonable accuracy. That job is relatively easy when we're deciding whether to cross the road or calculating life insurance premiums. But when it comes to the sort of predictions that dominate the news media, the best-seller charts, and the corporate lecture circuit—predictions about large-scale, highly complex, highly uncertain social phenomena over long periods of time—reliable forecasting is a challenge on par with climbing Mt. Everest barefoot. And that's when it's even *theoretically* possible, which it usually isn't. A good model to keep in mind is weather, which can be forecast with considerable accuracy a day out. Two days out, accuracy declines but it's still reasonably good. Three days, the forecasts are shakier. Two weeks out, weather forecasts are essentially useless. As scientists learn more about weather, as forecasting techniques are improved, as computing power grows, the horizon for accurate forecasts may be pushed forward, but these advances will be increasingly difficult. Like most of what's interesting in life, weather is subject to chaos and all sorts of nonlinear weirdness that limits how far we can peer into the future. Those limits will never be eliminated.

Knowing the world is fundamentally uncertain and unpredictable, and knowing that the brains we use to understand this uncertain and unpredictable world contain psychological biases and other trip wires that skew our judgment, a little humility is in order. The future is dark, and much as we might like to see in the dark, we cannot. Imagining otherwise is dangerous. Stride confidently forward in the dark and you're likely to feel quite pleased with yourself right up until the moment you walk into a wall.

That is how George W. Bush broke his nose. If one feature defined the former president of the United States more than any other, it was confidence. He was sure of himself. He knew invading Iraq was the right course of action. He knew Iraqis would welcome American soldiers as liberators, that the new Iraq would be stable and democratic, that the changes in Iraq would inspire positive reforms throughout the Middle East, that terrorism would diminish. He was certain of it, and so was his administration, which is why the White House ignored contingency planning done in the State Department and invaded Iraq with a force too small and ill-equipped to cope if things turned out differently than expected. The rest, as they say, is history. So while George Friedman is right that the United States invaded Iraq on the basis of a prediction, it's far more important to recognize that things might have gone considerably better for the president and everyone else if Bush had been much less confident of the accuracy of that prediction.

The same lesson can be seen in Friedman's point about people investing with Bernie Madoff. It's true that everyone who invested with Bernie Madoff predicted their investment would deliver a good return. It's the same whenever someone invests with anyone. But many of those who invested with Madoff did not merely think it *likely* the investment would deliver a good return. They were sure of it—so sure they gave Madoff their entire life savings. If they had been more uncertain of their prediction, if they had accepted that there are no sure things in life, they would not have handed over everything and they would not have been wiped out when Madoff was revealed to be a crook.

It should be obvious from this that being skeptical about predictions does not render people unable to make a decision; it just makes them cautious. This is not a bad thing, and, indeed in some circumstances, it can be a very good thing.

This is evident in the early-1970s debate about how governments should respond to the food crisis. William and Paul Paddock, authors of *Famine 1975!*, advocated a policy they called "triage": Rich nations should send all their food aid to those poor countries that still had some hope of one day feeding themselves; hopeless countries like India and Egypt should be cut off immediately. "To send food is to throw sand in the ocean," they wrote. The Paddocks knew countries that lost the aid would plunge into famine. They were quite explicit about that. But famine was going to come anyway, and this would at least improve the odds for countries that still had a chance. In *The Population Bomb,* Paul Ehrlich lavishly praised *Famine 1975!*—it "may be remembered as one of the most important books of our age"—and declared that "there is no rational choice except to adopt some form of the Paddocks' strategy as far as food distribution is concerned."

The Paddocks' proposal was not adopted, which is fortunate because the prediction of inevitable famines on which it was based was wrong. If the Paddocks' policy *had* been implemented, food shipments to India, Egypt, and elsewhere would have been cut off at a time when tens of millions of people stood at the brink of famine, and this would likely have pushed them over the edge: William and Paul Paddock, Paul Ehrlich, and all the other experts who were certain they knew what would happen in the future would have *created* the famines they predicted.

Ehrlich should have paid closer attention to something he wrote at the end of *The Population Bomb*. "Any scientist lives constantly with the possibility that he may be wrong," he wrote. Recognizing this, it's critical to ask, "What if my prediction doesn't pan out? What if I'm wrong? Will the course of action I've recommended still be a good one?" Ehrlich thought the answer in his case was obvious. "If I'm right, we'll save the world," he wrote. "If I'm wrong, people will still be better fed, better housed, and happier, thanks to our efforts." Even in 1968, it should have been clear this was glib nonsense. Cutting off food aid could tip nations into famine, and if the prediction of coming famines was indeed false, cutting off food aid would cause famines that would not otherwise happen. The logic was plain but Ehrlich didn't see it because he didn't seriously consider the possibility that he was wrong.

And yet, Ehrlich did have the right idea: While our decisions have to be made on the basis of what we think is going to happen, we must always consider how our decisions will fare if the future turns out to be very different. A good decision is one that delivers positive results in a wide range of futures.

Consider climate change. For the record, I accept that anthropogenic climate change is all too real. But as the reader may guess, I am skeptical of climate models that purport to forecast changes in the climate decades and even centuries out. Climate scientists are quite blunt that there is lots about climate that science does not understand, which is precisely why scientists find the field exciting to work in. Combine that ignorance with the almost indescribably complex interactions at work in the massive, nonlinear systems that make up climate and there are huge uncertainties woven into every climate prediction. This does not mean we should shrug and walk away, however. The models may over-estimate the extent of climate change and the damage it does. But they may also *underestimate* it, as seems to have already happened in some cases. Walking away would be foolhardy. We have to decide what to do.

In making that decision, we must seriously consider the possibility that we are wrong. That cuts both ways. For those who scoff at climate change, it means considering the possibility that decades from now, as ice caps melt and coasts flood and agricultural yields fall, only a stiff dose of hindsight bias will save them from the humiliation of recalling what they once believed. For those who think climate change is real, it means imagining a future where people who look back at the hand-wringing about climate change today are as amazed and amused as we are when we look back at scary predictions from the 1970s. These are radically different futures. Is there anything we can do now that will look good in either future, or in the many possible futures that lie some-where between those two extremes?

Some proposals definitely flunk this test. Expensive schemes for "carbon sequestration"—pumping carbon dioxide emissions back underground—would be a waste of money if climate change is a dud. But many others pay off no matter what. Capturing methane emitted from landfills not only stops a potent greenhouse gas from entering the atmosphere, it delivers a fuel that may be burned to generate electricity. That's a winner in any future. As are improvements in energy effi-ciency that not only reduce carbon dioxide emissions but also save money. The same can be said of many other choices, including the big climate change proposal endorsed by most economists: a stiff carbon tax with the revenues returned to the economy in the form of cuts to other taxes. Would it deliver benefits even if climate change turns out to be bunk? Absolutely. Carbon taxes raise the effective cost of fossil fuels, making alternative energy more competitive and spurring research and development. And reducing the use of fossil fuels while increasing the diversity of our energy sources would be wonderful for a whole host of reasons aside from climate change. It would reduce local air pollution, reduce the risk of catastrophic oil spills, buffer economies against the massive shocks inflicted by oil price spikes, and lessen the world's vulnerability to instability in the Middle East and elsewhere. It would also reduce the torrent of cash flowing from the developed world to the thuggish governments that control most major oil-producing nations, including Saudi Arabia, Iran, and Russia. And of course there's peak oil. If the peaksters turn out to be right, finally, how much of our economy is fueled by oil will determine how badly we will suffer—so carbon taxes would steadily reduce that threat too.

For Americans, in particular, there's some unfortunate history to keep in mind. In the 1970s, when oil prices were surging and most experts agreed oil was only going to get much more expensive, huge advances were made in conservation and the development of alternative energy. But in the mid-1980s, when the price crashed, the advances slowed or stopped; at least they did in the United States. While Americans rejoiced at the return of cheap gas, most northern European countries kept the price high with stiff taxes. As a result, Europe got dramatically more energy efficient than the United States. In 2008, with oil prices soaring to previously unimaginable highs, the conservative American columnist Charles Krauthammer fumed that a quarter of a century earlier he and many others had called for an energy tax in order to curtail consumption "and keep the money at home." It didn't happen. And so, "instead of hiking the price ourselves by means of a gasoline tax that could be instantly refunded to the American people in the form of lower payroll taxes, we let the Saudis, Venezuelans, Russians, and Iranians do the taxing for us—and pocket the money that the tax would have recycled back to the American worker." But the United States did do *something* in the twenty years between the fall of oil prices in the 1980s and the surge in the first decade of the twenty-first century: It massively escalated its military involvement in the Persian Gulf region, which was done primarily to protect the flow of oil that is the global economy's lifeblood. Two wars and trillions of dollars later, the cost of that approach, in both treasure and blood, is staggering. Seen in this light, Jimmy Carter's dire oil forecast of 1977 and his call for the "moral equivalent of war" look very different. The forecast was wrong, but Carter's call for a concerted national effort to improve energy efficiency and develop alternative energy was exactly right. If the United States had kept at it in the 1980s and 1990s, it would have been far more secure in the twenty-first century. Tragically, it did not. It abandoned Carter's direction after his forecast collapsed, and so, almost three decades after Carter's famous speech, the United States was still addicted to oil—a fact bemoaned by environmentalists, economists, generals, national security experts, and politicians ranging from George W. Bush to Barack Obama.

What all this means, very simply, is that accurate prediction often isn't needed in order to make good decisions. A rough sense of the possibilities and probabilities will often do. We can't predict earthquakes, but we do know where they are more and less likely and we make building codes less or more strict accordingly. That works. Similarly, it wasn't necessary to predict the 9/11 terrorist attack in order to know that having reinforced cockpit doors on jets is a good idea. In the 1990s, several incidents, including the stabbing of a Japan Airlines pilot by a deranged man, convinced many safety advocates and regulators that reinforced doors were a wise investment. They weren't in place on 9/11 because the airlines didn't want the extra cost and they successfully lobbied politicians to block the proposal. It was politics, not unpredictability, that left planes vulnerable that fateful morning. Commodity speculation is another model. Every day, traders buy and sell futures contracts, which, as the name suggests, are based on what people predict future prices of commodities will be. This might look like people making money by predicting the future, but the traders' maxim "Cut your losses and let profits run" hints at what's really going on. Traders aren't so foolish as to think they can predict the future. Instead, they make a large number of bets. When one goes bad, they quickly sell it off. The loss is minimal. But the profit from a good call is likely to be substantial. As a result, the traders make money even if the overwhelming majority of their forecasts are wrong—which they fully expect they will be.

Accepting uncertainty stops us from striding confidently through the darkness, but it's still possible to make decisions and take actions: We can stretch out our hands and cautiously grope our way through the darkness, always alert to the possibility of surprise. This may not be as thrilling as believing we possess a map to the future and setting out boldly for some distant El Dorado, but it is considerably less likely to end in a collision of one's nose and reality.

DOING IT BETTER

Alan Barnes wasn't satisfied. His unit churned out forecasts about political and economic events but he didn't know how good they were. He and his staff had a sense, of course. "It happened anecdotally," he says. "You make a judgment about something and six months later it blows up in your face. Something happens that you said wasn't going to happen. Your colleagues make it clear." But aside from collegial ribbing or boasting when someone nailed a big call, there was nothing to go by. The accuracy of the unit's forecasts had never been systematically analyzed because the people who used the unit's forecasts had never asked if they were any good. If they wouldn't hold the unit accountable, Barnes would.

Barnes's unit is part of the Privy Council Office of the Canadian government. The sort of questions it handles—who will win the Russian election? will China strike a deal to develop Nigerian oil reserves?—is standard stuff in intelligence circles. The problem Barnes faced is also typical. Intelligence agencies don't track the accuracy of their forecasts. Instead, they use process standards. The Central Intelligence Agency, for one, has a checklist of best practices its analysts should follow. Did you examine other hypotheses? Did you consider contrary evidence? If all the boxes are ticked, the analyst's forecast is considered sound. Whether events actually unfold as the analyst expected is considered irrelevant in judging the quality of the forecast.

Barnes thought this was a mistake. His unit was constantly issuing reports saying it was unlikely that this or that would happen in the Russian election and probable that China would sign that Nigerian oil deal. But nobody knew how often the outcome matched the forecast, and if he wanted to improve his unit's judgments, he first had to know how good those judgments were.

To do that, Barnes had to overcome the problem of language. What does *probably* mean? To one person, in one context, it may mean there's a slightly better than fifty-fifty chance of something—say, 55 or 60 percent. But to another person, or in another context, it may mean that thing has a very good chance—something like 75 or 80 percent. The language of forecasting is riddled with this ambiguity, so Barnes created a numerical scale from 0 to 10 that attached precise numbers to key terms. *Probably* means 7 or 8 out of 10. So does *likely. Almost certain* and *highly likely* are a 9 out of 10. At the other end of the scale, *very unlikely* and *little prospect* are a 1 while *unlikely* is a 2 or 3. This cut the ambiguity and made statistical analysis possible.

The problem in assessing probability judgments is that it's impossible to say if any one such judgment is right or wrong. Most people would consider a forecast of "It is likely that X will happen" to be right if X does happen. But what if X *doesn't* happen? Was the forecast wrong? No—because the forecast implicitly said, "Although X is likely to happen, X may not happen." The same is true if the probabilities are expressed in numbers. But if numbers are used, and many different forecasts are collected, the numbers can be crunched and the "calibration" of the judgments determined. If the forecasts are perfectly accurate, the probability calls they make should match the probabilities that actually played out: So events that are said to be 90 percent likely should happen 90 percent of the time; 70 percent of the 70 percent calls should happen; and so on. With the help of David Mandel, a psychologist who studies judgment with the Canadian Department of National Defense, Barnes got to work.

Barnes and Mandel gathered data from fifty-one intelligence memoranda issued by Barnes's unit over an eighteen-month period. In all, they were able to compare 580 predictions with real-world outcomes. In order to avoid skewing the results by the difficulty of the predictions being made, they subdivided the calls into three categories of difficulty and calculated each separately.

The results were impressive: Overall, there was almost none of the overconfidence that is usually found in these sorts of tests. "The calibration value for that sample was 0.014, which is a very high degree of calibration," Mandel says. That's almost as good as the results obtained from the one professional group that has long been shown to have the best calibration—meteorologists—and the analysts were looking much further into the future than meteorologists ever do, even as far ahead as a year. And, of course, the analysts were dealing with people—complex, self-aware, unpredictable people. As expected, when the results of the three difficulty levels were broken out, the analysts did best on the easiest calls and worst on the hardest. But that didn't explain the overall result. "The calibration index for the hardest level of judgments was still 0.05," Mandel says, "which is still very good calibration."

But how did they do it? Barnes's first response when asked this question is revealing. "To a certain extent," he says, "I would have to express some skepticism about the outcome." That's right. After careful testing revealed his team has far better judgment than most, Barnes didn't boast about the results and cite them as proof that he and his analysts are uniquely insightful people. Instead, he suggested the methodology of the testing may have been somewhat flawed and his team might not be as good as the tests made them out to be.

So we discussed Barnes's concern about the methodology. It was modest. Even if correct, it didn't overturn the general results. As Barnes put it, "I'm not convinced that what we've done is accurate to three decimal points. There is still a significant fudge factor in this. I think it's broadly indicative but I wouldn't be quite as confident in the level of precision."

The very fact that Barnes's first instinct was to express doubt is essential to understanding why his team did so well, because doubt is the hallmark of the fox.

Recall that people whose thinking style marks them as "foxes," in Philip Tetlock's terms, are modest about their ability to forecast the future, comfortable with complexity and uncertainty, and very self-critical—they are always questioning whether what they believe to be true really is. Foxes also reject intellectual templates, preferring to gather ideas and information from as many sources as they can get their hands on.

When I summarized "fox-thinking" with Alan Barnes, he nodded. "That's fundamental to how we approach analysis."

Three key elements explain why foxes' cognitive style improves the accuracy of their forecasts. First is *aggregation*. Heaps of research show that combining multiple sources of information is more likely to produce good results than using a single source of information. This fundamental fact was popularized by journalist James Surowiecki in *The Wisdom of Crowds*, which is an unfortunate phrase because crowds in a literal sense are not wise. In fact, they tend toward conformity and "groupthink," which makes them a terrible structure for decision making. What is "wise" is the combined judgment of large numbers of people making decisions independently. In these circumstances, the mistakes of any one person are likely to be canceled out by the countervailing mistakes of others while the solid information each person brings is combined with that brought by others. The net result: a collective judgment that will almost certainly be superior to the judgment of any one person. Even combining the judgments of laypeople is likely to produce a better judgment than that of one expert, however well informed. This powerful phenomenon is the basis for "prediction markets," like the famous Iowa Presidential Election Markets, in which people bet on political predictions in much the same way they buy and sell stocks.

And it's not only the judgments of individuals that can be aggregated. Combining poll results is a good way to produce an aggregate poll that is more accurate than any of the polls that went into it.

By grabbing on to whatever information is available, from whatever source, foxes aggregate. They may not do it as well as a prediction market, but the fundamental process is the same, and it helps make their judgment superior to that of hedgehogs who know One Big Thing and aren't interested in finding out more. Alan Barnes's analysts are urged to aggregate, and they're given every opportunity to do so, first by selecting the topics they wish to work on, then with access to classified and unclassified information, and finally by being allowed the time they need to do the job. And that's just the first step. After they come to a conclusion, they talk it over with Barnes, and then it's sent to external experts for comment. The conclusion is constantly revised in light of new information and new views, so the final judgment is the product of a wide array of inputs—which is to say, it is the product of aggregation.

The second element at work is what psychologists call *metacognition.* This is simply thinking about thinking. Alan Barnes constantly pushes his analysts to reflect on their conclusions, to question them, to ask themselves where they came from and whether they really make sense or not. "I find that in the more instinctive way of drafting these kinds of reports . . . people quite often make judgments without even really consciously thinking about making those judgments," Barnes says. "It just sort of flows out as part of the drafting process. It just feels right." Requiring analysts to explain their judgments forces them to think consciously about them, and conscious thought is the only way to catch the mistakes intuition often makes. Barnes has also found that attaching numbers to probability statements such as "unlikely" also helps because the precision of the number forces analysts to pause and think a little more carefully.

None of this is likely to work, however, without knowledge of the psychological traps people can fall into. "The biggest problem is not the bias per se," observes David Mandel. "It's the ease with which we pro-

ceed with those biases and are unaware of their impact on our judgment." Overcoming biases is a major challenge because, as psychologists
have shown, people taught to watch out for psychological biases readily
spot their pernicious influence in the thinking of other people. But we
perceive our own judgment to be objective and factual. This, too, is a
psychological bias. It goes by the clever name "bias bias." It is why
Barnes's analysts are not only required to learn about "confirmation
bias" and the many other hazards identified by psychology, they are
asked to use techniques designed to catch and correct cognitive biases.
The learning part is easy. Putting it to work is much harder. A basic
method for overcoming confirmation bias, for example, is to draft a list
of reasons that your belief may be wrong, but the analysts "are reluctant
to use even that extremely simple tool," Barnes says. "Even myself, when
I am drafting a paper, I must admit I don't use it as often as I should. It's
just not a normal way of thinking." But such measures are essential in
order to catch mistakes and make sound judgments.

The last of the three key elements at work is *humility*. "I think when
you're dealing with future events, pretending that you have absolute certainty is doing the reader a great disservice," Barnes says. His unit will
use the far ends of the probability scale if, after rigorous consideration,
they think that's where the evidence points. But they'll also deliver middling probability calls, even though people want to hear "This *will* happen," not "There is an 80 percent chance this will happen." Barnes will
even draw people's attention to the simple fact that when his unit says
something is "very likely to happen," it may not—which is necessary
because even very sophisticated people often treat a forecast of 80 percent as if it were 100 percent. When they do, Barnes has to remind them
of some old and wise advice: "Don't put all your eggs in one basket,
because the world is ultimately unpredictable," he says.

It's not only the strutting certainty of the TV talking head that Barnes
avoids, it's predictions that are impossible. That means, among other
things, not trying to peer too far into the future. A narrow question in
a time frame of six months or a year, fine. But Barnes and his analysts

don't predict the fate of China decades out. They don't forecast the price of oil in 2020. And they wouldn't dream of imagining what the world will look like when a baby boy born this year becomes a father. That may be the stuff of best sellers, but in a complex, nonlinear world, it's beyond human judgment. And Barnes knows his limits, as do all foxes. It's an essential feature of the species. "Whenever I start to feel certain I am right," one fox-expert told Philip Tetlock, "a little voice inside tells me to start worrying."

The billionaire financier George Soros is a classic fox. As a young man, he studied philosophy with Karl Popper, who taught him the value of introspection, humility, and pluralism. As far removed as Popperian philosophy might seem from the cutthroat world of finance, this was practical training. In a career spanning almost six decades, Soros has made an uncountable number of predictions about matters of enormous complexity, and his record—far from perfect but much better than most—is testament to the quality of his judgment. So is his wealth. Soros can also boast that he saw the real estate bubble building long before it popped in 2008, and that he had correctly warned about instability in the financial system. But Soros is not the sort of man who boasts. In January 2009, as the world plunged into the crisis Soros had long feared, a reporter asked him, in effect, why he's so good at what he does. Few would have objected if he had said, "It's because I'm so much smarter than everyone else." But he did not. Instead, he repeated his favorite theme. "I think that my conceptual framework, which basically emphasizes the importance of misconceptions, makes me extremely critical of my own decisions," he said. "I know that I am bound to be wrong, and therefore am more likely to correct my own mistakes." Soros's old teacher would have smiled. "Instead of posing as prophets we must become the makers of our fate," Karl Popper wrote. "We must learn to do things as best we can, and to look out for our mistakes." The student learned well.

Another man who saw the explosion of 2008 coming was Vince Cable. Formerly chief economist at Shell, Cable became a member of the

British Parliament and chief spokesperson on economics for the Liberal Democrats, and it was in this role that he furiously sounded the alarm on the real estate and finance bubbles. Like Soros, he was vindicated by the crash but he did not boast. Indeed, in his 2009 book *The Storm: The World Economic Crisis and What It Means,* Cable insisted he is no Nostradamus. "When I was paid for attempting to predict future economic developments for a leading multinational company," he wrote, "I was frequently reminded of the Arabic saying: 'Those who claim to foresee the future are lying, even if by chance they are later proved right.' The extraordinary speed with which the crisis has unfolded and overwhelmed the unready should underline the need for caution in anticipating the next few months, let alone years. It is perhaps more helpful to think of plausible scenarios than likely developments, and to frame any policy proposals in a spirit of humility, recognizing that no one fully understands what has happened or how the current drama will play out."

In his book *The Sages,* former banker Charles R. Morris looks at Soros, esteemed former chairman of the Federal Reserve Paul Volker, and legendary investor Warren Buffett. The quality all three share, according to Morris—who knows Soros and Volker personally—is "humility in the face of what one does not know." That is no accident. When Socrates was told that the Oracle of Delphi had deemed him the wisest man in Athens, he was characteristically skeptical. He felt he really didn't know much, while all around him were smart people who were confident they knew lots. So Socrates wandered about, questioning people to determine what they really knew. He discovered they were as ignorant as he. But unlike everyone else, Socrates knew he was ignorant, and this meant, Socrates decided, that he really was the wisest man in Athens.

That's how foxes think. They may eventually be convinced by the evidence that they are somewhat better than others at predicting the future, but only somewhat. As any fox worthy of the name would quickly add, their ability to predict is modest and strictly limited. The world is infinitely complex and the human mind fallible, so the future will forever be uncertain.

And foxes are just fine with that.

A FINAL OBJECTION

I have to acknowledge that in an important sense my skepticism about predictions is itself based on a prediction. Chaos theory and nonlinearity set strict limits on our ability to see into the future, as does our imperfect understanding of human consciousness and decision making. But this is only true based on what we know now. What about the future? Scientific theories are occasionally overthrown. What is unknown sometimes becomes known. Isn't it possible that, as scientists explore and computing power grows, we may one day be able to do what today is theoretically and practically impossible? Isn't that, after all, a good summary of the history of science? As scientist and author Arthur C. Clarke sagely observed, "When a distinguished but elderly scientist states that something is possible, he is almost certainly right. When he states that something is impossible, he is very probably wrong."

I must concede this point. Work on a vast array of theoretical issues and forecasting models continues at a furious pace. Occasionally, it produces stumbles, such as the very impressive models developed by political scientists which revealed in the spring of 2000 that the presidential election later that year would be won in a landslide by Al Gore. And it was, let us not forget, the latest and greatest modeling that told economists nothing especially bad was going to happen in 2008. But still, real progress has been made. Prediction markets, for example, are a genuine advance. And on a more theoretical level, skeptics like me have to accept the possibility that the bases for their skepticism may be overturned because scientific knowledge is always subject to revision in light of new evidence. It is never fixed and final. "The normal state of affairs in science is unsettled and uncertain," writes geophysicist Henry Pollack, "and no amount of new research will completely eliminate uncertainty."

So I have to accept that someone, someday, may be able to do what people have tried and failed to do for millennia. Which is why, when that claim is made, it deserves our attention, and why we should have a quick look at the work of Bruce Bueno de Mesquita.

"Politics is predictable," Bueno de Mesquita declared in *The Predictioneer's Game,* his 2009 best seller. For decades, Bueno de Mesquita has been a respected political scientist with a sideline running a consulting firm whose clients include global corporations and intelligence agencies. They want to know what will happen in the future and he tells them.

Bruce Bueno de Mesquita is very much a hedgehog. The idea that is the foundation of all his thinking is that people do what they believe is in their self-interest. He's not the only one to embrace this foundation, of course. Over the last several decades, most economists have treated it as axiomatic, although that view is waning thanks to advances in the study of decision making and the failure of events—notably the crash of 2008—to conform to the "rational man" model. But Bueno de Mesquita is faithful to his One Big Idea and he uses it, along with concepts springing from the related field of "game theory," to predict what people, corporations, and nations will do. In practice, Bueno de Mesquita enlists experts to help him identify who has a stake in the matter at hand, what they want, how badly they want it, and how much clout they have. Everything else is ignored. Cultural traditions, historical background, and personalities are all irrelevant. Bueno de Mesquita then takes his key information, plugs it into a computer programmed to run the algorithm he invented, and out pops the future.

Bueno de Mesquita is sure his method works, and in *The Predictioneer's Game* he regales readers with fascinating stories full of drama and amazing outcomes. He also has plenty of client testimonials. And he has a statistic, which he repeats like a mantra: "According to a declassified CIA assessment, the predictions for which I've been responsible have a 90 percent accuracy rate." Many people find this evidence impressive. "Some of you may be skeptical," an official of the Carnegie Council said in an introduction that began with a list of Bueno de Mesquita's predictive hits. "But be forewarned. Professor Bueno de Mesquita claims a ninety percent accuracy rate in his use of game theory to predict political trends, and his fans include many Fortune 500 companies, the CIA, and the Department of Defense."

This sort of credulity is all too common when people assess predictions and the judgment of those who make them. Bueno de Mesquita has made thousands of predictions and even if he made them all flipping a coin, some would have been right. Anecdotes are suggestive only. And nice words from clients are not terribly compelling when we keep in mind the long list of smart people who believed dumb things. George Washington swore by the Perkins Metallic Tractor—a contraption said to draw out any disease when it was waved over the afflicted body part—but the patronage of that great man didn't change the fact that the Perkins Metallic Tractor was junk. The whole point of modern science is to get beyond the illusory insight of anecdotes and testimonials, and since Bueno de Mesquita claims his methods are strictly scientific, it seems especially retrograde to fall back on such "evidence" here.

Then there is that "90 percent" figure. As Philip Tetlock wrote in a review of Bueno de Mesquita's book, we need to know much more before accepting it as compelling evidence. "A 90 percent hit rate is, for example, no great achievement for meteorologists predicting that it will not rain in Phoenix. And it is no big deal to achieve a 100 percent hit rate of predicting X—no matter what X may be—if doing so comes at the cost of an equally high false-alarm rate. Anyone can predict every war from now until eternity by simply predicting war all the time." A reviewer for *The New York Times* who located the document that is the source of Bueno de Mesquita's number was even less impressed. "The passage in question describes forecasts about political outcomes in 30 countries between October 1982 and October 1985. It says: 'Forecasts done with traditional methods and with Policon'—Bueno de Mesquita's system—'were found to be accurate about 90 percent of the time. . . . Both traditional approaches and Policon often hit the target, but Policon analyses got the bull's eye twice as often.'" Summing up, the reviewer noted that the passage "refers to a small sample of analyses done long ago on limited problems and with not overwhelming success. It also didn't come from some super-secret document written by the head of the agency: It came from an analyst whose last prominent appearance in the press was for his post-CIA adventure running a sausage company."

The ability to consistently and reliably predict major events in the future could do incalculable good for humanity—it certainly would have helped in 1914—and so it's no exaggeration to say it would be at least as valuable as a cure for cancer. And what does a rational person demand when someone claims to have invented a cure for cancer? Evidence, naturally. Not anecdotes and testimonials, but proper scientific testing, whether it's the gold standard of double-blind trials conducted by disinterested third parties or one of the many other testing methods. Unless and until the person making the claim produces such evidence, we wouldn't take him seriously.

That's the rational way of handling big claims about important matters, but that's not how we deal with predictions. We don't think carefully and demand evidence. If the prediction *feels* right, we go with our gut. As a result, there is little or no accountability in the prediction business. Many practitioners find that state of affairs quite acceptable. Those who don't are not given the resources to do better and so, like Alan Barnes, they are forced to make do with what they have, producing results that fall below the level of rigor they would like to demand of themselves. "Our clients have been too willing to accept analyses that are not as good as they could be and should be," Barnes says. "And because we're not getting that kind of pressure, there's not much incentive to improve the way we do business." Philip Tetlock has proposed that major consumers of forecasting—big corporations and intelligence agencies—fund carefully conducted research that would rigorously assess forecasting methods, but there hasn't been much interest.

A SPOONFUL OF SKEPTICISM

Skepticism is a good idea at all times, but when the news is especially tumultuous and nervous references to uncertainty are sprouting like weeds on the roof of an abandoned factory, it is essential. The 1970s were one such time. As I write, we are in another.

The crash of 2008 was a shock. The global recession of 2009 was a torment. Unemployment is high, economies weak, and government debt steadily mounts. The media are filled with experts telling us what comes next. We watch, frightened and fascinated, like the audience of a horror movie. We want to know. We *must* know.

For the moment, what the experts are saying is, in an odd way, reassuring. It's bleak, to be sure. But it's not apocalyptic, which is a big improvement over what they were saying when the crash was accelerating and the gloomier forecasters, such as former Goldman Sachs chairman John Whitehead, were warning it would be "worse than the Great Depression." To date, things aren't worse than the Great Depression, nor are they remotely as bad as the Great Depression. Naturally, the gloomsters would be sure to add "so far." And they would be right. Things change. The situation may get very much worse. Of course it may also go in the other direction, slowly or suddenly, modestly or sharply. The range of possible futures is vast.

As it always is. Anyone who reads history with sufficient imagination to overcome hindsight bias knows this. What appears most likely, or even certain, does not happen, while what happens is something quite unexpected. It was true for my grandfather's generation. It was true for my mother's. It is true for mine. And it will be true for my children's, which is one of the few grand-scale predictions I am comfortable making. As journalist James Fallows observed, "What looks like tomorrow's problem is rarely the real problem when tomorrow rolls around."

Fallows's point was proved by the very article in which he wrote those words. It was a book review published in the bleak and frightening year of 1974, and the subject of the review was Robert Heilbroner's crushingly grim *An Inquiry into the Human Prospect*. Fallows didn't care for the book, but it wasn't the pessimism that put him off. It was Heilbroner's "over-inflated certainty," a quality that, Fallows noted, Heilbroner occasionally shared with optimists like Herman Kahn. It's a mistake to be so sure we know what's coming, Fallows wrote. A little humility is in order. Almost four decades later, it's hard to read *An Inquiry into the Human Prospect* without laughing, and even harder not to think Fallows was a smart man.

In fact, Fallows was a smart *young* man at the time he wrote that review. Three years later, at the beginning of the Carter administration, he became the youngest person ever to hold the post of chief presidential speechwriter. He left after two years to begin a long and distinguished career in journalism, and so it was that in the bleak and frightening year of 2009 a considerably older James Fallows attempted, like Robert Heilbroner before him, to peer into the future. But it was not the human prospect Fallows grappled with. It was America's.

All the talk is of American decline, Fallows noted. Is it true? Do the best days of the United States lie in the past? Plenty of experts are sure they know the answer. It's no, say George Friedman and others. "Wrong," respond Chris Hedges, author of *Empire of Illusion,* and many more pundits. And Fallows? He starts by putting the question in perspective. Even in the colonies that would later become the United States, he notes, blasts against a society that had lost its way were routinely heard and they have been a fixture of American life ever since. In the modern era, fears surge and ebb, jeremiads come and go, but in literally every decade, there have been substantial numbers of experts proclaiming that the United States is a setting sun. "Through the entirety of my conscious life," Fallows wrote, "America has been on the brink of ruination, or so we have heard, from the launch of *Sputnik* through whatever is the latest indication of national falling apart or falling behind. Pick a year over the past half century, and I will supply an indicator of what at the time seemed a major turning point for the worse." Fallows then canvasses a wide array of factors working in America's favor, from the quality of top-tier university research to the country's continued ability to attract the best and brightest from around the world. It seems as if Fallows will side with Friedman and predict sunny days ahead.

But then, as foxes always do, Fallows considers the opposite perspective. The fact that decline was predicted in the past and did not come does not mean all predictions of decline must fail, he cautions. Only that they *may* fail. America's problems are real. And substantial. Fallows lists many, putting particular emphasis on a sclerotic federal government that may be incapable of making the changes necessary to prevent decline.

Fallows's conclusion? He refuses to draw one. The "only sensible answer" to the question of whether the United States is Rome in the waning days of the empire, he writes, is "maybe." To a mind craving certainty, that's not an answer at all. But it is the *correct* answer. What will happen to the United States is contingent on innumerable choices that will be made by more than three hundred million Americans, individually and collectively. It is further contingent on the individual and collective choices of billions of others on the planet. And it is contingent on factors in the natural world about which human understanding and ability to predict are strictly limited. That's a lot of contingencies. Gather them together, pile them one on top of the other, and you get a very thick deck of cards. Shuffle and deal. What hand will the United States draw? Experts who think they can answer that are fooling themselves and those who listen to them. We'll know when we see the cards.

Whatever disagreements one may have with the particular analyses offered by Fallows, his essay is a model of how a fox works his way forward in the darkness of the future. It is informed by the past, it is revealing about the present, and it surveys a wide array of futures. It is infused with metacognition ("Maybe I'm biased," Fallows cautions at one point). It offers hopeful visions of what could be; it warns against dangers that also could be. It explores our values by asking us what we want to happen and what we don't. And it goes no further. It raises issues, questions, and choices, and it suggests possibilities and probabilities. But it does not peddle certainties, and it does not predict.

What I've just described may sound commonplace. "No serious futurist deals in 'predictions,'" Alvin Toffler wrote in the introduction to *Future Shock.* "These are left for television oracles and newspaper astrologers." Similar statements can be found in countless essays and books about the future. "It is impossible to predict the future, and all attempts to do so in any detail appear ludicrous within a very few years," wrote Arthur C. Clarke in the introduction to *Profiles of the Future,* published in 1962. "This book has a more realistic yet at the same time more ambitious aim. It does not try to describe *the* future, but to define the boundaries within which possible futures must lie." But as common as statements like this are, so is what follows: predictions about *the* future. "The gas engine is on its way out, as any petroleum geologist will assure you in his more unguarded moments," Clarke wrote a mere forty-eight pages after announcing that he would not attempt to predict the future. Also finished, according to Clarke, were ships and cars. They would be replaced by hovercraft. Clarke even knew what "the characteristic road sign of the 1990s" would say: NO WHEELED VEHICLES ON THIS HIGHWAY.

It's easy to say, in the abstract, that the world is unpredictable. But it's a struggle to live by that belief. Medieval monks would test the strength of their commitment to celibacy by lying in bed, naked, with a woman, and anyone who contemplates the future faces a similar temptation. Embracing uncertainty may be the cold intellectual ideal, but it's the soft, warm sensation of certainty we crave.

So what will happen in our future? To repeat a phrase that appears often in this book, I don't know. No one does. The future will be determined by an almost infinite array of what the philosopher Michael Oakeshott called "interlocking contingencies." Certainty about the outcome is seductive. It's also ridiculous. The best that we can do is study, think, and choose as best we can in the spirit of building toward the future, as James Fallows put it. Then hope for a little luck. That's not a satisfying conclusion. It's even a little frightening. But, if it's any consolation, we can remember that it was no different for earlier generations, whether they knew it or not.

At the end of that 1975 episode of *All in the Family,* Mike despairs for the child he is about to bring into the world. A friend gives him a newspaper clipping. Chastened, he hands it to Gloria, who reads it aloud. It's something Alistair Cooke wrote, she says.

"Who?" her father, Archie, whispers to his wife. "Alice the cook," says the confused Edith.

"In the best of times our days are numbered anyway," it begins. "And so it would be a crime against nature for any generation to take the world's crisis so solemnly that it put off enjoying those things for which we were designed in the first place. The opportunity to do good work, to fall in love, to enjoy friends, to hit a ball, and to bounce a baby."

A wise person, that Alice.

Notes

CHAPTER 1

Page

2. John Bates Clark, "Recollections of the Twentieth Century," *The Atlantic Monthly*, January 1902.
3. G. P. Gooch, *History of Our Time 1885–1911*, 1911.
3. Quoted in "Europeans Are from Venus," *New York Times*, February 10, 2008.
3. Quoted in "Europeans Are from Venus."
4. Richard Overy, *The Twilight Years: The Paradox of Britain Between the Wars*, 2009.
5. Overy, *The Twilight Years*.
5. Quoted in John Mueller, "The Catastrophe Quota," *Journal of Conflict Resolution*, September 1994.
5. Quoted in John Mueller, *Overblown*, 2006.
5. Quoted in John Mueller, *Atomic Obsession*, 2009.
5. Quoted in Mueller, "The Catastrophe Quota."
6. Robert Fogel, Working Paper 11125, National Bureau of Economic Research, February 2005.
6. Fogel, Working Paper 11125.
8. Fogel, Working Paper 11125.
10. Overy, *The Twilight Years*.
10. "The Futurists: Looking Toward A.D. 2000," *Time*, February 25, 1966.

11. Jonathan Schell, *The Fate of the Earth,* 1982.

12. James Bonner, *Science,* August 25, 1967.

12. Daniel Yergin, *The Prize,* 1992.

12. *Time,* December 7, 2009.

13. *The Walrus,* May 2010.

13. IMF Working Paper WP/00/77.

14. Charles Morris, *The Sages,* 2009.

20. David Wallechinsky et al., *The Book of Predictions,* 1980.

21. *The Economist,* June 3, 1995.

CHAPTER 2

Page

32. *The New Republic,* February 25, 1978.

33. Daniel Yergin, *The Prize,* 1992.

33. Robert Sherrill, "The Case Against the Oil Companies," *New York Times,* October 14, 1979.

33. Author's interview with Peter Schwartz, November 2009.

34. James Akins, *Foreign Affairs,* April 1973.

34. Ron Alquist and Lutz Kilian, Center for Economic Policy Research Discussion Paper DP6548.

35. Anthony Parisi, *New York Times,* September 1, 1977.

36. Quoted in Oona Strathern, *A Short History of the Future,* 2007.

38. Quoted in John Cox, *Storm Watchers,* 2002.

38. James Crutchfield, Doyne Farmer, Norman Packer, and Robert Shaw, "Chaos," *Scientific American,* December 1986.

41. William H. McNeill, "Passing Strange: The Convergence of Evolutionary Science with Scientific History," *History and Theory,* February 2001.

42. Quoted in Justin Fox, *The Myth of the Rational Market,* 2009.

43. John Lewis Gaddis, "International Relations Theory and the End of the Cold War," *International Security,* Winter 1992/93.

43. David Robson, "Disorderly Genius: How Chaos Drives the Brain," *New Scientist,* June 29, 2009.

44. Spyros Makridakis, Robin Hogarth, and Anil Gaba, *Dance with Chance,* 2009.

46. "The Gipper or the Guard," *New York Times,* November 3, 2009.

46. The classic illustration of small things making huge differences is based

on what is likely an apocryphal tale: Mark Antony, it is said, gazed for so long at a statue of Cleopatra, and in particular the statue's striking nose, that he was late to arrive at the battle that decided the fate of the Roman Empire. Thus, the philosopher Blaise Pascal reasoned, history turned on Cleopatra's nose. Stodgier historians like to cite "Cleopatra's nose" as a way of belittling the notion that great events can be traced to trivial sources. Great events must have great causes, they insist. But if it is possible for a butterfly's flap to cause a tornado, it is possible for a monkey's bite to cause a war, and the insistence that great events come from great sources is nothing more than a prejudice. The story of Cleopatra's magnificent proboscis may not be true, but Pascal had the right idea.

47. "Projecting the Unknowable" in *World Population to 2300*, United Nations.

48. Robert Sencourt, "Population and the Future," *The Atlantic Monthly*, April 1925.

49. Richard Overy, *The Twilight Years*, 2009.

49. Michael S. Teitelbaum and Jay M. Winter, *The Fear of Population Decline*, 1985.

49. Overy, *The Twilight Years*.

49. "The Future of Population" in *What the Future Holds*, 2002.

49. See *America Alone* by Mark Steyn for a particularly hysterical example.

50. "Go Forth and Multiply a Lot Less," *The Economist*, October 31, 2009.

50. Joel Cohen, "The Future of Population" in *What the Future Holds*. Cohen notes that one researcher found the number was revised up eleven times and down six times, while two others counted thirteen changes up and four down. "Evidently there is some uncertainty about the uncertainty," he dryly concluded.

52. "The Future of Population" in *What the Future Holds*.

52. Jack Davis, "Why Bad Things Happen to Good Analysts" in Roger Z. George and James B. Bruce, eds., *Analyzing Intelligence*, 2008.

53. Charles Kurzman, *The Unthinkable Revolution in Iran*, 2005.

55. Clark C. Abt, "The Future of Energy" in *What the Future Holds*, 2002.

55. Noel Grove, "Oil, the Dwindling Treasure," *National Geographic*, June 1974.

56. *Energy: Global Prospects 1985–2000*, Workshop on Alternative Energy Strategies, 1977.

56. Nassim Taleb, *The Black Swan*, 2007.

56. "Forbes Predicts Oil Will Drop to $35 Within a Year," *Daily Telegraph,* August 31, 2005.

56. "Oil's End," *New York Times,* March 5, 2008.

57. David Olive, *Toronto Star,* July 27, 2009.

57. "Warning: Oil Supplies Are Running Out Fast," *The Independent,* August 3, 2009.

57. COMPAS Inc., June 8, 2009.

CHAPTER 3

Page

59. All biographical details from William H. McNeill, *Arnold J. Toynbee: A Life,* 1989.

59. Arnold J. Toynbee, "What the Book Is For," reprinted in Ashley Montagu, ed., *Toynbee and History,* 1956.

60. Quoted in *Arnold J. Toynbee: A Life.*

62. "Testing the Toynbee System" in *Toynbee and History.*

62. "Much Learning . . ." in *Toynbee and History.*

62. Quoted in "Herr Spengler and Mr. Toynbee," H. Michell, *Toynbee and History.*

64. *Time,* April 20, 1953.

64. "The Napoleon of Notting Hill" in *Toynbee and History.*

65. "The Menace of Overpopulation" in Fairfield Osborn, ed., *Our Crowded Planet,* 1962.

66. A very generous observer might argue that the global preeminence of the United States, particularly as it existed in 2002, is akin to a "universal state." I don't think that's reasonable. Toynbee's conception of a universal state is literal, and no matter how powerful the United States was, and is, it is not a literal empire—a fact amply demonstrated in 2002, when the U.S. government exerted all the pressure it could muster on foreign governments to support its invasion of Iraq. Most refused. Even Canada and Mexico balked. The United States may have been the world's sole superpower, but it was not its governor.

66. *Time,* November 17, 1952.

66. Arnold Toynbee, "Is a World-Wide State Feasible?" in *Change and Habit: The Challenge of Our Time,* 1992.

66. Arnold Toynbee and Kei Wakaizumi, *Surviving the Future,* 1971.

69. Gary Marcus, *Kluge: The Haphazard Construction of the Human Mind,* 2008.

71. "Want to Keep Your Wallet? Carry a Baby Picture," *The Times,* July 11, 2009.

71. "Inferential Correction" in Thomas Gilovich, Dale Griffin, and Daniel Kahneman, eds., *Heuristics and Biases: The Psychology of Intuitive Judgment,* 2002.

72. Paul Rozin and Carol Nemeroff, "Sympathetic Magical Thinking" in *Heuristics and Biases: The Psychology of Intuitive Judgment.*

72. Researchers even found that the accuracy of people throwing darts at a dartboard significantly declines when the board has a photo of a baby pinned to it.

74. Laura A. King, Chad M. Burton, Joshua A. Hicks, and Stephen M. Drigotas, "Ghosts, UFOs, and Magic: Positive Affect and the Experiential System," *Journal of Personality and Social Psychology,* vol. 92, no. 5, 2007.

74. See, for example, "Impressions of Baby-Faced Adults," Leslie Z. McArthur and Karen Apatow, *Social Cognition,* 1983. Baby faces have even been found to have an influence on the outcome of small-claims cases: Leslie A. Zebrowitz and Susan M. McDonald, "The Impact of Litigants' Baby-facedness and Attractiveness on Adjudications in Small Claims Court," *Law and Human Behavior,* December 1991.

74. The original calculation can be read at www.actuaries.org.uk/__data/assets/pdf_file/0016/26053/0481.pdf.

75. "His Heart Belongs to (Adorable) iPod," *New York Times,* October 19, 2006.

75. J. M. Henslin, "Craps and Magic," *American Journal of Sociology,* 1967.

76. Ellen J. Langer, "The Illusion of Control," *Journal of Personality and Social Psychology,* 1975.

76. "Heads I Win, Tails It's Chance," *Journal of Personality and Social Psychology,* 1975.

77. Paul K. Presson and Victor A. Benassi, "Illusion of Control: A Meta-Analytic Review," *Journal of Social Behavior and Personality,* 1996.

77. "Bull in Bull Markets," *Forbes,* April 6, 1987.

78. Richard Dawkins, *Unweaving the Rainbow,* 2000.

80. George Wolford, Michael B. Miller, and Michael Gazzaniga, "The Left

Hemisphere's Role in Hypothesis Formation," *The Journal of Neuroscience,* 2000.

81. Michael Gazzaniga, *The Mind's Past,* 1998.

82. *The NewsHour with Jim Lehrer,* June 23, 1999.

83. Baruch Fischhoff, Paul Slovic, and Sarah Lichtenstein, "Knowing with Certainty: The Appropriateness of Extreme Confidence," *Journal of Experimental Psychology,* 1977.

83. Sarah Lichtenstein, Baruch Fischhoff, and Lawrence D. Phillips, "Calibration of Probabilities: The State of the Art to 1980" in *Judgment Under Uncertainty: Heuristics and Biases,* 1982. Also Max Henrion and Baruch Fischhoff, "Assessing Uncertainty in Physical Constant," *American Journal of Physics,* 1986.

83. Craig R. M. McKenzie, Michael J. Liersch, and Ilan Yaniv, "Overconfidence in Interval Estimates: What Does Expertise Buy You?" *Organizational Behavior and Human Decision Processes,* 2008.

83. Stuart Oskamp, "Overconfidence in Case-Study Judgments" in Daniel Kahneman, Paul Slovic, and Amos Tversky, *Judgment Under Uncertainty: Heuristics and Biases,* 1982.

83. Claire I. Tsai, Joshua Klayman, and Reid Hastie, "Effects of Amount of Information on Judgment Accuracy and Confidence," *Organizational Behavior and Human Decision Processes,* 2008.

85. Charles G. Lord, Lee Ross, and Mark R. Lepper, "Biased Assimilation and Attitude Polarization: The Effects of Prior Theories on Subsequently Considered Evidence," *Journal of Personality and Social Psychology,* 1979.

85. Raymond J. Nickerson, "Confirmation Bias: A Ubiquitous Phenomenon in Many Guises," *Review of General Psychology,* 1998.

86. Michael J. Mahoney, "Publication Prejudices: An Experimental Study of Confirmatory Bias in the Peer Review System," *Cognitive Therapy and Research,* 1977.

86. R. G. Collingwood, *The Idea of History,* 2005.

87. A. J. P. Taylor, "Much Learning . . ." in *Toynbee and History.*

CHAPTER 4
Page

91. "Geopolitical Thoughts: Requiem for the American Empire," *The Nation,* January 11, 1986.

92. Robert Reich, "Is Japan Out to Get Us?" *New York Times,* February 9, 1992.

93. Also in the early 1990s, Thurow predicted that the value of natural resources, which had fallen substantially over the previous twenty years, would continue to fall for another twenty years. Nations will not "be rich on the basis of natural resources" in the future, Thurow said in 1991 at a major conference of the Liberal Party of Canada. This was a big worry for Canadians, as the Canadian economy was heavily dependent on the country's huge natural resource base. But Thurow was wrong. The price of most natural resources soared in the first decade of the twenty-first century and Canada made a killing. See David Crane, "Canada Given Stern Warning."

94. Paul Kennedy, *The Rise and Fall of the Great Powers,* 1988.

94. Ignacio Ramonet, "Lessons of a Non-war," *Le Monde diplomatique,* March 1, 1998.

95. World Development Indicators, World Bank.

96. Marguerite Kramer and Bruce Russett, "Images of World Futures," *Journal of Peace Research,* 1984.

99. Deutsche Bank Research, "Global Growth Centres 2020," March 23, 2005.

104. Dan Gardner, *Risk,* 2008.

105. Cass R. Sunstein, *Risk and Reason,* 2002.

106. John S. Carroll, "The Effect of Imagining an Event on Expectations for the Event: An Interpretation in Terms of the Availability Heuristic," *Journal of Experimental Social Psychology,* 1978.

107. "Challenging the Crowd in Whispers, Not Shouts," *New York Times,* November 1, 2008.

108. Robert S. Baron, Joseph A. Vandello, and Bethany Brunsman, "The Forgotten Variable in Conformity Research: Impact of Task Importance on Social Influence," *Journal of Personality and Social Psychology,* 1996.

110. Sam Cole, "The Zeitgeist of Futures?" *Futures,* August 2008.

112. Derek J. Koehler, "Explanation, Imagination, and Confidence in Judgment," *Psychological Bulletin,* 1991; Steven J. Sherman, Robert B. Cialdini, Donna F. Schwartzman, and Kim D. Reynolds, "Imagining Can Heighten or Lower the Perceived Likelihood of Contracting a Disease: The Mediating Effect of Ease of Imagery," *Personality and Social Psychology Bulletin,* 1985.

114. See, for example, Paul J. H. Schoemaker, "Forecasting and Scenario Planning: The Challenges of Uncertainty and Complexity," in Derek Koehler and Nigel Harvey, eds., *Blackwell Handbook of Judgment and Decision Making,* 2007.

116. Robert Fogel, *Foreign Policy,* January/February 2010.

117. David M. Levy and Sandra J. Peart, "Soviet Growth in American Textbooks," December 3, 2009, http://ssrn.com/abstract=1517983.

CHAPTER 5

Page

119. Tom Morgenthau, *Newsweek,* July 2, 1979.

119. Daniel Horowitz, *Jimmy Carter and the Energy Crisis of the 1970s,* 2005.

119. Kevin Mattson, *What the Heck Are You Up To, Mr. President?* 2009; Bruce J. Schulman, *The Seventies.*

123. Mattson, *What the Heck Are You Up To, Mr. President?*

123. Schulman, *The Seventies: The Great Shift in American Culture, Society, and Politics.*

124. *The Public Perspective,* The Roper Center for Public Opinion Research, April/May 1997.

125. *New York Times,* January 4, 1981.

125. *The Public Perspective.*

125. *Time,* July 6, 1981.

125. Interview with author, *Ottawa Citizen,* January 18, 2004.

126. Leonard Silk, "A World Depression?" *New York Times,* June 18, 1974.

126. "The End of an Era," *New York Review of Books,* June 27, 1974.

128. Schulman, *The Seventies: The Great Shift in American Culture, Society, and Politics.*

129. *New York Times,* April 22, 2008.

129. "Follow-up on the News," *New York Times,* October 19, 1975.

130. "Nearing the Limits: II," *New York Times,* October 4, 1973.

131. "Rome: Can the World Organize to Save Itself?" *New York Times,* November 10, 1974, and "On the State of Man," November 4, 1974.

132. "Population Control of Hobson's Choice" in L. R. Taylor, ed., *The Optimum Population for Britain,* 1969.

132. "Four Pressing Problems Shape Global Crisis," *Salt Lake Tribune,* December 8, 1974.

133. Independent Commission on International Development Issues (the Brandt Commission), *North South: A Program for Survival*, 1980.

134. Ellen Langer and Judith Rodin, "Long-term Effects of a Control-Relevant Intervention with the Institutionalized Aged," *Journal of Personality and Social Psychology*, 1977.

134. See, for example, Sir Michael Marmot's "Whitehall" studies of British civil servants, which found that those who felt they had no control at work were substantially more likely to develop heart disease. Also, James Geer and Gerald Davison, "Reductions of Stress in Humans Through Nonveridical Perceived Control of Aversive Stimulation," *Journal of Personality and Social Psychology*, December 1970.

135. Arnoud Arntz, Marleen van Eck, and Peter de Jong, "Unpredictable Sudden Increases in Intensity of Pain and Acquired Fear," *Journal of Psychophysiology*, 1992.

135. Quoted in John Conroy, *Unspeakable Acts, Ordinary People*, 2000.

136. B. Malinowski, *Magic, Science, and Religion*, 1954.

136. Gioria Keinan, "Effects of Stress and Tolerance of Ambiguity on Magical Thinking," *Journal of Personality and Social Psychology*, 1994.

136. Gioria Keinan, "The Effects of Stress and Desire for Control on Superstitious Behavior," *Personality and Social Psychology Bulletin*, 2002.

136. Jennifer A. Whitson and Adam D. Galinsky, "Lacking Control Increases Illusory Pattern Perception," *Science*, October 3, 2008.

136. "Sporting Rituals," *British Psychological Association Research Digest*, October 5, 2009.

136. Michaela C. Schippers and Paul A. M. Van Lange, "The Psychological Benefits of Superstitious Rituals in Top Sport: A Study Among Top Sportspersons," *Journal of Applied Social Psychology*, 2006.

137. Stephen M. Sales, "Threat as a Factor in Authoritarianism: An Analysis of Archival Data," *Journal of Personality and Social Psychology*, 1973.

137. Vernon R. Padgett and Dale O. Jorgenson, "Superstition and Economic Threat," *Personality and Social Psychology Bulletin*, 1982.

137. Stewart J. H. McCann, "Threatening Times and Fluctuations in American Church Memberships," *Personality and Social Psychology Bulletin*, 1999.

138. Schulman, *The Seventies: The Great Shift in American Culture, Society, and Politics*.

138. George Johnson, "A Menace or Just a Crank?," *New York Times*, June 18, 1989.

139. "What You Don't Know Makes You Nervous," *New York Times*, May 20, 2009.

140. Roy F. Baumeister, Ellen Bratslavsky, Catrin Finkenauer, and Kathleen D. Vohs, "Bad Is Stronger Than Good," *Review of General Psychology*, 2001.

142. "Portrait of the 1980s," *New York Times*, December 24, 1989.

CHAPTER 6
Page

143. "My Media: Norman Lamont," *The Guardian*, October 11, 1999.

150. Donald H. Naftulin, John E. Ware, and Frank A. Donnelly, "The Dr. Fox Lecture: A Paradigm of Education Seduction," *Journal of Medical Education*, July 1973.

150. M. Lefkowitz, R. R. Blake, and J. S. Mouton, "Status Factors in Pedestrian Violations of Traffic Signals," *Journal of Abnormal and Social Psychology*, 1955.

150. "The Perceptual Distortion of Height as a Function of Ascribed Social Status," *Journal of Social Psychology*, 1968.

151. Stanley Milgram, *Obedience to Authority*, 1974.

151. C. K. Holfling et al., "An Experimental Study of Nurse-Physician Relationships," *Journal of Nervous and Mental Diseases*, 1966.

151. Robert Cialdini, *Influence*, 1984.

151. If the reader is wondering, yes, I am guilty of doing this myself. It's hard not to be impressed by the aura of a great university, or to make use of it.

153. Wendy M. Williams and Stephen J. Ceci, "'How'm I Doing?' Problems with Student Ratings of Instructors and Courses," *Change Magazine*, September/October 1997.

153. Harvey London, Philip J. Meldman, and A. Van C. Lanckton, "The Jury Method: How the Persuader Persuades," *Public Opinion Quarterly*, 1970.

153. P. Zarnoth and J. A. Sniezek, "The Social Influence of Confidence in Group Decision Making," *Journal of Experimental Social Psychology*, 1997.

153. Brian L. Cutler, Steven D. Penrod, and Thomas E. Stuve, "Juror Decision Making in Eyewitness Identification Cases," *Law and Human Behavior,* 1988.

153. Paul C. Price and Eric R. Stone, "Intuitive Evaluation of Likelihood Judgment Producers: Evidence for a Confidence Heuristic," *Journal of Behavioral Decision Making,* 2004.

154. J. F. Yates, P. C. Price, J. Lee, and J. Ramirez, "Good Probabilistic Forecasters: The 'Consumer's' Perspective," *International Journal of Forecasting,* 1996.

154. Yates et al., "Good Probabilistic Forecasters: The 'Consumer's' Perspective"; Price and Stone, "Intuitive Evaluation of Likelihood Judgment Producers: Evidence for a Confidence Heuristic," *Journal of Behavioral Decision Making,* January 2004.

155. "My Media: Norman Lamont." The columnist in question was Lord William Rees-Mogg.

156. Joseph R. Radzevick and Don A. Moore, "Competing to Be Certain (But Wrong): Social Pressure and Overprecision in Judgment," January 14, 2009, draft, in press.

158. Yates et al., "Good Probabilistic Forecasters: The 'Consumer's' Perspective."

163. Pierre Desrochers and Christine Hoffbauer, "The Post War Intellectual Roots of the Population Bomb," *Electronic Journal of Sustainable Development,* 2009.

164. "Paul Ehrlich: Crusading Now to Change the Future," *St. Petersburg Times,* March 7, 1970.

165. Stuart Blackman, "Promises, Promises." *The Scientist,* vol. 23, no. 11, 2009.

165. Robert Lempert, "Can Scenarios Help Policymakers?" in *Blindsided,* 2007.

165. Blackman, "Promises, Promises."

166. "A Guessing Game?" *Online NewsHour,* PBS, June 23, 1999.

166. Paul Wells, "Wells's Rules, Annotated," *Inkless Wells* (blog on www.macleans.ca), May 21, 2009.

167. National Research Council, *Severe Space Weather Events—Understanding Societal and Economic Impacts Workshop Report,* 2008.

167. Michael Brooks, "Gone in 90 Seconds," *New Scientist,* March 21, 2009.

168. Nick Davies, *Flat Earth News,* 2008.

169. See www.cl.cam.ac.uk/~rja14/Papers/y2k.html for the original paper and the media release.

170. Michael Lind, "Shocking News: The World Is Stable!" *Salon,* December 8, 2009.

171. http://web.archive.org/web/20010211165926/kunstler.com/mags_y2k.html.

172. *Weekly Standard,* March 17, 2003.

172. *Weekly Standard,* March 17, 2003.

172. *The Guardian,* November 21, 2006.

175. Glen McGregor, "Web Disaster Prophecy a High School Project," *Ottawa Citizen,* September 14, 2001.

175. And it continues. Despite the indisputable origins of the verse, and the dedicated efforts of debunking Web sites, Marshall's words continue to be cited in cyberspace as proof of Nostradamus's dazzling powers.

176. See www.skepdic.com/dixon.html.

177. "Not with a Bang but a Gasp," *New York Times,* December 15, 1969.

178. "On the State of Man," *New York Times,* November 4, 1975.

178. Robert Paarlberg, *Starved for Science,* 2008.

178. "Ignore All the Iran Experts," *Foreign Policy,* June 2009.

178. Davies, *Flat Earth News.*

178. "The Coming Oil Crisis," *Newsweek,* June 29, 2009.

179. "Rubin, Oil Predictor, Sees $100 Crude in 2010," *BusinessWeek,* January 7, 2010.

179. "Economist Predicts $1.50 a Litre for Gasoline," *Toronto Star,* January 11, 2008.

179. Two books that appeared in the same period were *Dow 40,000* by David Elias and *Dow 100,000* by Charles Kadlec.

183. Personal correspondence with the author.

184. "Bertram R. Forer, "The Fallacy of Personal Validation: A Classroom Demonstration of Gullibility," *Journal of Abnormal Psychology,* 1949.

185. John Durant, *Predictions: Pictorial Predictions from the Past,* 1956.

186. "Not with a Bang but a Gasp."

187. www.youtube.com/watch?v=8Cz-6tYHK8I.

187. Kirk Shinkle, "Permabear Peter Schiff's Worst-Case Scenario," *U.S. News and World Report,* May 30, 2008.

188. Brian O'Keefe, "Peter Schiff: Oh, He Saw It Coming," *Fortune*, January 23, 2009.

188. Shinkle, "Permabear Peter Schiff's Worst-Case Scenario."

188. "Peter Schiff—and Shawn Tully—Were Right," Executive Suite, *New York Times* blog, December 3, 2008.

188. See the dedication to Peter Schiff's best-selling 2007 book *Crash Proof.* "To my father, Irwin Schiff," it reads, "whose influence and guidance concerning basic economic principles enabled me to see clearly what others could not." Irwin Schiff's views are spelled out in the 1976 book *The Biggest Con: How the Government Is Fleecing You.* The younger Schiff was not exaggerating. His beliefs, and the predictions he generates with them, are remarkably similar to those expressed by his father more than thirty years earlier.

190. See, for example, Victor Davis Hanson's essay "Tomorrow's Wars" in the Winter 2010 edition of *City Journal.* I'm embarrassed to admit I also repeated the calumny, both in newspaper columns and a first draft of this book. My thanks to political scientist John Mueller for setting me straight.

191. Martin Ceadel, *Living the Great Illusion: Sir Norman Angell, 1872–1967,* 2009.

191. Both letters quoted in an appendix to Norman Angell, *The Great Illusion 1933,* reprint 2006.

192. Robert W. Merry, "Sands of Empire," *New York Times,* June 26, 2005.

CHAPTER 7

Page

199. R. E. Know and J. A. Inkster, "Post-decision Dissonance at Post-Time," *Journal of Personality and Social Psychology,* 1968.

200. Lee Ross, Mark R. Lepper, and Michael Hubbard, "Perseverance in Self-Perception and Social Perception: Biased Attributional Processes in the Debriefing Paradigm," *Journal of Personality and Social Psychology,* 1975.

200. Lee Ross and Craig Anderson, "Shortcomings in the Attribution Process," in D. Kahneman, P. Slovic, and A. Tversky, eds., *Judgment Under Uncertainty: Heuristics and Biases,* 1982.

202. Christopher H. Achen and Larry M. Bartels, "It Feels Like We're Thinking: The Rationalizing Voter and Electoral Democracy," paper prepared

for presentation at the Annual Meeting of the American Political Science Association, 2006.

202. Danielle Shani, "Knowing Your Colors: Can Knowledge Correct for Partisan Bias in Political Perceptions?" paper presented at the Annual Meeting of the Midwest Political Science Association, 2006.

202. Doris Kearns Goodwin, *No Ordinary Time*, 1994.

204. Carol Tavris and Elliot Aronson, *Mistakes Were Made*, 2007.

206. On the foibles of memory, see Daniel Schacter, *The Seven Sins of Memory*, 2002.

206. Daniel Offer, Marjorie Kaiz, Kenneth Howard, and Emily Bennett, "The Altering of Reported Experiences," *Journal of the American Academy of Child and Adolescent Psychiatry*, 2000.

207. Tavris and Aronson, *Mistakes Were Made*.

209. Baruch Fischhoff, "Hindsight Does Not Equal Foresight: The Effect of Outcome Knowledge on Judgment Under Uncertainty," *Journal of Experimental Psychology*, 1975.

209. Neal J. Roese and Sameep D. Maniar, "Perceptions of Purple: Counterfactual and Hindsight Judgments at Northwestern Wildcats Football Games," *Personality and Social Psychology Bulletin*, 1997.

211. "My Y2K—A Personal Statement," April 1999, http://webarchive.org/web/20010211165926/kunstler.com/mags_y2k.html.

213. Kunstler's point about hypercomplexity is interesting and, obviously, worthy of exploration. But it's also important to know that it's not new. "Vast concentrations of human beings are involved in systems that are now so complicated that they are becoming uncontrollable," wrote Roberto Vacca in the 1973 book *The Coming Dark Age*. Soon, Vacca predicted, the advanced nations would experience "an apocalypse that is impersonal, casual, and unpremeditated." Hundreds of millions would die. Industrial production and scientific research "would come to a complete stop." The very foundations of modern civilization would crumble. "We cannot know whether future historians will fix on 1960, 1970, or some later date for its beginning: it would seem from many signs that the era of breakdown may have started already." But Vacca hoped the full plunge into the abyss wouldn't happen for a few more years—"sometime between 1985 and 1995," he wrote.

217. An elaboration Heilbroner shared with *New York Times* columnist

Anthony Lewis. See "Rome: Can the World Organize to Save Itself?," *New York Times,* November 10, 1974.

220. "Looking across the main developments of the last decade or two," Heilbroner wrote in the 1995 book *Visions of the Future,* "it is difficult to imagine any mood other than apprehension and anxiety that would reflect the experiences we have lived through." Bloodshed in Yugoslavia. "The descent into desperation of Soviet society, following the dissolution of its empire." War in central Africa. Skinheads in Germany and neofascists in Italy. And "the breakdown of civil society" in the United States. "Each of these events, in itself, would have been traumatic; taken together, they have hypnotized and horrified the public imagination to a degree unimaginable some 40-odd years ago." One would think the avoidance of mass starvation, the peaceful conclusion of the Cold War, and the end of authoritarian rule across a vast swathe of Europe and Asia would qualify as countervailing good news. But no. It was all so bad it would have been "unimaginable" in the past, which is really quite an extraordinary statement coming from a man who had declared twenty-two years earlier that humanity's only options were extinction or dictatorship, and who, thirty-six years before—in *The Future as History,* in 1959—had described that era as "a period of historic assault such as we have never known before."

224. Human Security Centre, University of British Columbia, Human Security Report 2005.

224. RAND MIPT database. After 2000, the trend started up again, but only when incidents in South Asia and the Middle East are included. Elsewhere, the rate continued to decline.

225. Francis Kinsman, *Future Tense: A Prophetic Consensus for the Eighties,* 1980.

226. "Population Control or Hobson's Choice" in L. R. Taylor, ed., *The Optimum Population for Britain,* 1969.

227. The world birthrate also fell, particularly from the 1980s on. It was thirty-three at the time Ehrlich wrote *The Population Bomb.* By 1980 to 1985, it was twenty-seven; 2005 to 2010, twenty.

228. "The Population Bomb Revisited," *The Electronic Journal of Sustainable Development,* 2009.

228. *On disease:* It is narrowly true, as Ehrlich said, that he predicted there would be novel diseases, but there are *always* novel diseases appearing as

a result of unknown viruses and bacteria emerging from the wild, and known viruses and bacteria evolving. What Ehrlich actually predicted in *The Population Bomb* was something much more precise. "As population density increases, so does the per capita shortage of medical personnel, so do problems of sanitation, and so do populations of disease-harboring organisms such as rats," he wrote. "In addition, malnutrition makes people weaker and more susceptible to infection. With these changes and with people living cheek by jowl, some of mankind's old enemies, like bubonic plague and cholera, may once again be on the move." Or something new may emerge, Ehrlich wrote. There could be a terrifying new "super flu," like the Spanish flu pandemic of 1918. Or worse. "What if a much more lethal strain should start going in the starving, more crowded population a few years from now? This could happen naturally or through the escape of a special strain created for biological warfare." It is a stretch to see this as forecasting the emergence of AIDS in the 1980s. *On climate change:* It's also true that Ehrlich raised the possibility of climate change in *The Population Bomb* and elsewhere. He even mentioned carbon dioxide emissions and the greenhouse effect. But Ehrlich didn't limit himself to one hypothesis. In *The Population Bomb,* his worries about carbon dioxide emissions were matched by his fear that supersonic jets leaving icy contrails in the upper atmosphere could either warm the planet by adding to the greenhouse effect or cool it by reflecting the sun's rays back out into space. In the 1971 book *How to Be a Survivor,* Ehrlich worried that dust and solid particles kicked up by agriculture and industry could decrease "the ability of sunlight to penetrate the atmosphere" and cause global cooling. In a paper that same year, Ehrlich and co-author John Holdren discussed how nuclear energy and the burning of fossil fuels generate heat as a by-product, so if population and economies continue to grow, they could heat the atmosphere like lightbulbs in an Easy-Bake oven ("Overpopulation and the Potential for Ecocide" in *Global Ecology: Readings Toward a Rational Strategy for Man,* 1971). In a 1969 paper, he warned there are "several ways in which a new ice age could be rapidly generated," including jet contrails—which he deemed "a major threat to humanity"—a "veil of pollution," or a sudden outward slipping of the Antarctic ice sheet—which would also cause a tsunami so vast it would wipe out the United Kingdom ("Population Control or Hobson's Choice," in L. R. Taylor, ed., *The Optimum Population for Britain*, 1969). So the most that can be said about Ehrlich's climate change predictions is that he predicted the climate could change.

228. And there's a final reason to be skeptical: Just how accurate is Ehrlich's number? In speaking with me, Ehrlich repeated this argument but he said the number who died of hunger was "two hundred million," not three hundred million. So I asked Ehrlich for the source of his number. He emailed this response: "Starvation number is all over the web [e.g., www.jesus-is-savior.com/Disturbing%2Truths/18000_kids_die.htm] but that's likely low because many deaths of children and adults are ascribed to diseases that wouldn't have killed them if they weren't immune compromised by mal- and undernutrition." The fact that the number is "all over the web" didn't strike me as compelling evidence of its accuracy, so I contacted UN agencies and development researchers and discovered that official death-by-hunger statistics do not exist because it's too hard to define, identify, and count such deaths. His number, it seems, is the guesswork of persons unknown.

229. Ehrlich, *The End of Affluence*.

230. Even the less hyperbolic predictions in *The End of Affluence* fared poorly. Between 1970 and 1998, the proportion of income spent on food by the average American fell from 23 percent to 14 percent (U.S. Census Bureau, *Statistical Abstract of the United States*). Over the same period, the number of hours the average American had to work to buy a color television fell from 174 to 23; the hours worked to buy a VCR went from 365 to 15; for a microwave, they went from 97 to 15; and for a calculator, 31 hours to 46 minutes ("Time Well Spent" in the Annual Report of the Federal Reserve Bank of Dallas, 1997). Americans may have had problems in those years but buying stuff wasn't one of them.

230. See "Ecofables/Ecoscience: The Two Simon Bets" on the Web site of Ehrlich's Center for Conservation Biology at www.stanford/edu/group/CCB/Pubs/Ecofablesdocs/thebet.htm.

231. See, for example, the Bank of Canada's Commodity Price Index, which tracks the price of twenty-three commodities. In 1999, the index registered 96.02. It peaked in 2008 at 249.03 and declined to 171.25 in 2009. The "Industrial Materials" subcategory of the index, which tracks metals, went from 95.13 in 1999 to 151.99 in 2009.

232. http://crowhill.net/blog/?p=7234&cpage=1.

232. "Ehrlich's Erroneous Predictions Proved Him a Visionary," *Las Vegas Review-Journal*, January 28, 2010.

CHAPTER 8
Page

234. "I Know a Hawk from a Handsaw" in M. Szenberg, ed., *Eminent Economists: Their Life Philosophies*, 1991.

236. A long-term prediction that looks a little better in hindsight is found in John Maynard Keynes's 1930 essay "Economic Possibilities for Our Grandchildren." Great progress has been made, Keynes writes, and there's no reason it can't continue. Extending the trend line out a hundred years, and factoring in the power of compound interest, Keynes foresees the standard of living in 2030 being "between four and eight times as high as today." It was a very simple and narrow analysis and it is roughly on track, so far. But then Keynes ponders what such an increase in wealth would mean and the train flies off the rails: People will be free of "pressing economic concerns"; making money will no longer be of "high social importance"; the love of money will be regarded as "a disgusting morbidity"; and the greatest problem people will face is figuring out what to do with their boundless leisure time. There are still twenty years left on Keynes's clock but things will have to change in a hurry if these forecasts are not to produce wry smiles in 2030.

237. Richard Overy, *The Twilight Years*, 2009.

239. William Vogt, *The Road to Survival*, 1948.

239. "The more things change, the more they stay the same."

240. George Eaton, "Q & A: George Friedman," *New Statesman*, August 27, 2009.

242. The extent to which it was pricey gas or the lower speed limit that caused the decline in fatalities is debated. For my purposes, it doesn't matter, as both factors were unexpected.

243. James Fallows, "Blind into Baghdad," *The Atlantic Monthly*, January/February 2004.

245. And Ehrlich had more than the usual reasons to consider that possibility, because the two books that deeply influenced his views and shaped the

course of his life—*Road to Survival* and *Our Plundered Planet*—contained predictions that looked shaky even in 1968, when Ehrlich was writing *The Population Bomb*. Unless the United States is "willing to place 50 million British feet beneath our dining room table, we may well see famine once more stalking the streets of London," William Vogt wrote in *Road to Survival*, which was published in 1948. "And hand-in-hand with famine will walk the shade of that clear-sighted English clergyman, Thomas Robert Malthus." Vogt said the same about Japan. Instead of seeing that things might be more complicated than they appeared, Ehrlich repeated both forecasts, foreseeing hunger in the United Kingdom in his 1969 paper "Population Control or Hobson's Choice?" and the same for Japan in the 1974 book *The End of Affluence*.

245. A similar threat to good decision making is the product of hindsight bias, and it can also be illustrated with the 1970s food crisis: It is a matter of record that global demand for food almost outstripped supply and the world came dangerously close to starvation on a massive scale. It could well have happened if events had been even a little different. But that's not how it feels in hindsight. There was no starvation on a massive scale and so it *feels* as if it was highly likely, even certain, that there would not be. Unfortunately, that feeling contributed to the sense that the world's food supply wasn't a serious concern, and that, in turn, contributed to drastic cuts governments and donors made to agricultural research—the very research that had averted disaster—during the 1980s and 1990s. As a result, agricultural advances slowed, which was a big reason that, in 2008, the world experienced substantial food shortages, and food riots, for the first time since the 1970s.

246. It's worth noting the contradiction in the position of many climate change activists. They often cite the predictions of climate change models as if it were a near certainty the future will unfold as described. But on the subject of geo-engineering—such as proposals to spray aerosols into the Arctic atmosphere in the expectation that they would increase sunlight reflection and decrease warming—they are opposed on the grounds that we know so little about the complex interactions of the atmosphere that we cannot possibly predict the outcome of such schemes. They can't have it both ways.

246. Something many scientists have been admirably clear about. They

include John Beddington, the chief scientific adviser to the UK government, who acknowledged that the uncertainties in climate predictions are "quite substantial" (see Haroon Siddique, "UK's Top Scientist Urges Care in Presenting Results of Climate Change," *The Guardian,* January 27, 2010).

247. See the "Copenhagen Diagnosis," a statement released by twenty-six climate scientists in November 2009.

247. Charles Krauthammer, "At $4, Everybody Gets Rational," *Washington Post,* June 6, 2008.

248. Max H. Bazerman and Michael D. Watkins, *Predictable Surprises,* 2004.

248. Charles F. Doran, "Why Forecasts Fail," *International Studies Review,* 2002.

253. Andreas Graefe, Alfred G. Cuzan, Randall J. Jones Jr., and J. Scott Armstrong, "Combining Forecasts for U.S. Presidential Elections: The PollyVote," 2009.

255. Chrystia Freeland, "The Credit Crunch According to Soros," *Financial Times,* January 30, 2009.

255. Karl Popper, *The Open Society and Its Enemies,* 1963.

257. Adam Clymer, "And the Winner Is Gore, If They Got the Math Right," *New York Times,* September 4, 2000.

257. Henry N. Pollack, *Uncertain Science . . . Uncertain World,* 2003.

259. www.cceia.org/resources/transcripts/0220.html.

259. Martin Gardner, *Fads and Fallacies in the Name of Science,* 1957.

259. "Reading Tarot on K Street," *The National Interest,* September/October 2009.

260. "Reading Tarot on K Street."

261. Reuters, "Whitehead Sees Slump Worse Than Depression," November 12, 2008.

261. James Fallows, "How Do You Protect the Environment Without Interfering with Privacy?," *New York Times,* May 12, 1974.

262. James Fallows, "How America Can Rise Again," *The Atlantic Monthly,* January/February 2010.

Bibliography

Angell, Norman. *The Great Illusion 1933*. Manchester, NH: Ayer, 2006.

Asimov, Isaac, ed. *Living in the Future*. New York: Beaufort Books, 1985.

Attali, Jacques. *Millennium*. New York: Times Books, 1991.

Batra, Ravi. *The Crash of the Millennium*. New York: Harmony Books, 1999.

Batra, Ravi. *The Downfall of Capitalism and Communism*. Dallas: Venus Books, 1990.

Batra, Ravi. *The Great American Deception*. New York: Wiley, 1996.

Batra, Ravi. *The Great Depression of 1990*. New York: Simon and Schuster, 1987.

Batra, Ravi. *The New Golden Age*. New York: Palgrave Macmillan, 2007.

Batra, Ravi. *Surviving the Great Depression of 1990*. New York: Dell, 1988.

Bazerman, Maz, and Michael Watkins. *Predictable Surprises*. Cambridge: Harvard Business School Press, 2004.

Bell, Daniel, and Stephen Graubard, eds. *Toward the Year 2000*. Cambridge: MIT Press, 1997.

Brown, Harrison. *The Challenge of Man's Future*. New York: Viking Press, 1954.

Brown, Lester, et al. *Running on Empty*. New York: Norton, 1979.

Bueno de Mesquita, Bruce. *The Predictioneer's Game*. New York: Random House, 2009.

Burger, Edward, and Michael Starbird. *Coincidences, Chaos, and All That Math Jazz*. New York: Norton, 2005.

Burstein, Daniel. *Yen!* New York: Fawcett Columbine, 1990.

Burton, Robert. *On Being Certain.* New York: St. Martin's Press, 2008.

Cable, Vince. *The Storm.* London: Atlantic Books, 2009.

Canton, James. *The Extreme Future.* New York: Plume, 2007.

Ceadel, Martin. *Living the Great Illusion.* Oxford, UK: Oxford University Press, 2009.

Cerf, Christopher, and Victor Navasky. *The Experts Speak.* New York: Villard, 1998.

Cerf, Christopher, and Victor Navasky. *Mission Accomplished!* New York: Simon and Schuster, 2008.

Cialdini, Robert. *Influence.* New York: Collins Business Essentials, 2007.

Clarke, Arthur. *Profiles of the Future.* Popular Library, 1977.

Cohen, Joel. *How Many People Can the Earth Support?* New York: Norton, 1995.

Collingwood, R. G. *The Idea of History.* Oxford, UK: Oxford University Press, 2005.

Commoner, Barry. *The Closing Circle.* New York: Knopf, 1971.

Cooper, Joel. *Cognitive Dissonance.* London: Sage, 2007.

Cooper, Richard, and Richard Layard. *What the Future Holds.* Cambridge: MIT Press, 2002.

Corn, Joseph, and Brian Horrigan. *Yesterday's Tomorrows.* Baltimore: Johns Hopkins University Press, 1984.

Crichton, Michael. *Rising Sun.* New York: Ballantine Books, 1992.

Damasio, Antonio. *Descartes' Error.* New York: Penguin, 1994.

Davidson, James Dale, and William Rees-Mogg. *Blood in the Streets.* New York: Summit Books, 1987.

Davidson, James Dale, and William Rees-Mogg. *The Great Reckoning.* New York: Summit Books, 1991.

Davidson, James Dale, and William Rees-Mogg. *The Sovereign Individual.* Clearwater, FL: Touchstone, 1997.

Durant, John. *Predictions.* New York: A. S. Barnes and Company, 1956.

Ehrlich, Paul. "Ecocatastrophe!" in *Eco-Catastrophe*, editors of Ramparts. San Francisco: Canfield Press, 1970.

Ehrlich, Paul. *The Population Bomb.* San Francisco: Sierra Club, 1969.

Ehrlich, Paul. *The Population Bomb.* Cutchogue, NY: Buccaneer Books, 1971.

Ehrlich, Paul, and Anne Ehrlich. *Betrayal of Science and Reason*. Washington, DC: Shearwater, 1996.

Ehrlich, Paul, and Anne Ehrlich. *The End of Affluence*. New York: Ballantine, 1974.

Ehrlich, Paul, and Anne Ehrlich. *Extinction*. New York: Random House, 1981.

Ehrlich, Paul, and Richard Harriman. *How to Be a Survivor*. New York: Ballantine, 1971.

Falk, Richard. *This Endangered Planet*. New York: Vintage, 1972.

Figgie, Harry. *Bankruptcy 1995: The Coming Collapse of America and How to Stop It*. Boston: Little, Brown, 1993.

Festinger, Leon, Henry Riecken, and Stanley Schacter. *When Prophecy Fails*. London: Pinter and Martin, 2008.

Friedman, George. *The Next 100 Years*. New York: Doubleday, 2009.

Friedman, George, and Meredith Lebard. *The Coming War with Japan*. New York: St. Martin's Press, 1991.

Friedman, Thomas. *Hot, Flat, and Crowded*. New York: Farrar, Straus and Giroux, 2008.

Fukuyama, Francis, ed. *Blindside*. Baltimore: Brookings Institution Press, 2007.

Gardner, Martin. *Fads and Fallacies in the Name of Science*. New York: Dover Publications, 1957.

Gazzaniga, Michael. *The Mind's Past*. University of California Press, 1998.

Gilovich, Thomas, Dale Griffin, and Daniel Kahneman. *Heuristics and Biases: The Psychology of Intuitive Judgment*. Cambridge, UK: Cambridge University Press, 2002.

Gilovich, Thomas, Dacher Keltner, and Richard Nisbett. *Social Psychology*. New York: Norton, 2006.

Goldsmith, Edward, et al. *A Blueprint for Survival*. London: Tom Stacey, 1972.

Gordon, Adam. *Future Savvy*. New York: American Management Association, 2009.

Greer, John Michael. *The Long Descent*. Gabriola Island, BC: New Society Publishers, 2008.

Hacker, Andrew. *The End of the American Era*. New York: Atheneum, 1980.

Hedges, Chris. *Empire of Illusion*. Toronto: Knopf Canada, 2009.

Heilbroner, Robert. *The Future as History*. New York: Harper and Row, 1959.

Heilbroner, Robert. *An Inquiry into the Human Prospect*. New York: Norton, 1995.

Heilbroner, Robert. *Visions of the Future*. New York: Oxford University Press, 1995.

Heinberg, Richard. *Peak Everything*. Gabriola Island, BC: New Society Publishers, 2007.

Homer-Dixon, Thomas. *The Ingenuity Gap*. Toronto: Vintage Canada Edition, 2001.

Homer-Dixon, Thomas. *The Upside of Down*. Toronto: Knopf Canada, 2006.

Horowitz, Daniel, ed. *Jimmy Carter and the Energy Crisis of the 1970s*. Boston: Bedford, 2005.

Independent Commission on International Development Issues (the Brandt Commission). *North-South: A Program for Survival*. Cambridge: MIT Press, 1980.

Ishihara, Shintaro. *The Japan That Can Say No*. New York: Simon and Schuster, 1989.

Jacobs, Jane. *Dark Age Ahead*. Toronto: Vintage Canada, 2005.

Janis, Irving. *Victims of Groupthink*. Boston: Houghton Mifflin, 1972.

Jevons, W. Stanley. *The Coal Question*. Gloucester, UK: Dodo Press, 2008.

Kahn, Herman. *The Next 200 Years*. New York: Morrow, 1976.

Kahn, Herman, and Anthony Wiener. *The Year 2000*. New York: Macmillan, 1967.

Kahneman, Daniel, Paul Slovic, and Amos Tversky, eds. *Judgment Under Uncertainty: Heuristics and Biases*. New York: Cambridge University Press, 1982.

Kennedy, Paul. *Preparing for the Twenty-first Century*. New York: Random House, 1993.

Kennedy, Paul. *The Rise and Fall of the Great Powers*. Waukegan, IL: Fontana Press, 1988.

King-Hele, Desmond. *The End of the 20th Century?* New York: Macmillan, 1970.

Koehler, Derek, and Nigel Harvey, eds. *Blackwell Handbook of Judgment and Decision Making*. Malden, MA: Blackwell Publishing, 2007.

Kotkin, Joel. *The Next Hundred Million: America in 2050*. New York: Penguin, 2010.

Kunstler, Howard. *The Long Emergency*. New York: Grove Press, 2006.

Langdon-Davies, John. *A Short History of the Future*. New York: Dodd, Mead and Company, 1936.

Leeb, Stephen. *The Coming Economic Collapse*. New York: Business Plus, 2006.

Leeb, Stephen, *Game Over*. New York: Business Plus, 2009.

Leeb, Stephen, and Roger Conrad. *The Agile Investor*. New York: HarperCollins, 1997.

Lindsey, Hal. *The Late Great Planet Earth*. Grand Rapids: Zondervan, 1970.

Lindsey, Hal. *The 1980s: Countdown to Armageddon*. New York: Bantam, 1981.

Lovelock, James. *The Revenge of Gaia*. New York: Basic Books, 2006.

Makridakis, Spyros, et al. *Dance with Chance*. Oxford, UK: Oneworld, 2009.

Marcus, Gary. *Kluge*. New York: Houghton Mifflin, 2008.

Mason, Colin. *A Short History of the Future*. London: Earthscan, 2006.

Mattson, Kevin. *What the Heck Are You Up To, Mr. President?* New York: Bloomsbury, 2009.

McKibben, Bill. *Eaarth*. Toronto: Knopf Canada, 2010.

McNeill, William H. *Arnold J. Toynbee: A Life*. New York: Oxford University Press, 1989.

Meadows, Dennis, et al. *The Limits to Growth*. New York: Signet, 1972.

Mitchell, Melanie. *Complexity*. New York: Oxford University Press, 2009.

Mlodinow, Leonard. *The Drunkard's Walk*. New York: Vintage, 2008.

Montagu, Ashley, ed. *Toynbee and History*. Boston: Porter Sargent, 1956.

Moynihan, Michael. *The Coming American Renaissance*. New York: Simon and Schuster, 1996.

Orlov, Dmitry. *Reinventing Collapse*. Gabriola Island, BC: New Society Publishers, 2008.

Orrell, David. *The Future of Everything*. New York: Thunder's Mouth Press, 2007.

Osborn, Fairfield. *The Limits of the Earth*. Boston: Little, Brown, 1953.

Osborn, Fairfield, ed. *Our Crowded Planet*. London: George Allen and Unwin, 1963.

Osborn, Fairfield. *Our Plundered Planet*. New York: Pyramid Books, 1970.

Overy, Richard. *The Twilight Years*. New York: Viking, 2009.

Paddock, William, and Paul Paddock. *Famine 1975!* Boston: Little, Brown, 1967.

Paddock, William, and Paul Paddock. *Time of Famines*. Boston: Little, Brown, 1976.

Popper, Karl. *The Open Society and Its Enemies.* New York: Harper Torch-books, 1963.

Popper, Karl. *The Poverty of Historicism.* London and New York: Routledge, 1957.

Prestowitz, Clyde. *Trading Places.* Tokyo: Charles E. Tuttle Company, 1988.

Roberts, Paul. *The End of Food.* New York: Houghton Mifflin, 2008.

Roberts, Paul. *The End of Oil.* Boston: Mariner Books, 2005.

Rosenthal, Jeffrey. *Struck by Lightning.* New York: HarperCollins, 2005.

Rubin, Jeff. *Why Your World Is About to Get a Whole Lot Smaller.* Toronto: Random House Canada, 2009.

Ruff, Howard. *Famine and Survival in America.* Salt Lake City: Publishers Press, 1974.

Ruff, Howard. *How to Prosper During the Coming Bad Years.* New York: Warner Books, 1979.

Ruff, Howard. *How to Prosper During the Coming Bad Years in the Twenty-first Century.* New York: Berkley Books, 2008.

Ruff, Howard. *How to Prosper During the Hard Times Ahead.* Washington, DC: Regnery, 1999.

Ruff, Howard. *Survive and Win in the Inflationary Eighties.* New York: New York Times Books, 1981.

Sauvy, Alfred. *Fertility and Survival.* New York: Criterion Books, 1961.

Schacter, Daniel. *The Seven Sins of Memory.* Boston: Houghton Mifflin, 2001.

Schell, Jonathan. *The Fate of the Earth.* New York: Knopf, 1982.

Schiff, Irwin. *The Biggest Con.* Hamden, CT: Freedom Books, 1977.

Schiff, Peter. *Crash Proof 2.0.* Hoboken, NJ: Wiley, 2009.

Schnaars, Steven. *Megamistakes: Forecasting and the Myth of Rapid Techno-logical Change.* The Free Press, 1989.

Schulman, Bruce. *The Seventies: The Great Shift in American Culture, Society, and Politics.* New York: Da Capo Press, 2001.

Schumacher, E. F. *Small Is Beautiful.* Vancouver, BC: Hartley and Marks, 1999.

Schwartz, Peter. *Inevitable Surprises.* New York: Gotham Books, 2003.

Schwartz, Peter, Peter Leyden, and Joel Hyatt. *The Long Boom.* Reading, MA: Perseus, 2000.

Shapiro, Robert. *Futurecast.* New York: St. Martin's Griffin, 2008.

Sherden, William. *The Fortune Sellers.* New York: Wiley, 1998.

Shiller, Robert. *Irrational Exuberance.* New York: Currency Doubleday, 2005.

Simon, Julian, *The Ultimate Resource.* Princeton, NJ: Princeton University Press, 1981.

Simon, Julian. *The Ultimate Resource 2.* Princeton, NJ: Princeton University Press, 1996.

Smith, F. E. (the earl of Birkenhead). *The World in 2030 A.D.* London: Hodder and Stoughton, 1930.

Soros, George. *The Crash of 2008 and What It Means.* Philadelphia: Public-Affairs, 2009.

Soros, George. *Staying Ahead of the Curve.* New York: Wiley, 1995.

Spengler, Oswald. *The Decline of the West.* New York: Alfred A. Knopf, 1926.

Sterling, Bruce. *Tomorrow Now.* New York: Random House, 2003.

Steyn, Mark. *America Alone.* Washington, DC: Regnery, 2006.

Strathern, Oona. *A Brief History of the Future.* New York: Carroll and Graf, 2007.

Strauss, William, and Neil Howe. *The Fourth Turning.* New York: Broadway Books, 1998.

Sunstein, Cass. *Laws of Fear.* New York: Cambridge University Press, 2005.

Sunstein, Cass. *Risk and Reason.* New York: Cambridge University Press, 2002.

Surowiecki, James. *The Wisdom of Crowds.* New York: Anchor Books, 2005.

Suzuki, David, and Holly Dressel. *From Naked Ape to Super Species.* Vancouver: Greystone, 2004.

Szulc, Tad. *The Energy Crisis.* New York: Franklin Watts, 1974.

Taleb, Nassim Nicholas. *The Black Swan: The Impact of the Highly Improbable.* New York: Random House, 2007.

Tavris, Carol, and Elliot Aronson. *Mistakes Were Made.* New York: Harcourt, 2007.

Taylor, Gordon Rattray. *Rethink.* Harmondsworth, UK: Pelican Books, 1974.

Teitelbaum, Michael, and Jay Winter. *The Fear of Population Decline.* Orlando: Academic Press, 1985.

Tetlock, Philip. *Expert Political Judgment.* Princeton, NJ: Princeton University Press, 2005.

Thurow, Lester. *Head to Head.* New York: Harper Business, 2003.

Toffler, Alvin. *Future Shock.* London: Bodley Head, 1970.

Toffler, Alvin, ed. *The Futurists.* New York: Random House, 1972.

Toynbee, Arnold. *Change and Habit.* London: Oneworld, 1992.

Toynbee, Arnold. *A Study of History.* New York: Oxford University Press, 1987.

Toynbee, Arnold. *Surviving the Future.* New York: Oxford University Press, 1971.

Vacca, Roberto. *The Coming Dark Age.* New York: Doubleday, 1973.

Vogt, William. *Road to Survival.* New York: Sloane, 1948.

Wallechinsky, David, et al. *The Book of Predictions.* New York: Morrow, 1980.

Wells, H. G. *The Shape of Things to Come.* New York: Penguin, 2005.

Workshop on Alternative Energy Strategies. *Energy: Global Prospects 1985–2000.* New York: McGraw-Hill, 1977.

Yergin, Daniel. *The Prize.* New York: Free Press, 1992.

Zubrin, Robert. *Energy Victory.* Amherst, NY: Prometheus Books, 2007.

Index